SLAYING DRAGONS

DANIEL KOLENDA

CHARISMA
HOUSE

Most CHARISMA HOUSE BOOK GROUP products are available at special quantity discounts for bulk purchase for sales promotions, premiums, fund-raising, and educational needs. For details, call us at (407) 333-0600 or visit our website at www.charismahouse.com.

SLAYING DRAGONS by Daniel Kolenda
Published by Charisma House
Charisma Media/Charisma House Book Group
600 Rinehart Road
Lake Mary, Florida 32746

Library of Congress Cataloging-in-Publication Data

Names: Kolenda, Daniel, author.
Title: Slaying dragons / Daniel Kolenda.
Description: Lake Mary, Florida : Charisma House, 2020. | Includes
    bibliographical references.
Identifiers: LCCN 2019012178 (print) | LCCN 2019980915 (ebook) | ISBN
    9781629996578 (trade paper) | ISBN 9781629996585 (ebook)
Subjects: LCSH: Spiritual warfare.
Classification: LCC BV4509.5 .K65 2020 (print) | LCC BV4509.5 (ebook) |
    DDC 235/.4--dc23
LC record available at https://lccn.loc.gov/2019012178
LC ebook record available at https://lccn.loc.gov/2019980915

20 21 22 23 24 — 9 8 7 6 5
Printed in the United States of America

CONTENTS

FOREWORD

I'VE HAD THE privilege of knowing Evangelist Daniel Kolenda for several years, and I have been able to grasp his passion to see nations and lives transformed by the gospel and our beloved Lord and Savior, Jesus Christ. The experiences shared in *Slaying Dragons* will certainly bless many. This book provides deep revelation of the spiritual realm that will empower the reader to step into a higher level of faith.

After reading through *Slaying Dragons*, I am convinced that its content regarding spiritual warfare will enable the reader to access a new level of faith and authority in Jesus Christ. In these times we must strive to deepen our knowledge and understanding of the spiritual realm like never before. Satan and his army are tirelessly working to deceive believers. It is imperative that we are fully clothed with God's armor in order to effectively fight back and take authority over all darkness and evil spirits. We are reminded in Luke 10:19 of the authority Jesus Christ has given us over all the power of darkness.

I fervently encourage every reader to embrace this book's deep revelation of the spiritual realm. Genuine and true revelation can only lead us to be more like Jesus. Furthermore remember there are millions of lost souls waiting for you to be the bearer of good news and present Jesus to them. Be encouraged and believe that God wants to use your life.

—CARLOS ANNACONDIA

THE GREAT DRAGON, THAT OLD SERPENT

There he lay, a vast red-golden dragon, fast asleep; a thrumming came from his jaws and nostrils, and wisps of smoke, but his fires were low in slumber. Beneath him, under all his limbs and his huge coiled tail, and about him on all sides stretching away across the unseen floors, lay countless piles of precious things, gold wrought and unwrought, gems and jewels, and silver red-stained in the ruddy light. Smaug lay, with wings folded like an immeasurable bat, turned partly on one side, so that the hobbit could see his underparts and his long pale belly crusted with gems and fragments of gold from his long lying on his costly bed.

—J. R. R. TOLKIEN, *THE HOBBIT*

THE IMAGE OF the dragon is as old as human consciousness. The terrifying legends of great serpentine, fire-breathing monsters come from virtually every ancient culture on earth. The word *dragon* comes from the Greek word *drakōn*, which means gazer. It comes from a verb that means to see clearly. The word came to describe ancient monsters, typically intelligent, reptilian, snakelike beings.

One author writes, "In the mythology of the ancient Greeks, such fantastical 'chimeric' beasts were created by the Titans, in the distant 'Kronian Age' before the Olympian gods, and typically dwelled in the mysterious places at the far reach of the world-river 'Okeanos'—a metaphor for the most distant place a mortal could travel."[1]

The Egyptians had Akhekh, an enormous, four-legged serpent. Its name may have been derived from a dialect of the southeastern African Makua where "*Ikuka* is the great Python." In this area serpents have been found up to thirty-six feet long![2] In Europe the Drakon Kholkikos, with a three-forked tongue and magic teeth, was said to guard a golden fleece in the sacred grove of Ares in Kolkhis (present-day Georgia).[3] The Scandinavians had Fafnir, who began life as a dwarf but became a dragon through a curse.[4] The Yucatec Maya people (in present-day Mexico) worshipped Kukulkan, the "Feathered Serpent."[5] The people of India had Vritra, who was depicted as a dragon-like entity so large he was able to block rivers.[6] The Bhutanese had Druk, the Thunder Dragon, who is still depicted on the national flag of Bhutan today.[7] Similar dragons appear in Chinese, Japanese, Korean, Vietnamese, and other Asian mythology.

The Bible also uses dragon imagery. In the first story, in the beginning of the first book of the Bible, we are introduced to the dragon. Satan, in the form of a sentient, talking serpent, beguiles Eve and brings about the fall of mankind. The story ends with a prophetic promise that points to Jesus. God says to the serpent, "And I will put enmity between you and the woman, and between your offspring and hers; he will crush your head, and you will strike his heel" (Gen. 3:15).

Christ, the offspring of Eve, would crush the head of that old serpent. Christ's body was mortally wounded in the process, but He rose from the dead in victory! His death was but a strike to the heel. On the other hand, Satan was defeated over and over by Jesus during His earthly life. Then at the cross he was utterly conquered with no hope of ever rising again to victory. His head was totally crushed. Even now, as he continues to ravage the world with sickness, disease, temptation, and all kinds of evil, he is a completely vanquished and defeated foe. His only power is what we give him.

Although Satan's ultimate defeat came through the death and resurrection of Christ, Jesus beat the devil soundly at every turn throughout His earthly life. Jesus demonstrated for us what it is to walk in victory. He gave His disciples authority to walk in that same victory over sin, Satan, and evil. This is our inheritance as children of the light.

Psalm 91 is considered a Messianic psalm. That means it points to and is fulfilled most perfectly by Christ Himself. Satan quoted verses

11 and 12 of the psalm to Jesus in the wilderness. Luke tells us, "The devil led him to Jerusalem and had him stand on the highest point of the temple. 'If you are the Son of God,' he said, 'throw yourself down from here. For it is written: "He will command his angels concerning you to guard you carefully; they will lift you up in their hands, so that you will not strike your foot against a stone"'" (Luke 4:9–11). Ironically, the psalm's next verse perfectly describes what happened to Satan that day in the wilderness when Jesus overcame every temptation: "Thou shalt tread upon the lion and adder: the young lion and the dragon shalt thou trample under feet" (Ps. 91:13, KJV). Jesus is the ultimate dragon slayer! At every point, He trampled the devil underfoot as prophesied.

John Gill, writing about Psalm 91, says, "Some think the Messiah is meant; and that the psalm contains promises of protection and safety to him, as man, from diseases, beasts of prey, evil spirits, and wicked men, under the care of angels; and this not because that Satan has applied one of these promises to him, Matthew 4:6, but because they seem better to agree with him than with any other: and one part of the title of the psalm, in the Syriac version, runs thus, 'and spiritually it is called the victory of the Messiah, and of everyone that is perfected by him.'"[8]

I love that last phrase: "the victory of the Messiah, and of everyone that is perfected by him." As brethren of the great dragon slayer Himself, we are all called to trample serpents and scorpions, just as He did. His victory is ours! His authority is ours! His gifts and power are ours!

Matthew Henry, in his commentary on Psalm 91, says, "The devil is called *a roaring lion, the old serpent, the red dragon*; so that to this promise the apostle seems to refer in that (Rom. 16:20), *The God of peace shall tread Satan under your feet*. Christ has broken the serpent's head, spoiled our spiritual enemies (Col. 2:15), and through him *we are more than conquerors*; for Christ calls us, as Joshua called the captains of Israel, to come and set our feet on the necks of vanquished enemies. Some think this promise had its full accomplishment in Christ, and the miraculous power which he had over the whole creation, healing the sick, casting out devils, and particularly putting it into his disciples' commission that they should *take up serpents*, Mark 16:18."[9]

In Revelation, John describes Satan as "the great dragon...that old serpent, called the Devil, and Satan, which deceiveth the whole world" (Rev. 12:9, KJV). Here we see that the great dragon—warring against almighty God, battling Michael the archangel and other mighty angels (v. 7), persecuting the church, and fighting against believers—is none other than "that old serpent." He's the same one who beguiled Eve in the Garden of Eden and whose head was crushed by the Messiah. We battle against him still today. But we fight from a position of victory, not defeat.

In Luke chapter 10 Jesus sent seventy-two disciples out two by two to every place He was about to go. He gave them authority and told them to heal the sick and tell them that the kingdom of heaven is near. They returned to Jesus, rejoicing that the demons were subject to them in His name. Jesus responded, "I saw Satan fall like lightning from heaven. I have given you authority to trample on snakes and scorpions and to overcome all the power of the enemy; nothing will harm you. However, do not rejoice that the spirits submit to you, but rejoice that your names are written in heaven" (vv. 18–20).

What an amazing scripture! Jesus, the One who was prophesied of old to crush the head of the serpent, has given us authority to trample on the serpent as well! And yet there is a more glorious promise. No matter what happens to us in this life, our names are written in heaven! No matter what, we win! We fight from a place of victory. This is why Jesus promises, "In this world you will have trouble. But take heart! I have overcome the world" (John 16:33).

AN OVERVIEW

In this book we will look at what the Bible teaches about spiritual warfare. First, we will examine what the Bible has to say about angels, demons, and the spiritual world. Are there different kinds of angels? What purpose do they serve? Who is Satan, and where did he come from? How are angels and demons similar? How are they different? What are demons, and where do they come from? How can demons influence humans? What authority do demons have in this world? What kinds of evil spirits are mentioned in Scripture? What does it mean to be "demon-possessed" or "demonized"?

I will write about the cosmic battle we are engaged in. It's easy to lose sight of the big picture in our day-to-day lives. The small battles we face are part of a much bigger war. Understanding where we fit in God's cosmic strategy will help us to take our individual assignments more seriously. Also, understanding what our enemy is trying to accomplish will help us recognize his devices and resist him with wisdom.

I will also do my best to demystify spiritual warfare. Often Christian books and teachings have presented highly superstitious ideas about spiritual warfare. Some of it has become spooky and weird—closer to a Harry Potter novel than anything in the Bible. I will teach biblical principles about spiritual warfare that are both doctrinally sound and practical.

I will write about the armor that God has provided us, and the mighty weapons of our warfare. I will cover casting out demons, both from Scripture and from my own experience. Finally, I will give you some parting words of wisdom that will help you to walk in victory every day. My prayer is that through this book you will be equipped to slay every dragon you encounter—not only in the world but also in your life.

CHAPTER 1

ANGELS AND DEMONS IN THE BIBLE

How you have fallen from heaven, morning star, son of the dawn! You have been cast down to the earth, you who once laid low the nations! You said in your heart, "I will ascend to the heavens; I will raise my throne above the stars of God; I will sit enthroned on the mount of assembly, on the utmost heights of Mount Zaphon. I will ascend above the tops of the clouds; I will make myself like the Most High." But you are brought down to the realm of the dead, to the depths of the pit.

—ISAIAH 14:12–15

I T WAS A warm night in West Africa. The vast crowd in front of me stretched as far as the eye could see. It's a surreal sight but something that has become as normal to me as a pastor's church congregation. The air was hazy with an orange hue as our portable stadium lights on the crusade field filtered through a thick veil of dust kicked up by hundreds of thousands of dancing feet and the ever-present harmattan.[1] As usual I was preaching the gospel of Jesus Christ. If memory serves me well, I was preaching about the blood of Jesus that night and the power it has to save, heal, and deliver.

A well-known witch doctor in the region was visiting that night. She was famous because it was said that her curses had the ability to kill their victims. I didn't know all of this at the time, but later the local pastors gave me the details, which they were familiar with. One

1

pastor said that he was personally aware of nearly a dozen people who had died after coming under her curse. As you can imagine, people were terrified of her and her dark arts.

She had come to the service that night not to hear the gospel but to put a curse on me, the evangelist, and to kill me right there on the platform. Now, you might wonder why someone would want to do such a thing to a nice guy like me. But the truth is she was not the first witch doctor to hate us, nor will she be the last. We are bad for their business. Whenever I come into a region where voodoo and animism are practiced, both of which are quite common in West Africa, I confront these demonic systems without hesitation. They bind many people in darkness and fear. Sometimes the locals will not even dare to utter the name of local demonic spirits or curses out of fear that they will come upon them. I defy them with utter contempt. I will often get a list from the local pastors of the names of these spirits and their curses, which are all well known to and held in fear by the people, and I read them aloud from the platform and break their power in Jesus' name! The people often gasp at first—amazed I didn't die on the spot. Then they rejoice in freedom as we burn idols, fetishes, amulets, charms, and all witchcraft juju that people want out of their lives and homes.

I tell the people that once they belong to Jesus, they don't need to be afraid of any demonic curses. Jesus Christ has the power to protect them and to provide whatever they need. Witch doctors go out of business as a result of losing all their clientele to Christianity. In one city the local witch doctor had large stones at his house that were said to have magical powers. People would pay him to stand on those stones and hear what they believed were the voices of their dead ancestors. But after our gospel crusade this witch doctor was angry with us because his stones were no longer "speaking"! I have seen on several occasions how the witch doctors themselves have become Christians and surrendered their juju to be burned, confessing Jesus as Lord!

The woman who came to the meeting to kill me, however, was apparently on another level. Even the pastors acknowledged her power. But I didn't even know she was in the meeting. I was just preaching Jesus as I always do. She stood off to the right side of the stage, out in front of one of the two massive towers that suspend our line array speakers. She had brought some strange charms to conduct her business. While I was preaching, she began to conjure some curse to hurl against me. Suddenly—and this is when I became aware of her presence—she let out a bloodcurdling scream and fell to the ground. There she lay, writhing like a snake and foaming at the mouth. I ignored her. With a crowd of half a million people or more, I wasn't about to stop to address one demon. Hundreds of thousands of people were listening to the gospel. I kept preaching. But we have a team trained to address such occurrences. They carried this woman behind the platform to a tent we had set up for deliverance. We call it "The Snake Pit."

The deliverance team cast the demons out of her, and she came to her right mind and received Jesus as her Savior. Then they brought her to me on the platform, and she shared her story with me as the massive crowd looked on. The people gasped when they saw her, knowing very well who she was. Even the local pastors on the platform

The Bible is absolutely clear that the spirit world is not only real but even more real than what we can see.

seemed uncomfortable. She told me how she had come to kill me. She told me that when she went to put the curse on me, she was suddenly struck to the ground. She told me how the demons had been cast out of her and she was free. Then she told me how she had surrendered her life to Jesus as well because, in her words, "Jesus is more powerful than my witchcraft."

This is the reality I live in. I often encounter people who are demonized. I have seen things that would give grown men nightmares (and actually have). If you don't believe demonic spirits are real, I guarantee one trip with me would change your mind. One thing I know for sure. The spirit world is real. Angels are real, and demons are real. God is real, and Satan is real. We are in the midst of a cosmic battle between good and evil that has been going on for millennia and continues to rage all around us. Some people prefer to ignore it and pretend the visible world is all there is, but no Christian is justified in having such a worldview. The Bible is absolutely clear that the spirit world is not only real but even more real than what we can see. The spirit world is where the battle is raging, and all followers of Jesus need to be sober and vigilant.

In this chapter we will explore some of the basics regarding angels, demons, and the spiritual realm. This will give us a foundation upon which to discuss spiritual warfare in the following chapters.

WHAT ARE ANGELS?

What comes to mind when you read that question? Do you think back to childhood images of little babies flying around with little wings and harps? Or does a more religious symbol come to mind, such as a medieval painting of humanlike figures with golden wings, long hair, a robe, and a halo? Perhaps you picture a more contemporary rendition, such as those found in Christian bookstores: a superhero-sized man with flowing hair, shining armor, powerful wings, and a huge sword. Or you may be one of those who have seen angels in a vision or in person, so the picture that comes to your mind may not be a mere interpretation—it may be the real deal.

Whatever comes to our minds, the Bible offers its own portrait of angels. But it is not a simple one. There is more to angels than can be captured in any one painting or vision. Scripture spreads many allusions to angels throughout its pages, like pieces to a giant puzzle scattered on a table. We have to put them all together to see the full picture.

Let's begin with the term itself. The word *angel* means messenger. It can actually refer to a human messenger sent to bring news to others (e.g., Gen. 32:3; Num. 20:14; 21:21). The Bible even refers to prophets as angels. The name Malachi means my angel—the Lord called him "My messenger" (Mal. 1:1, AMP).[2] These "angels" are not heavenly spirits. The Bible applies the word to them in the purely practical sense of messenger.

On the other hand, the same word clearly refers to nonhuman, spiritual entities who are God's messengers (e.g., Gen. 19:1, 15; Dan. 3:28; Zech. 1:9; Matt. 1:20; 2:13; Luke 1:26, 28; Rev. 1:1; 5:2; 7:2). God sends them to bring special news (like the angels of the Christmas story) or to accomplish special tasks (like the angels who destroyed Sodom and Gomorrah). Scripture describes angels as powerful spiritual beings who enjoy access to God's presence (Job 1:6; Matt. 18:10; Luke 1:19), obey His commands (Ps. 103:20–21), worship Him (Ps. 148:2; Rev. 5:11–14), protect His people (Ps. 91:11–12), and minister to their needs (1 Kings 19:5; Matt. 4:11; Heb. 1:14).

But the biblical portrait of angels is more complex than this. This chapter will expand on it by looking at several names that apply to angelic beings throughout Scripture. We begin in the Old Testament.

OLD TESTAMENT NAMES FOR ANGELS

Not only does the Old Testament speak often of angels (e.g., Ps. 91:11), but its depictions are also fascinating and sometimes shocking. In fact, *angel* is only one term among several that describe these spiritual beings.[3] God created several different kinds of angelic creatures that attend Him and perform His will. This section will look at some of the terms in the Old Testament.

The council of the Lord

First, we will look at a broader term that encompasses all kinds of angelic beings. The Old Testament is framed in a worldview that sees the Lord seated on His throne, atop His heavenly mountain, surrounded by a great assembly of the heavenly host. He is utterly unique, but He is not alone. God is surrounded by a massive throng of spiritual beings that constitute a great heavenly assembly—an assembly Jeremiah calls "the council of the Lord" (Jer. 23:18; see also v. 22).

> God has taken his place in the divine council; in the midst of the gods he holds judgment.
> —Psalm 82:1, esv

> And so the heavens will praise your wonderful deed, O Yahweh, even your faithfulness, in the assembly of the holy ones. For who in the sky is equal to Yahweh? Who is like Yahweh among the sons of God, a God feared greatly in the council of the holy ones, and awesome above all surrounding him?
> —Psalm 89:5–7, leb

Both of these passages refer to a great heavenly council ruled by God and attended by angels. It is a place of spectacular worship. But it

5

is also a place of legislation and decrees. Several prophets had a vision of this gathering. Indeed, they themselves stood with angels on this council. Isaiah's vision is probably the most well known. He saw the Lord on His throne surrounded by angelic beings. After his confession of sin and his cleansing, Isaiah heard the call for a volunteer to go for "us"—a pronoun that included the Lord and the entire angelic council (Isa. 6:1–8).

Daniel saw this same council sitting in judgment over wicked nations (Dan. 7). God, "the Ancient of Days," presided over the court (v. 9). There were other thrones and multiplied thousands of angelic beings in attendance. The council ruled against the rebellious nations and transferred their dominion to "one like a son of man" (v. 13).

The prophet Micaiah probably gives us the most fascinating glimpse into this council (1 Kings 22:1–40; 2 Chron. 18). Like Isaiah did, he saw the Lord on a throne surrounded by the heavenly host.

God uses His heavenly host for the same reasons He uses redeemed people. He is full of love and does not want to execute His plan alone.

After decreeing that King Ahab would die in battle, the Lord asked His council how to coax Ahab into that battle. A debate among the council members followed! "One suggested this, and another that" (1 Kings 22:20; 2 Chron. 18:19). Then one "spirit" stepped forward before the Lord and volunteered his services. He suggested going out as "a deceiving spirit in the mouths of all his [false] prophets" (1 Kings 22:22; 2 Chron. 18:21). The prophets would encourage Ahab to go into the battle, prophesying he would be successful. God said the idea would work and sent the spirit to do the job. The plan did work— Ahab died in battle.

It seems strange that God would like the idea of a lying spirit. It may seem even stranger that God would consult with lesser beings at all. Why does God need the counsel of lesser spirits when He has all knowledge and power? But this is exactly why it is so important to understand angels and the council of the Lord. God uses His heavenly host for the same reasons He uses redeemed people. He is full of love and does not want to execute His plan alone. He wants all kinds of children—in heaven and on earth—to work with Him and for Him.

This vision of heaven's council shows us that God has servants other than humans. They have ranks in His kingdom and various functions in God's family. God loves and respects them. They are part of His household, assisting Him as He governs creation. Further, the existence of this council—with its various kinds and levels of spirits—helps us understand the origin of demons and why they have different evil characteristics. And finally, the council gives us greater clarity about Jesus' lordship. His life, death, resurrection, and ascension mean He is exalted to the highest place of a universe filled with powerful spirit beings. Jesus helps preside over this huge, heavenly council *as a man*. The eternal Son of God, who is also now the chief human being, is "superior to the angels" (Heb. 1:4)! This is what Jesus means when He says, "All authority *in heaven* and on earth has been given to me" (Matt. 28:18, emphasis added). In light of all this let's look at a few more names the Old Testament gives these angelic beings.

Elohim

You may already be familiar with this Hebrew word. It can be translated either "God" or "gods." Its Hebrew form is plural, but it can have a singular meaning (like *sheep* in English).[4] That's the way the Old Testament writers most often use it. *Elohim* usually refers to the one eternal God of Israel. But in other contexts the same word can be a plural reference either to false gods (e.g., Exod. 20:3) or to angelic beings (Ps. 8:5). Psalm 82:1 describes the angelic beings on the divine council. According to the Old Testament, these angels are, in one sense of the word, *elohim*.

Context must always determine which meaning is used.[5] When the Bible applies the word *elohim* to angelic beings, of course it is not saying they are literally gods to be worshipped, served, or obeyed (though the ungodly nations see them this way). Instead it is using the word to highlight the fact that they are not humans. They are instead powerful, supernatural creatures who inhabit the spiritual realm.[6] As such, they sit on the Lord's heavenly council and help administer His justice among the nations (Ps. 82). The term *elohim* also brings attention to the authority these beings have in the world as God's agents. He presides over them and even judges them when they rebel. "God [*elohim*] stands in the divine assembly; he administers judgment in the midst of the gods [*elohim*]" (Ps. 82:1, LEB).[7]

The sons of God

There is only one eternal Son of God. Jesus Christ is the Father's "one and only Son," equal to the Father and Spirit in divinity (John 1:14, 18). He is fully human, fully divine, and greater than all angels (Heb. 1). But did you know the Bible speaks of other "sons of God" besides Jesus and redeemed humans? The unique phrase "sons of God" is yet another way the Old Testament refers to angelic beings who dwell in the heavens. The term means something similar to elohim. In fact, Psalm 82 identifies the elohim with the "sons of the Most High" (v. 6). It seems these divine sons are the same as the elohim. Both terms are general descriptions of the supernatural beings who stand on the Lord's council and exercise authority in the world on God's behalf.

So why refer to angelic beings as sons of God? Because it draws out other important aspects of angels we must understand. First, angelic beings are in some sense God's children. Even though they do not reproduce their own children like humans (Matt. 22:30), they are still God's offspring. He made them; they are His sons. The

Angels are not spiritual robots. They have the power of choice. It is possible for them to make the choice to abandon their God-given place and operate in ways contrary to God's will.

Father carefully, creatively, and compassionately created each and every angelic being for His pleasure. He is the One who gave them existence. They are part of His heavenly family and therefore part of His massive household (Eph. 3:15).

Second, the phrase "sons of God" means these spiritual beings are supernatural and powerful. Though they can enter the earthly realm, even appearing and functioning within it, this world is not their natural habitat. Heaven is. They are, after all, God's own sons. As His spiritual kin—His children—they stand on the royal council and share God's dominion in the world.

And finally, "sons of God" bear God's image. Though they are not humans, they have powerful abilities, intellects, and emotions. They also possess free will. Angels are not spiritual robots. They have the power of choice. It is possible for them to make the choice to abandon their God-given place and operate in ways contrary to God's will (Jude 6). As we will see later, some have done this. Most of them, however, have remained loyal to their Father and Lord and continue to serve Him on His council.[8]

Cherubim and seraphim[9]

These spiritual creatures seem to comprise the highest order of God's angelic sons. Some scholars would even say we should not call them angels.[10] But even though the use of terms can be debated, it is clear that these extraordinary creatures belong to a highly specialized class of angelic beings. Descriptions of them strike us as quite peculiar and even bizarre. Modern movies that create outlandish, CGI space creatures don't even come close to these *real*, extraterrestrial creatures who abide close to God's throne.

The prophets give us our most poignant descriptions of cherubim and seraphim.[11] Some also come from the stories of the tabernacle and temple,[12] and a few references occur in the psalms.[13] *Seraph* means "fiery serpent."[14] The verb form of this Hebrew word means to burn, and the noun means serpent, so most translators simply combine the meanings. In some places in the Old Testament, *seraph* denotes a literal snake. When used in judgment against God's people in the wilderness, their venom is their fire (Num. 21:6, KJV). Yet in that same story, the Lord tells Moses to "make a snake [seraph]" out of bronze (v. 8). When the bitten Israelites look at the bronze figure, they are healed.

The prophet Isaiah sees seraphim as angelic figures on the council of the Lord (Isa. 6:1–4). They are close to the throne, shouting, "Holy, holy, holy!" to one another. Both stories give us clues to the function of the angelic seraphim. From Isaiah's story it is clear these angelic creatures help steward God's presence (along with the cherubim, discussed below). They must cover their faces at the sheer, unapproachable brilliance of the Lord's light. And they must warn one another neither to look nor to perhaps come too close (e.g., Exod. 19:12–22). That is why Isaiah experienced such terror. He was *not* covering his face, and he "saw the Lord" (Isa. 6:1).

The Moses story seems to indicate seraphim are also related to

God's restoring powers. That is why a bronze fiery serpent is a symbol of healing for the Israelites in the wilderness. Even Jesus compares His being lifted on the cross to Moses' lifting the serpent in the wilderness (John 3:14). Isaiah's experience confirms this idea. When he confesses his sin, one of the seraphim brings a burning coal to touch his lips. This act restores Isaiah, enabling him to go forth on a mission (Isa. 6:5–8). Seraphim seem to attend the Lord's throne as guardians and to administer the Lord's restoring power.

The word *cherub* comes from a Semitic word that means "to bless, praise, adore."[15] Ezekiel sees four cherubim beneath the throne of God. Each has four faces, four wings, human hands, and calves' feet (Ezek. 1:6–8). With giant, whirling wheels next to each of them, they seem to "carry" God on His throne (vv. 15–28). Yahweh sits atop these beings like He's riding a glory chariot through the skies (Ps. 18:10). All of this indicates that the cherubim are also stewards of the Lord's presence. They attend and escort Him. This is why two cherubim flank the top of the ark of the covenant. And it is why the tabernacle curtains and the holy place in Solomon's temple have several images of cherubim in them. The Lord sits on a throne between the cherubim, and He speaks to people from that position (Exod. 25:22).

Cherubim also act as guardians for the Lord. He placed cherubim and a flaming sword on the east side of the Garden of Eden to prohibit Adam from returning (Gen. 3:24). The cherub whom the Lord expelled from His holy mountain, an apparent reference to the angelic being who became Satan, was "anointed as a guardian cherub" (Ezek. 28:14, 16).

The Bible mentions cherubim almost one hundred times. They are much more prominent than seraphim, yet they seem to have similar roles as guardian stewards of God's holy presence. The seraphim offer protection between the holy God and an unholy world, but they can also serve to bring restoration to penitent humans when that border is crossed. Meanwhile the cherubim act as protective escorts of their holy King. These extraordinary angelic beings stand on the Lord's council as stewards of His presence and throne.

Princes

Angelic beings called princes appear mainly in the Book of Daniel (10:13, 20–21; 12:1). This term refers to a group of high-ranking angelic leaders over nations.[16] The biblical worldview sees spiritual govern-ments in the heavens as parallel to and ruling over earthly governments (e.g., 1 Kings 22:19–23; Ps. 82; Isa. 34:4–5; Dan. 2:21; 7; Rev. 16:14). The angelic princes in the Book of Daniel have a level of authority over various nations. Michael, for example, is called the prince of Daniel's people, Israel (Dan. 10:21; 12:1), while two rebellious princes are called the "prince of Persia" and the "prince of Greece" (10:20). All three are princes, yet only one is loyal to the Lord. The other two fight against Him. That means the rebellious princes previously served as high-ranking angels on God's council but have since revolted and used their authority for evil purposes. Further, Michael is called "one of the chief princes" and "the great prince" (10:13; 12:1). That means there is a hierarchy with higher-ranking princes leading military contingents. (See Matthew 26:53 and Revelation 12:7.)

The heavenly conflicts in Daniel correspond to earthly conflicts. Just as the Persian kingdom ruled before giving way to Alexander the Great's Greek kingdom, so the messenger in Daniel had to fight the spiritual prince of Persia while the prince of Greece was on the way (Dan. 10:20). All of this means that some members of the original angelic council were called princes because they had authority over nations. Among the princes there were various ranks and probably hosts of military angels under their command.

ANGELS IN THE NEW TESTAMENT

The Old Testament sketches a complex but stunning portrait of angelic beings. The New Testament uses that portrait as its backdrop, assuming its description of the Lord's council with its various kinds of angelic members. But it subsumes most of these members under one simple name: *angels*. In the New Testament, then, the word *angels* refers to the various spiritual beings that convene on the Lord's council. This section will look at some functions of New Testament angels in light of the Old Testament categories.

Elohim and sons of God

Jesus refers to angels as elohim when He quotes a psalm using the same phrase (Ps. 82:6; John 10:34).[17] The same reference also implies that Jesus sees angels as the sons of God (John 10:35–36). His use of

11

these terms affirms His adoption of the Old Testament's worldview. Angels in the New Testament are nonhuman, heavenly entities God created as His spiritual children. They bear God's image, sit on His heavenly council, and assist Him in governing the universe.

Messengers

When angels appear in the New Testament, most of the time they carry messages to humans or accomplish tasks for the Lord. Angelic messengers famously appear to Zechariah, Mary, Joseph, and the shepherds to announce the births of John the Baptist and King Jesus (Matt. 1:20–2:23; Luke 1:11–20, 26–38; 2:8–15). They give commands, warnings of danger, and physical guidance. Angels rescue people, watch over churches and individuals, and carry out various acts of judgment (Matt. 18:10; Acts 5:19; 12:7–10, 23; Rev. 2:1). Whatever the case, this role of angels as messengers is the most prominent in the New Testament. As in the Old Testament, angels are spiritual beings who do not possess natural, earthly bodies but can appear in human form (Heb. 13:2).

Angels in the New Testament also have crucial roles as messengers in the end times. Thus angelic activity will increase on the earth as the day of the Lord approaches. Angels help the Lord Jesus reap the last-days harvest and "weed out" people from the church who look like Christians but are not (Matt. 13:39–41). One of the reasons God created the heavenly host was to assist in the renewal of the earth at the end of the age, no doubt to unite His heavenly and earthly families (Eph. 3:15). In the end these spiritual messengers will be subject to humans and after the judgment will help them take care of the new, glorious world in the age to come (1 Cor. 6:2–3; Heb. 1:14; 2:5–18).

Council of the Lord

The New Testament, like the Old Testament, describes scenes of the angelic council of the Lord (which also includes humans in both Testaments). The most vivid example occurs in the Book of Revelation. The Father sits on a throne that gleams with color and is encircled by twenty-four elders on thrones, four living creatures, myriads of angels, and the Lamb (Rev. 4–5; see also Dan. 7:9–10). This council is convened for the unrolling of the great scroll and God's last-days judgments.

The other New Testament mention of the council occurs in Hebrews 12:22–24. The author describes the council to encourage Jewish believers that their church gatherings carry tremendous significance in the spiritual realm. When they assemble, they join a larger council in the "heavenly Jerusalem" on Mount Zion. In attendance are myriads of angels, the broader church, God, the perfected spirits of righteous people, and Jesus.[18]

Both New Testament visions of the council include humans with angels, and both include Jesus as coleader of the council with the Father. It is no wonder the author of Hebrews begins his epistle insisting that Jesus is "much superior to the angels" (Heb. 1:4). He stands on the great angelic council, not as a prophet or even merely an earthly ruler but as the *Lord* of the council. He is uniquely

In the end these spiritual messengers will be subject to humans and after the judgment will help them take care of the new, glorious world in the age to come.

and eternally God's Son; therefore, all the angels—the entire council—worship and serve Him the way they do the Father (Heb. 1).

Cherubim and seraphim

Though these creatures are not mentioned by name in the New Testament, it appears the cherubim appear in Revelation as "the four living creatures" (Rev. 4:6–8). They bear some striking similarities to Ezekiel's cherubim, although they also have some differences. Some Bible teachers see them as the same beings appearing in different forms.[19] Still others identify them with the seraphim of Isaiah.[20]

Princes

One of the princes from Daniel also appears in the New Testament. Michael, the prince who looks after the nation of Israel, is called an "archangel" in the New Testament (Jude 9). He is also pictured in a battle with "his angels" against "the dragon and his angels" (Rev. 12:7). The Greek prefix *arch* can mean first, beginning, ruler, or prince. So *archangel* clearly refers to a chief angel. Michael's description in Revelation shows us that he is a chief or prince angel because he oversees other princes, as well as other angels in his military contingent. He also has oversight over the nation of Israel.[21] Further, in Jude, Michael disputes with the devil (v. 9), which implies his level of authority in the hierarchy of angels. Michael and the devil probably had similar ranks before the rebellion.

WHAT ARE DEMONS?

What happens when any of these powerful angelic creatures rebel against the Most High? These angels, after all, are the "sons of God." God created them as His spiritual kindred, giving them the ability to choose loyalty to Him and obedience to His word. But not all made that choice. The angelic beings who did not choose to obey God were cast away from their heavenly sphere. They remained spirits, of course, and therefore continue to populate the spiritual realm. But by choosing to go their own way, they lost their intimate connection with God as well as their place in the atmosphere of His glory. I see two major consequences to such a fall. First, these angels experience a perversion of their original attributes. Different types of angels who had various abilities and responsibilities in heaven now, after rebellion, have distorted versions of their original characters. The expulsion and perversion of these fallen angels turns them into what the New Testament calls demons.

Second, without the atmosphere of glory for which they were made, they need another environment in which to express themselves and fight against God. That new environment is the earth. Specifically, they must work through human agency. This is because God designed humans to rule and take care of the earth. Demons must usurp humanity's role as rulers of the earth. But they also must create a kind of partnership with humans as hosts for their mission against God.

THE FALL OF ANGELS

The prophet Ezekiel offers an interesting proclamation of judgment and lamentation against the king of Tyre (Ezek. 28:1–19). The arrogance of this evil, human prince inspired him to claim invincibility and equality with God, so the prophet rebuked him. But as Ezekiel unfolds his prophecy, he clearly switches into another mode and begins to speak of a supernatural being. Remember that human princes correspond to spiritual princes. (See Daniel 10:13, 20.) For Ezekiel's prophecy about

Tyre's king to slide into a parallel description of a supernatural being should offer no surprise.

The prophet says this spiritual entity used to be "an anointed guardian cherub" who dwelled "on God's holy mountain," was covered with precious stones, had the seal of perfection, was "full of wisdom and perfect of beauty," walked among the stones of fire, and was "in Eden, the garden of God" (Ezek. 28:12–14, LEB). Such a list clearly describes a member of God's angelic council who appeared even in Eden. But the prophet goes on to say, "Your heart was proud because of your beauty; you ruined your wisdom because of your splendor" (v. 17, LEB). Further, and leaving no room for doubt that he addresses a fallen angelic being, the Lord says, "You sinned; and I cast you as a profane thing from the mountain of God, and I expelled you, the guardian cherub, from the midst of the stones of fire" (v. 16, LEB).[22]

It is logical, then, that we would encounter an evil, spiritual being in the Garden of Eden (Gen. 3:1–7). The serpent was the former cherub prince who wanted to rise to the highest place of the Lord's council, even making himself "like the Most High" (Isa. 14:14). He was a high-ranking council member that now appeared in the garden to seduce Eve and steer Adam into human rebellion and death. The New Testament identifies this serpent with none other than "the devil" and "Satan" (Rev. 12:9; see also 2 Cor. 11:3, 14). His rebellion inspired other angelic beings to follow suit. They also were expelled from the heavenly council (Rev. 12:9; see also Matt. 25:41).

Was this all one rebellion? Or were there several rebellions of other council members at different times? Scripture gives various references to angelic rebellion. Genesis tells us that "sons of God" took human wives for themselves (Gen. 6:1–4). These seem to be the same "angels who did not keep to their own domain but deserted their proper dwelling place, [that are now] kept in eternal bonds under deep gloom for the judgment of the great day" (Jude 6, LEB). Psalm 82 reveals that some of the sons of God who stood on the Lord's council became corrupt, while other sons of God clearly remained loyal to Him (Job 1:6; 2:1). These rebellious sons in Psalm 82, called elohim, refused to use their authority among the nations to help the weak, poor, and fatherless. Finally, Revelation tells us that the dragon's tail "swept away a third of the stars from heaven and threw them to the earth" (Rev. 12:4,

LEB). Clearly we find different references to angelic rebellion, which may have occurred at different times. But whether these are separate events or not, they clearly show us that demonic beings are former members of the angelic council who rebelled against the Lord.

VARIOUS KINDS OF DEMONS

A large portion of the angelic host rebelled. Whatever characteristics they bore in their previous state, they bear a twisted form of them now. Former high-ranking angels—cherubim, seraphim, and princes—are now dark forms of their prior selves. They still carry authority over nations, but they now use their authority to pervert justice, oppress people, resist God's plan, and create war and death on the earth. These are the principalities and powers to which Paul and Peter refer in their epistles (Eph. 1:21; 6:12; 1 Pet. 3:22). The demons' former power stations carry over into present rank-and-file positions. We read of "rulers...authorities...powers of this dark world...spiritual forces of evil in the heavenly realms" (Eph. 6:12). We also find words such as *lordships*, *names*, *thrones*, and *angels* (Eph. 1:21, LEB; 3:10; Col. 1:16; 1 Pet. 3:22). These are all references to hierarchical positions originally on the Lord's council. But they became evil positions on the satanic council.

In any hierarchical system, higher and lower ranks exist. Lower-ranking angels who rebelled became something like ground soldiers in the satanic army. These are usually called demons in the Gospels. They wreak havoc in people's lives in various ways. Previously they operated beneath higher-ranking angels and carried out certain assignments. Now they do the same for their overseers in the demonic realm. Previously they had various areas of expertise. Now they use perverted versions of those skills to exert the devil's oppressive power over people.

For instance, an angel originally tasked with various kinds of communication may now have become a "demon that [is] mute" (Luke 11:14). An angel assigned to extend beauty may now be a demon that causes blindness (Matt. 12:22). One given to steward the purity of worship may now be "an impure spirit" right in the middle of a synagogue service (Luke 4:33)! Popularly we may call such a demon a religious spirit. It camouflages gross impurity behind false piety. On a larger scale a seraph initially given extensive power to restore may now be a high-ranking prince with power to inflict the worst kinds of diseases on many people.

Demons cover a large spectrum of rank and power, and they work together. Jesus makes that clear (Matt. 12:26). Obviously they do not unite out of love. They unite out of fear. If they do not pool their resources around their common evil cause, they have no hope to succeed. Therefore, as in the case of Legion, lower-ranking demons can conglomerate to yield greater power over a region (Mark 5:1–20). The cluster of unclean spirits, Legion, demonizes a man *and* keeps a ten-city area under its dominion. This story reveals both planes of demonic activity: bondage over an individual but also government over a region.[23] This Legion, the name given to a detachment of as many as four thousand to six thousand demons, must also have worked under the authority of higher-ranking princes.[24]

DEMONS' NEED FOR REST

Jesus teaches, "When an impure spirit comes out of a person, it goes through arid places seeking rest and does not find it. Then it says, 'I will return to the house I left'" (Luke 11:24). Why do demonic spirits seek rest? As fallen spirits without the comfort and compatibility of their original environment, they must have some semblance of a "house" in this world where they can reside and through which they can express their agitated need for evil. Demons need hosts. Even the swine were better to Legion than the prospect of being disembodied, leaving their region, or heading to the premature judgment of the abyss (Matt. 8:29; Mark 5:10; Luke 8:31).

On the other hand, higher-ranking spirits inhabit heavenly regions, also called "the kingdom of the air" (Eph. 2:2). They do not seem to need individual humans to inhabit. But they do still need human regimes through which to express their dominion. They also seem to work through a chain-link connection that extends from lower-level evil activity on the ground up to higher-level government in the heavens. Again, this is what Legion seemed to be doing.

This human connection is the "rest" demonic forces need. Added to this is the fact that God designed us humans to live by His Spirit.

Adam naturally lived when the breath of life entered him (Gen. 2:7). And believers supernaturally live when we receive the Spirit of God and Christ (Rom. 8:9). God created us to be inspired by His Spirit. But if we do not have *His* Spirit, we will have a cavity in our hearts longing for some other kind of spirit. We must have spirit.

Meanwhile, demonic spirits traverse the earth needing hosts. These two dark requirements find one another like a match made in hell. This is why Paul says we were subject to "the spirit that is now working in the sons of disobedience" when we were sinners (Eph. 2:2, NASB). Without the Holy Spirit, humans must have some kind of connection with spirit—whether direct demonization or a general inspiration from the spirit of the world. Some people are more influenced by specific spirits than others.

This is why there seem to be different depths of demonic influence over people. Demons need rest, and people need spirit. The degree of mutual cooperation, as well as other factors, determines the degree of influence. In extreme cases demonic beings express themselves openly through human speech or behavior. The New Testament calls this being demon-possessed or demonized or having a demon (Matt. 8:16; Mark 9:17).[25] This does not mean that everyone without Christ is demonized. But it does mean everyone without Christ comes under the influence of the spirit of the world.

JESUS CHRIST IS LORD!

But Jesus has defeated every rebellious angelic spirit! His life, death, resurrection, and ascension did more than give us a way to be forgiven of sins. *His victory overthrew the entire host of dark powers.* When Jesus took His throne as the perfect Son of God and Son of Man, He specifically took dominion over the entire network of fallen angels. That is a huge part of what the Bible means when it says that Jesus is Lord! It is not even possible to understand this great confession fully without a worldview that sees a hierarchy of evil spirits ruling individuals and nations but now subjugated to Christ!

When we turn to the Lord and receive His Spirit, our vacuum for spirit is filled by the Holy Spirit. That means we are brought from spiritual death to eternal life. It also means we are raised to the place of dominion with Christ (Eph. 1:19–2:6). No longer are we subject to the spirit of the world, living under the tyranny of wicked forces. We are both liberated and elevated. In the man Christ Jesus, the original design for humans to rule the earth has been restored. We can walk in victory over these evil powers now, and one day we will rule with Christ over all creation. Jesus Christ is Lord.

QUESTIONS FOR DISCUSSION

- Why do you think God has created so many different kinds of creatures in heaven and on earth?

- Why does God use human and angelic agents rather than doing everything Himself?

- Why do demons need/want human hosts?

- Have you ever had an encounter with a demonized person? Have you ever seen an angel or a demon?

CHAPTER 2

WHERE THE DRAGON GETS HIS POWER

*It is prudent never to place one's entire trust in
things which have deceived us even once.*

—RENÉ DESCARTES, *MEDITATIONS ON FIRST PHILOSOPHY*

*I have no reason to suppose, that he, who would take away my liberty,
would not, when he had me in his power, take away every thing else.*

—JOHN LOCKE, *SECOND TREATISE OF GOVERNMENT*

HAVE YOU EVER been out for a walk, or perhaps working outside, and come across a snake? It's a chilling moment. A friend of mine recently shared how he was hiking with his family and had one of his four kids perched on his shoulders. He turned a corner and nearly stepped on a black serpent blocking his path. He wanted to scream. But he stifled his urge so he would not terrify his kids. Instead he uttered a noise that would be impossible to reproduce here in writing. But trust me when I tell you it was ridiculous. As you can imagine, with a child on his shoulders and three more tagging close behind him, he was somewhat less mobile than he would have liked, so he backed up slowly. Once at a safe distance he stamped his feet to scare the snake away.

It was not a particularly sophisticated strategy. I'm sure he would have smashed it with a rock or thrown a ninja star if he could have. He's cool like that. But in the moment, how cool he looked didn't matter. By his own admission, he didn't look, or sound, like a triumphant hero. His kids still imitate the high-pitched, half-whimper, half-warning throat-gargle-sounding-sound he made and then peal with laughter. But in retrospect all of that is irrelevant. The snake was gone, the path was clear, and they went on their merry way.

It would have been better if our first ancestors, Adam and Eve, had chosen a similar tactic all those years ago in Eden. Maybe they would have felt silly. Slowly backing away and stamping their feet may have appeared beneath their station as guardians of God's paradise, but they would have been better for it.

The first two chapters of Genesis paint a picture of a brand-new world created by God with humanity, male and female, bearing His image and ruling as earth's rightful overseers. God intended for humanity to govern the earth and have their own needs met by "every seed-bearing plant throughout the earth and all the fruit trees for your food" (Gen. 1:29, NLT). There was only one exception. God told the first man, Adam, and the first woman, Eve, "You may freely eat the fruit of every tree in the garden—except the tree of the knowledge of good and evil. If you eat its fruit, you are sure to die" (2:16–17, NLT).

The ensuing temptation centers on this command. God had given man everything in the garden except *one* tree, and that is the area where the temptation would come. In fact, this issue of temptation and choice is crucial for all of us. It is a theme that will reoccur throughout this book. It's important that we pause here and say a few things about the nature of sin and temptation. Why did God command Adam and Eve not to eat from a tree that He made available? Was He motivated by a sadistic curiosity to see whether they would fall for an arbitrary trap? Of course not. James tells us, "When tempted, no one should say, 'God is tempting me.' For God cannot be tempted by evil, nor does he tempt anyone" (Jas. 1:13). Still, on the surface of the Eden story, it might seem that God is setting Adam and Eve up to fail. After all, He puts them in a garden that seems perfect until we discover it comes with both a poisonous tree and a smooth-talking dragon.

FREE WILL

The way theologians have generally explained the presence of the tree of the knowledge of good and evil, as well as the fact that God seemed to allow *that old serpent* to tempt Adam and Eve, is with the concept of free will. This explanation is quite common. Yet for many the original question of God's arbitrariness persists. I think that is because the concept of free will as a philosophical and theological abstraction is one thing. But to apply these ideas to our actual, day-to-day lives seems less assuring.

Often people have desires and proclivities that by biblical standards they must not carry out. It's as if in the garden of their lives there is a tree they have been told is off limits. It just so happens to be the tree they want to partake of the most. Someone might ask, Why would God make me with certain desires and then tell me I can't fulfill them? It seems unfair, perhaps even a bit cruel. This is the dilemma I'm referring to. "Free will" is a solid theological answer in theory. But in the practice of everyday life it seems harder to swallow.

When a lion stalks a gazelle and tears it apart limb from limb, it may be horrifying to watch. But no one would say that the lion is evil. It is acting only in accordance with its nature. The lion is no more evil for eating a gazelle than a gazelle is for eating grass. Both are simply acting in accordance with their natures. In fact, when a lion kills the cub of another lion, even then we would attribute its actions to instinct and never describe them as evil. Killing comes naturally to a lion. He can't help it.

Likewise, how can something that comes natural to a human be condemned as evil? How can God expect us to deny our nature? What's more, if the Bible is true and God is real, then He is the One who created us. The way many people see it, God created us one way and then expects us to behave contrary to that very nature! This seems unfair.

The idea that our natural proclivity for certain behavior justifies that behavior belongs to the zeitgeist of the modern Western world. In other words, it belongs to the spirit of our age, the mood or value system that defines our times. Many people use it to defend their lifestyle choices or explain certain behaviors. For example, this is one of the main arguments used by homosexual activists. Their basic claim is that they were born with their sexual preferences. Therefore what they do is not only okay, but also they are virtuous for being authentic. This is why when someone comes out as gay or transgender, he or she is hailed as a hero. This is why Caitlyn Jenner, for example, won *Glamour* magazine's Woman of the Year award. It is considered laudable to "be true to yourself" against traditional conventions and norms. A recent article in *USA Today* says, "For decades, 'born this way' has been the rallying cry of the mainstream gay rights movement, a simple slogan cited as the basis for both political change and cultural acceptance."[1] Lady Gaga even wrote a song about it.

But this is not uniquely an LGBT issue at all. This is something every human being deals with. We are all born with certain proclivities and desires that are contrary to what we find in God's Word. For example, some scientists claim that heterosexual men seem biologically predisposed to want to seek out sexual relationships with multiple women. When you look at the statistics of the number of married men that have affairs at some point in their lives and add to that the number of men who have had multiple sexual partners either before marriage or through divorce and remarriage, it seems pretty clear that sexual promiscuity is a predisposition for humans. And yet the Bible's ideal is for one man and one woman to be married for life, with all sexual activity confined to that marriage relationship. Again, this all seems to be against our nature.

So that brings us back to the question. If God created us the way we are, how can He be displeased when we satisfy our natural proclivities the same way animals do? I understand the Christian response. God didn't create us with a sinful nature. That came as a result of the fall. But that still begs the question, Why did God create a world where sin is even a possible option? After all, Adam and Eve made the choice to disobey God before the fall.

Without launching into a prolonged thought experiment, I think it is reasonable to suggest that a world where people are free not to choose God and free to disobey Him is the best of all possible worlds. In such a world evil will exist, yes. But so will love, freedom, and true choice.

C. S. Lewis explains it like this:

God created things which had free will. That means creatures which can go either wrong or right. Some people think they can imagine a creature which was free but had no possibility of going wrong; I cannot. If a thing is free to be good it is also free to be bad. And free will is what has made evil possible. Why, then, did God give them free will? Because free will, though it makes evil possible, is also the only thing that makes possible any love or goodness or joy worth having. A world of automata—of creatures that worked like machines—would hardly be worth creating. The happiness which God designs for His higher creatures is the happiness of being freely, voluntarily united to Him and to each other in an ecstasy of love and delight compared with which the most rapturous love between a man and a woman on this earth is mere milk and water. And for that they must be free.[2]

One thing is clear from Scripture—this issue of free will is important to God. He created us with the ability to choose in general and the ability to choose Him specifically. This is important because God created us for Himself, to have a love relationship with Him. Without the ability to choose, a love relationship would not have been possible. If someone has to force himself on someone else in order to experience "love," then that isn't love at all. It is abuse, the main

Without the ability to choose, a love relationship would not have been possible.

mode of selfishness. God did not want a bunch of preprogrammed robots acting on computer code, nor did He want animals acting on instinct. Humankind was created with the ability to choose. But that ability must also come with the companion ability to reject God. Otherwise it could not be truly *free* will. If there are no consequences to wrong choices, then there is no free will. And if there is no free will, there is no genuine love.

So far everything I'm laying out is a standard freewill argument. Most of you will be familiar with this. But here is the part you may not have considered. Let's take it a step further. Free will is meaningful only in the presence of viable options. In other words, we often talk about the importance of freedom of choice, but we don't often talk about the value of that choice—the amount of meaningful worth that your freedom to choose entails.

For example, let's say I'm going to give you the choice between two options. You can either spend the day at a spa in Hawaii with all expenses paid, or I can stab you in the eye with a sharp stick. What kind of choice is that? Even though I might technically be giving you two options, there's really no choice, is there? No one in his right mind would pick the sharp stick in the eye over the vacation in Hawaii.

If God created human beings with the ability to choose but put them in a world where all of the variables were arranged toward only one viable option (Him), the ability to choose would be superfluous. There really would be no meaningful choice to be made. What's more, to choose God under those circumstances does not indicate true love—the very motive God desires in His human creation.

On the contrary, God allows us to remain in a fallen world where every condition has been stacked against Him. Yet He asks us to choose Him. That means a person who chooses God in this world has made a real and meaningful choice. When we choose God, our choice is meaningful for three important reasons.

1. He is not the most naturally visible choice.

The famous atheist Richard Dawkins was asked what he will say if he discovers upon death that there really is a God. His response was to quote Bertrand Russell who said he would ask God, "Sir, why did you take such pains to hide yourself?"[3] If it were true that God hides Himself, I might agree with Dawkins and Russell. If it were impossible to perceive God and there were no more evidence for His existence than for a flying spaghetti monster, it would be completely rational to reject the idea.

In reality, however, God has gone to great lengths to *reveal* Himself. He has revealed Himself throughout all of nature and creation. Paul says, "For since the creation of the world God's invisible qualities—his eternal power and divine nature—have been clearly seen, being understood from what has been made, so that people are without excuse" (Rom. 1:20). Not only has He put His fingerprint on all we see around us, but He has also put it on all we feel within us. He has "set eternity in the human heart" (Eccles. 3:11), giving us an inner awareness of the transcendent. We know we were made in His image.

But beyond the testimony of creation and the witness of our own conscience, God has revealed Himself through His Son. He came into the world and gave His life for ours. God's gift to us, the gift of His Son, is not merely a spiritual reality. Jesus came as flesh and blood into the real world. His life is a matter of historical record, and the evidence for the resurrection is overwhelming. One has to be resolved not to notice God to think He is hiding Himself.

God has revealed Himself in such a way that those who want to find Him can, and those who don't won't have to.

On the one hand, God has revealed Himself for those who are humble and seeking. But on the other hand, He has hidden Himself from the proud and hard-hearted. As the French mathematician and philosopher Blaise Pascal said, "[God] wished to render himself perfectly recognizable to those...who seek him with their whole heart, and hidden from those who shun him with all their heart...that he has given signs of himself which are visible to those who seek him and obscure to those who seek him not."[4]

Imagine if God suddenly appeared in the sky and His voice thundered throughout the earth, "I am God—worship Me." Everyone would probably choose to do so. But again, it wouldn't really be a choice, would it? God has revealed Himself in such a way that those who want to find Him can, and those who don't won't have to. Let me put it this way—if God were outwardly visible to the naked eye, choosing Him would not be meaningful. It would simply be the only option. Even those who don't love Him and don't want Him would still choose Him under the burden of a visible threat. But we who believe Him and choose Him—even when we don't see Him—have made a meaningful choice. As 1 Peter 1:8 says, "Though you have not seen him, you love him; and even though you do not see him now, you believe in him and are filled with an inexpressible and glorious joy."

2. He is not the most comfortable choice.

Scripture speaks of the broad road that leads to destruction (Matt. 7:13). It is full of people. But the narrow road leads to life. Few people travel by it. Why is the wide road to destruction so popular? Because it is wide—it is easy. Why is the narrow road so unpopular? Because it is narrow—it is hard. No one wants to walk a difficult road. If choosing God were the easiest, most comfortable, and most enjoyable option all the time, everyone would choose it. Yet that choice would be a selfish choice—indistinguishable from the self-serving desires through which sin comes.

3. He is not the most immediate choice.

The Lord says, "I have set before you life and death....Choose life" (Deut. 30:19). Why does God even need to say, "Choose life"? Life is obviously better than death. It seems to be one of those Hawaii-or-sharp-stick-in-the-eye options. But God knows that in our world the right choice will not always be the obvious choice. He says, "Choose life," because that choice is actually more demanding than it sounds on the surface. Very often the meaningful choice must be made between what feels good in the short term yet is destructive long term and what is painful in the short term yet rewarding in the long term. In other words, this choice is a choice between immediate or delayed gratification. And this should not be something entirely difficult to understand. Almost every meaningful choice in life must be made between what makes us feel good now and what will bring fulfillment and reward in the future.

Why then does God put us in a world where the choice is so difficult? Surely He could have arranged the world any way He wanted. Couldn't He have made it easier to choose Him? Why would he stack the deck against Himself?

I was watching a game show recently called *Deal or No Deal*. On the show the contestant is presented with a number of closed briefcases, each containing a certain amount of money. Most contain pretty small amounts. But some contain larger amounts, and one contains a huge jackpot. The contestant's goal is to get that jackpot. Why don't they put the jackpot in every briefcase and make it easier for him? Because, obviously, then the game would be meaningless.

If God is going to give us the ability to choose, then not only must the choice be meaningful, but the consequences and rewards must also be meaningful. To know God is the greatest treasure in the entire world. As God said to Abram, "I *am* thy shield, *and* thy exceeding great reward" (Gen. 15:1, KJV, emphasis added). It is only reasonable, then, that to gain Him, a meaningful choice must be made.

This is probably a natural place to mention the threat of hell and its place in this construct. Some might see the Christian ultimatum of heaven or hell as essentially the same as my Hawaii-or-sharp-stick-in-the-eye analogy. They would say God is not offering a real option at all. The best choice is too obvious. "Accept Christ or burn in hell" doesn't leave much room for nuance. And in one sense this is correct. The Christian gospel really is an ultimatum. There is no question which choice is better. However, because hell is a delayed consequence, many people will gladly risk it for an immediate reward—especially if they're not sure hell exists. The issues of heaven as reward and hell as punishment are similar to the issue of God's existence. We can deny them if we choose. God has arranged the world with these two realities hidden from the naked eye so our choice will be meaningful. In other words, God's arrangement has not overwhelmed our natural senses in a way that makes the choice automatic. The choice remains meaningful because the two options preserve our ability to choose.

In reality most people do not choose God simply because He is not the option that looks most attractive in the short term. They do not value the rewards of God's coming kingdom the way they value the rewards of this life. To choose Him requires sacrifice, self-denial, and delayed gratification in this world. But the renunciation of present fulfillment for eternal fulfillment simply does not appeal to most people.

THE NATURE OF EVIL

This thought inevitably leads to a consideration of the origin of evil itself. Earlier I quoted James 1:13, which says, "God cannot be tempted by evil, nor does he tempt anyone." But this raises the question: Why does evil exist in the first place? Perhaps choice and free will are good and necessary, but why can't our options be less extreme? Why can't we choose between good and less good or even two essentially good options? Why must it be good and evil, and why would God even create a world with evil to begin with?

A young man once told me that he had the argument that proved conclusively that Christianity was wrong. He said Christianity teaches that God created everything. Christianity also teaches that God is good. But if God created everything, then God also created evil. And if God created evil, then God cannot be good. This is one of those arguments that sounds good to a sixteen-year-old. As Francis Bacon said, "A little philosophy inclineth man's mind to atheism, but depth in philosophy bringeth men's minds about to religion."[5]

In fact, the Bible does not teach that God created everything with no exceptions. John says, "Without him nothing was made *that has been made*" (John 1:3, emphasis added). But many things were not made at all. For example, God did not create Himself. He is eternal and uncreated. If God is uncreated, so too are the various aspects of His essence. Love, for example, is uncreated, because "God is love" (1 John 4:8). Love is not merely something God has or gives but is an eternal aspect of His being. This brings to mind various other aspects of God's nature, such as joy, goodness, beauty, and

If you remove yourself from God's dominion, you will find that everything outside of it is contrary to His nature.

life. Such virtues are uncreated extensions of God Himself. By implication, then, even the essence of human life is uncreated. Yes, God formed Adam's body from the dust. But Adam's *life* was exhaled directly from God's nostrils. God extended His own living essence into humankind and continues to do so.

In the same way that love and life are uncreated, so evil and death must be uncreated. They are simply conditions opposed to God's nature. Indeed, evil and death are conditions brought about by the *absence* of God's love and life. Not only are they uncreated, but they are also entirely negative conditions. They are the results of subtraction or deficiency. You do not create darkness. You simply turn out light and darkness is automatic. You do not create cold. You simply eliminate heat and cold is inevitable. Likewise, evil is the absence of God's loving dominion. More specifically, for our purposes evil is the consequence of free will that chooses against God and is therefore devoid of His righteousness.

If you remove yourself from God's dominion, you will find that everything outside of it is contrary to His nature. If you remove yourself from God's light, you will be filled with darkness. If you remove yourself from God's life, you will be filled with death. If you remove yourself from God's love, you will be filled with fear. If you remove yourself from God's righteousness, you will be filled with evil. This, to me, is the most terrifying thing about hell. Often when people think about hell, they think about fire, torment, and eternal punishment. But hell is all of those things for one important reason. Hell is a place of separation from God. Hell is the absence of all that God is. That means there is no love, no joy, no light, no life, no peace, and no righteousness. There is no part of God's nature in hell. In fact, that is precisely what makes hell, hell.

This is why the choice we have is between two such extreme options. When we choose God and His will, it is good by definition. When we choose *anything* outside of Him, it is evil by definition. Just as darkness is all that remains when you turn off the light, evil is all that remains outside of God. There is simply no other alternative.

TEMPTATION

In light of these definitions of *free will* and *evil* we will now look at the nature of temptation. This is where our first parents fell, and the pattern still repeats itself today.

> The serpent was the shrewdest of all the wild animals the LORD God had made. One day he asked the woman, "Did God really say you must not eat the fruit from any of the trees in the garden?"
>
> "Of course we may eat fruit from the trees in the garden," the woman replied. "It's only the fruit from the tree in the middle of the garden that we are not allowed to eat. God said, 'You must not eat it or even touch it; if you do, you will die.'"
>
> "You won't die!" the serpent replied to the woman. "God

knows that your eyes will be opened as soon as you eat it, and you will be like God, knowing both good and evil."

The woman was convinced. She saw that the tree was beautiful and its fruit looked delicious, and she wanted the wisdom it would give her. So she took some of the fruit and ate it. Then she gave some to her husband, who was with her, and he ate it, too. At that moment their eyes were opened, and they suddenly felt shame at their nakedness. So they sewed fig leaves together to cover themselves.

—Genesis 3:1–7, nlt

Notice Satan's three-step technique:

1. Satan gets Eve to question God's words ("Did God really say…?").

2. Satan gets Eve to question God's truthfulness ("You won't die!").

3. Satan gets Eve to question God's motives ("God knows that your eyes will be opened as soon as you eat it, and you will be like God, knowing both good and evil").

These accusations against God's character planted seeds of doubt in Eve's mind. And this is exactly what the serpent does. In fact, his role is implied by his name, Satan. The original Hebrew phrase *the satan* can refer either to a human being or supernatural being that acts as an "adversary," "one who withstands," or one who "accuse[s]."[6] Over time the term became a proper name for the devil. Already, in this first encounter with the serpent in Genesis, we clearly see how he earned the title. The devil's strategy as revealed in this story is entirely one of deceptive accusation. He calls into question God's word and character.

This is the same strategy the enemy continues to use on people today. We will go into more depth on this in the next chapter. But even in this first encounter we can see how Satan operates and how we can defeat him when he tempts us.

Satan's first move was to get Eve to question what God actually said.

How did he do this? By distorting God's words when he posed his question to Eve. "Did God really say you must not eat the fruit from any of the trees in the garden?" (Gen. 3:1, NLT). That is absolutely not what God said. In fact, God said the complete opposite. God indeed showed extravagant generosity to Adam and Eve. He told them they could have *all* the trees and *all* the fruit—anything they wanted—except for the fruit of one tree. Satan's question was an implicit accusation. (Remember, he is the accuser.) He made God out to be a tyrant—a greedy miser who makes a paradise full of beautiful, tasty things, only to keep them all to Himself. "God doesn't want you to have fun. He doesn't want you to enjoy the garden. Your life here is one of rules and restrictions." And yet the truth was exactly the opposite.

Eve responded well at first, correcting the serpent's distortion. But his deception seems to have been effective enough in that Eve ended up introducing a little distortion of her own. She added an additional rule. "God said, 'You must not eat it or even touch it; if you do, you will die'" (Gen. 3:3, NLT). But again, this is not what God said. God did not tell them they could not touch the tree. This was Eve's additional regulation. And here we find the beginning of legalism. Religion often creates rules on top of rules. The Pharisees in Jesus' day were particularly skilled at this. Jesus said that through their traditions they had nullified the word of God (Mark 7:13).

Satan's second move was to get Eve to question God's truthfulness.

So maybe Eve knows what God said (or something close). But now Satan plants a seed of doubt in her mind about God's honesty: "You won't die!" (Gen. 3:4, NLT). In other words, "God is lying to you." Two voices now speak directly to Eve. One voice says, "You will die." The other voice says, "You won't die." They cannot both be right. Eve must choose which voice to agree with and heed. Will she choose to agree with the One who created her? Will she choose the words of the One whom she knew so well, with whom she walked in the cool of the day, and who had given her everything in her life to enjoy? Or will she agree with the words of a dragon whose authority was rooted in distortion and accusation? You might wonder why Eve would ever be susceptible to such a ruse. But as we are about to see, these accusations are part of a powerful strategy to poison Eve with a demonic thought pattern.

Finally, Satan accuses God of having selfish motives.

"God knows that your eyes will be opened as soon as you eat it, and you will be like God, knowing both good and evil" (Gen. 3:5, NLT). In other words, "God just wants to hold you down. He's trying to keep you from being all that you could be. He wants to keep something from you so you can't be like Him. God's motive is not your well-being but His own self-interest. He's threatened by your potential!" Not only was this an accusation against God's character, but it also came with an offer that Eve could not refuse: "you will be like God."

Satan had effectively projected his pattern of thinking onto Eve. Remember, Satan is the one who had been cast out of heaven for setting his eyes on the throne of God. He said, "I will make myself like the Most High" (Isa. 14:14). He wanted to be like God. Now he was passing on his twisted way of thinking to Eve—and she bought it.

You see, the fall of man was not just about one act of disobedience (although that act was the catalyst). In their fall Adam and Eve accepted the same satanic way of thinking that led to Satan's fall. I imagine he used a similar tactic on two-thirds of the angels in heaven that fell with him. Perhaps they didn't have a tree involved in their rebellion, but I'm sure the core issues were the same. They questioned God's word. They questioned God's truthfulness. And they questioned God's motives.

We see a vivid picture of this demonic thought pattern at work in Matthew 16. Jesus began to explain to His disciples that He was going to suffer and die and then be raised from the dead. This was the divine plan, but it was very different from what the disciples had envisioned. They thought Jesus would lead a political revolt to overthrow the Roman Empire and restore the kingdom to Israel in their lifetime. Now they were finding out that God's plan was quite different.

So "Peter took him aside and began to rebuke him. 'Never, Lord!' he said. 'This shall never happen to you!'" (Matt. 16:22). Peter thought he was doing the right thing. He was encouraging Jesus that such a terrible fate would never come to Him. But Jesus was not encouraged—He was indignant. "Get behind me, Satan! You are a stumbling block to me; you do not have in mind the concerns of God, but merely human concerns" (v. 23). We see some crucial points in this shocking exchange:

- Jesus calls Peter "Satan."
- Peter is not thinking as God thinks.
- Instead Peter is thinking as man thinks.

The inference from these points is clear: the way God thinks is contrary to the way man thinks. Man's way of thinking is, in fact, satanic. Satan has passed his way of thinking to man, and this is just where we return to the life cycle of sin that James describes.

> When tempted, no one should say, "God is tempting me." For God cannot be tempted by evil, nor does he tempt anyone; but each person is tempted when they are dragged away by their own evil desire and enticed. Then, after desire has conceived, it gives birth to sin; and sin, when it is full-grown, gives birth to death.
>
> —JAMES 1:13–15

The process that James describes looks like this:

Evil desires ➜ Temptation ➜ Sin ➜ Death

The process begins with evil desires. But where do these evil desires originate? In the garden Eve saw that the tree was beautiful and its fruit was delicious. Further, she wanted the wisdom the fruit would give her. These desires for beauty, delicious taste, and wisdom hardly seem evil in themselves. And of course they are not. Why would God make trees beautiful if not for man's enjoyment? Why would God make fruit delicious if not for man's pleasure? Why would God give man insatiable curiosity if He did not intend for it to be satisfied in a quest for wisdom? All these desires reflect God's good will toward humanity. However, once Satan effectively perverted Eve's way of thinking, her good desires also became twisted. She now looked for satisfaction in the one option contrary to God's word. The fruit she now desired was forbidden. The knowledge of good and evil was off limits, so she wanted it. Eve's desires, which otherwise would have been good, were now evil because they sought gratification outside of God's express command.

Eve's satanic way of thinking culminated when she decided that she and Adam could be like God. And it was acted out when she took the fruit and ate it. Disobedience to God's Word is essentially the elevation of our own will and desires over God's will and desires. We make ourselves god. No wonder such terrible consequences inevitably follow.

DEFENDING AGAINST TEMPTATION

With all of this in mind let's consider for a moment how we can defend ourselves against temptation and against this satanic way of thinking.

First, we must *know* God's Word.

We must know well what God has *actually* said. Otherwise the enemy will be able to make God say anything he wants. Satan will even try to convince us that God has said the complete opposite of what His Word really says. We know this because that is exactly what he tried to do with Eve. It is even more amazing that Satan had the nerve to use God's Word against Jesus Himself! In the wilderness Satan used the Scriptures to tempt Jesus. But Jesus could not be fooled because He knew God's Word, and He used it to combat Satan's temptations. If Jesus used the Scriptures in His spiritual warfare, I would say that sets a pretty solid precedent for us today.

If there is one thing every spiritual warrior needs, it is a love for the Scriptures. God's Word is called the sword of the Spirit for good reason. It is a powerful weapon against the enemy. Jesus Himself used it in the desert against His own temptations. The Word of God as the sword of the Spirit is the only offensive weapon Paul mentions among God's full armor (Eph. 6:14–17). It is no wonder that Satan is so interested in distorting and causing us to question God's Word right out of the gate. Without the Word we have been disarmed in our spiritual battle. Many intercessors and spiritual warriors spend time in prayer but little time in the Word. And while I realize there are different seasons, different gifts, and different callings upon people's lives, there is no way around this principle: if you go into a spiritual battle without the Word in your hand and your heart, you are basically an unarmed civilian in a war zone—a bad idea.

Second, we must not only know God's Word but also *believe* it.

Satan told Eve explicitly, "You will not surely die" (Gen. 3:4, NKJV). We can be sure of one thing: Satan will do everything in his power to cause us to doubt the truth of what God said. This principle is so vital to our spiritual warfare and survival that it must be emphasized. Satan's accusation that God's Word was not reliable, combined with his next accusation, led Eve to question God's character and opened her up to the satanic way of thinking that ushered in the fall.

Third, we must *trust* God's motives.

The message of an immensely popular worship song, "Good Good Father," is so simple and obvious. Why does the message that God is a good, good Father resonate with so many people? I believe it is because the enemy has targeted precisely this truth in the lives of so many people. He has tried to convince them that God is a selfish and cruel tyrant. The enemy has tried to get people to question whether God truly has their interests at heart. Beaten down by these lying accusations, when a child of God hears the simple words of timeless truth—that God is a good Father—the witness of the Holy Spirit on the inside leaps and shouts *yes!*

One of my favorite passages of Scripture says, "He who did not spare his own Son, but gave him up for us all—how will he not also, along with him, graciously give us all things?" (Rom. 8:32). In this verse Paul points to the cross as the ultimate evidence of God's love and goodwill toward us. This is something Eve did not have as a point of reference. But we who have experienced God's love through the cross are much better equipped. Paul is saying in effect, "When you see that wounded, mangled body hanging on a tree, just remember: God did that for you! If He would give you His only Son—the gift that cost God everything and bankrupted heaven—you can rest assured that He will give you anything else you need. If you ever question God's motives and His intentions toward you, just think about the cross. Forever the question has been answered."

Eve failed to trust that the motives behind God's commands were pure. And that failure left her vulnerable. Ephesians 6:16 tells us that faith is our shield. In Christianity faith is not simply belief, although belief is certainly a part of it. *Faith* is probably most simply defined as trust. Interestingly this is exactly what is missing

If you go into a spiritual battle without the Word in your hand and your heart, you are basically an unarmed civilian in a war zone—a bad idea.

in Eve's heart in this first temptation. It's bad enough that she doesn't fully *know* what God said. But it's even worse that she does not *trust* what He said. Therefore, without a shield the fiery darts of the enemy penetrate her naked soul without any resistance. Their poison penetrates her mind, and she becomes infected with the satanic way of thinking.

THE NAKED SNAKE

We don't know how long the first humans enjoyed the paradise of Eden. At some point they turned a proverbial corner and saw a serpent on the path. Without fanfare or explanation the narrator tells us, "The serpent was the shrewdest of all the wild animals the LORD God had made. One day he asked the woman, 'Did God really say you must not eat the fruit from any of the trees in the garden?'" (Gen. 3:1, NLT).

The Hebrew word translated as "shrewdest" is *'arum*. However, another Hebrew word with a similar spelling is translated as "naked" in Genesis 2:25.[7] The author uses wordplay here to connect these two different words that look and sound similar. The effect is powerful.

> Now the man and his wife were both naked [*'arummim* (plural of *'arum*)], but they felt no shame. The serpent was the shrewdest [most *'arum*] of all the wild animals the LORD God had made. One day he asked the woman, "Did God really say you must not eat the fruit from any of the trees in the garden?"
> —GENESIS 2:25–3:1, NLT

Adam and Eve were both naked but felt no shame. Similarly, using the wordplay, the snake was the "most naked" out of all the wild animals. The serpent's nakedness is distinct from Adam and Eve's in that it is compared to the wild animals. Just as today we may say that a clever person is "smooth," so too the author of Genesis connects the nakedness with intelligence. Wild animals are usually covered with fur, feathers, or thick hair. The snake, however, stands in contrast to the wild animals. Though wild animals are rough on the outside, they are innocent within. On the other hand, the snake's "surface speech is beguiling and flawless, hiding well his rough ulterior purposes."[8] In other words, he's smooth. He's "naked."

One of the saddest parts of the story of humanity's fall is how tame the whole scene is. Adam, standing with the love of his life, seems to stare blankly as the con proceeds. He doesn't even utter a bizarre, high-pitched, half-whimper, half-warning throat-gargle-sound like my friend in the story at the beginning of this chapter. The snake does not wield any amazing superpower. He offers no magic tricks or illuminating displays. He merely distorts God's word and calls into question His motives. As Dr. Ed Nelson writes,

> As far as the Torah shows, *ha-nachash* ["the serpent"] is virtually powerless in his rhetoric....His power, if it may be termed thus, is in his contradiction of God's word. He offers an alternative outlook to what God says, critical of God's knowledge as being selfish knowledge. He is utterly dependent on God's power, not his own, to reshape history and alter human destiny. God's commands, when broken, demand justice. "The serpent" forces the issue that God's judgment must occur for the humans. *Yahweh* must honor His spoken word to the man and the woman: "Dying, you shall die," He said. He is obligated to exercise His executive power under His promise of death to living if they ate of the banned fruit. He must be true to His word. The devil depended on it. It is his back-handed way of exerting power.[9]

The snake's scam worked. Adam and Eve chose self-elevation over love. When they took the fruit of the tree, they separated themselves not only from God's word to them but also from God Himself. The immediate result was "they suddenly felt shame in their nakedness. So they sewed fig leaves together to cover themselves" (Gen. 3:7, NLT).

Adam and Eve forfeited a shame-free life in exchange for pain, strife, toil, and death. But God still had mercy.

> The LORD God said, "Look, the human beings have become like us, knowing both good and evil. What if they reach out, take fruit from the tree of life, and eat it? Then they will live forever!" So the LORD God banished them from the Garden of Eden, and he sent Adam out to cultivate the ground from which he had been made. After sending them out, the LORD God stationed mighty cherubim to the east of the Garden of Eden. And he placed a flaming sword that flashed back and forth to guard the way to the tree of life.
> —GENESIS 3:22–24, NLT

Sin separated man from God. The intimacy and fellowship they shared were gone. Death entered, and paradise was lost. God sent them all out of the garden, each with his or her own curse. Finally, God positioned cherubim and a flaming sword in the way of the tree of life to guard it. God's concern: "What if they reach out, take fruit from the tree of life, and eat it? Then they will live forever."

The snake does not wield any amazing superpower. He offers no magic tricks or illuminating displays. He merely distorts God's word and calls into question His motives.

I always thought this final step—driving Adam and Eve out of the garden and then posting cherubim and a fiery sword to guard the way to the tree of life—was part of the punishment. I saw it as God's way of making sure they could never reverse the curse. But one day I realized this was perhaps one of the greatest displays of God's mercy. God knew that if Adam and Eve were to sneak back into the garden and eat of the fruit from the tree of life, they would make their separation from God permanent. The fruit of the tree of life could give them physical immortality, but it could not redeem them from their fallen state. Living forever in a permanent state of separation from God is not eternal life. In fact—as we discussed earlier—it is the very definition of *hell*!

That cherubim and blazing sword were protecting them. At the same time, I believe they were pointing away from that tree as if to say, "Don't come back here anymore. This tree cannot help you now. But don't worry—God will give you another tree." Thousands of years later God would give humanity another tree of life. It was not a beautiful tree with delicious fruit. It was a bloody tree where the twisted, mangled body of Jesus was crucified. But on that tree Jesus took the sin of Adam and Eve and of all their human children upon Himself at the same moment. He became sin for us that "we might become the righteousness of God" (2 Cor. 5:21).

But in the garden, for the moment, God clothed them. He covered their nakedness and shame as they waited, with all the earth, for the day the Redeemer would come. They had clothed themselves with fig leaves they had sewn together. But God rejected these inadequate garments—the work of their own hands (a picture of self-righteousness). He clothed them instead in animal skins—the ultimate sacrifice of an innocent substitute (a picture of Christ's sacrifice). The clothing itself was a picture of the redemption to come.

FROM A SNAKE TO A DRAGON

When we read the Genesis account of creation, we see God's handing the dominion of the earth realm to humankind (Gen. 1:27–29; 2:20). But later in the New Testament we discover that Satan is "the god of this world" (2 Cor. 4:4, ESV). How did this happen? We never read about God handing the authority over the world to Satan. There can be only one explanation. He got it from us! In one sense Adam and Eve gave it to him when they chose to yield to temptation and disobey God. In another sense the entire human race does this everyday as they continue to be deceived by that crafty serpent. Let me say it another way. Satan's only pathway to power is by deceiving us out of it. No wonder he has such an insatiable appetite for destroying humanity.

Satan leans on human agency not only out of preference but also out of necessity. Though he was already a fallen angel, in the garden he came under yet another curse that forever ties his fate to the fate of humanity.

> The LORD God said to the serpent, "Because you have done this, cursed are you more than all cattle, and more than every beast of the field; on your belly you will go, and dust you will eat all the days of your life; and I will put enmity between you and the woman, and between your seed and her seed; he shall bruise you on the head, and you shall bruise him on the heel."
> —GENESIS 3:14–15, NASB

This is the second time that dust is mentioned in Scripture. Earlier in Genesis we read, "The LORD God formed man of dust from the ground, and breathed into his nostrils the breath of life; and man became a living being" (Gen. 2:7, NASB). We can rest assured that the idea that man is made from dust was not lost on God when He cursed the serpent. "[The serpent] is commanded to live in the very substance from which man was made, in the elemental particles of creation. Figuratively, he shall eat this dry dust from which animals and man [were] formed by God. It is a sign of his fall and destined ruin to dwell in the ashes of animals and humanity."[10]

The accuser has been feeding on people—the dust—ever since. In one sense his survival is dependent on human casualties. He feeds on the rotting corpses of humanity, the casualties of his deception, the victims of the curse. The apostle Peter pulls on this image when he warns, "Stay alert! Watch out for your great enemy, the devil. He prowls around like a roaring lion, looking for someone to devour" (1 Pet. 5:8, NLT). Peter evidently had good cause to sound the alarm. Because of his constant, steady diet of dust the serpent has grown into what the apostle John described as "an enormous red dragon with seven heads and ten horns and seven crowns on its heads" (Rev. 12:3). Lest we should write off this extraordinary and terrifying image as a symbol for something else, John goes on.

> Then war broke out in heaven. Michael and his angels fought against the dragon, and the dragon and his angels fought back. But he was not strong enough, and they lost their place in heaven. The great dragon was hurled down—that ancient

serpent called the devil, or Satan, who leads the whole world
astray. He was hurled to the earth, and his angels with him.
—REVELATION 12:7–9

What a terrifying image—an enormous serpentine monster like
those depicted in myths the world over for millennia. It's a terror that
seems to lurk within the deepest recesses of the collective human
consciousness—and for good reason. It is humanity's great nemesis. A
prowler. A hunter. A predator.

But upon closer inspection we find a curious reality. The dragon has
no teeth—only a silver tongue. His power is not one of physical force
but of inner deception. If we don't yield to him, he has no strength.
What's more, Jesus Christ is the "last Adam" (1 Cor. 15:45) and succeeded where the first Adam failed. Through Christ, God has created
a new race of human beings—hybrids of sorts. They are made of the
dust as the first Adam was, but within them dwells the Spirit of God.
They are born and bred dragon slayers. The original Adam was a soft
target. His naked flesh was vulnerable and weak. He could have done
little more than stomp his feet on the ground and make half-whimper,
half-warning throat-gargle sounds. But these new humans are more
than a match for every serpent and scorpion in this world. They carry
weapons from another dimension. They are not naked but clothed with
invincible armor. The Bible describes them as children of the light who
pierce the darkness wherever they go (e.g., Matt. 5:14–16; John 12:36;
Eph. 5:8; 1 Thess. 5:5–8).

These are the champions for whom I write this book—the dragon
slayers!

QUESTIONS FOR DISCUSSION

- What modern-day pictures come to mind when you
  think of Satan, or the devil?

- How is the serpent described in Genesis? In Revelation?
  How do these images compare to modern images/char-
  acterizations of Satan, Lucifer, the devil, and evil?

- How is banishment from the Garden of Eden a demonstration of God's mercy?

- What are Satan's tools for holding power over humans? What do you imagine are God's tools given to humans for defeating the power of Satan?

- What is the satanic way of thinking? How do you see that played out in the world today? What about in your life?

- Why is God's gift of free will a good thing if there are truly evil options? How are Christians still challenged by such choices?

CHAPTER 3

HATH GOD SAID?

*God wants fit instruments for His power—wills surrendered,
hearts trusting, lives consistent, and lips obedient to His will;
and then He can use the weakest weapons, and make them
mighty through God to the pulling down of strongholds.*

—A. B. SIMPSON, *DAYS OF HEAVEN UPON EARTH*

*Doubt discovers difficulties which it never solves: it creates
hesitancy, despondency, despair. Its progress is the decay
of comfort, the death of peace. "Believe!" is the word which
speaks life into a man; but doubt nails down his coffin.*

—C. H. SPURGEON, *FAITH IN ALL ITS SPLENDOR*

HE CHINESE GENERAL Sun Tzu said in *The Art of War*, "If you know the enemy and know yourself, you need not fear the result of a hundred battles."[1] The apostle Paul, speaking to the Corinthians, exposed Satan's strategies "in order that Satan might not outwit us. For we are not unaware of his schemes" (2 Cor. 2:11). Knowing what your enemy is up to not only gives you a tactical advantage, but it also can be the difference between life and death. In this book we have been exposing Satan's strategy in the earth and showing how he can be defeated. In the last chapter we saw where the dragon gets his power. In short, he has no power except what we give him. He is a liar, a deceiver, and most importantly an accuser. He accuses God to us and accuses us before God. He has passed his twisted way of thinking to humanity, and through it he controls the fallen world. Understanding his strategy is crucial if we are going to battle it.

In this chapter we are going to examine more closely Satan's schemes and expose one of his most potent weapons against us. He used this weapon on Eve in the garden. Then he used it again on Jesus in the wilderness. I would argue that he uses this weapon on all of us, attempting to poison our minds with unbelief and impart his evil way of thinking. It is what often makes us susceptible to attack, and it's a technique he has used to destroy countless lives.

I recommend reading this chapter all in one sitting. This is not a collection of different thoughts; it is one cohesive revelation that can change your life.

A SNAKE IN THE GARDEN

In the third chapter of Genesis we read the story of the fall of Adam and Eve in the garden.

> Now the serpent was more subtil than any beast of the field which the LORD God had made. And he said unto the woman, Yea, hath God said, Ye shall not eat of every tree of the garden?
>
> And the woman said unto the serpent, We may eat of the fruit of the trees of the garden: But of the fruit of the tree which is in the midst of the garden, God hath said, Ye shall not eat of it, neither shall ye touch it, lest ye die.
>
> And the serpent said unto the woman, Ye shall not surely die: For God doth know that in the day ye eat thereof, then your eyes shall be opened, and ye shall be as gods, knowing good and evil.
>
> And when the woman saw that the tree was good for food, and that it was pleasant to the eyes, and a tree to be desired to make one wise, she took of the fruit thereof, and did eat, and gave also unto her husband with her; and he did eat.
>
> —GENESIS 3:1–6, KJV

This story is set in the pristine paradise of God's newly created Garden of Eden. Satan had been watching as God rolled up His sleeves and began creating a new world—a beautiful world. For the first few days it all seemed pointless. God was creating fish and birds and plants and trees, nothing of real consequence.

Suddenly God did something bizarre. Instead of simply speaking something into existence, He knelt down and scooped up a clump of dirt and began to fashion it and form it with His own hands into a creature after His own image. And then, amazingly, God bent down over the creature, put His mouth to its mouth, and began to breathe into it the breath of life, and man became a living soul.

Satan's blood pressure must have shot through the roof when he saw God taking His man on walks in the garden in the cool of the day. God was becoming personal and intimate with His protégé. Destiny was written all over man, and when God delegated to him dominion over the earth, Satan knew mankind would be his worst nightmare.

We are the gatekeepers to this world! Satan hates us because we are his archenemies and the ultimate threat to his plan for this world.

It's important to understand that Satan hates humanity because we are a direct threat to his plan and power. When God created mankind, He created us with a special status. He delegated to us authority and dominion over this planet. That was the purpose of Adam, and it has been passed down to us. We are the gatekeepers to this world! Satan hates us because we are his archenemies and the ultimate threat to his plan for this world. We will talk more about this in chapter 5.

Lurking behind the shrubs in the garden, Satan watched Adam and Eve and developed his strategy to bring them down and take the dominion God had given to them. One day Eve was strolling through the garden, and she decided to take a detour past the tree of the knowledge of good and evil. She knew that eating its fruit was forbidden, but perhaps the fact that it was off limits made the tree especially intriguing to her. She had no intention of eating the fruit, but it wouldn't hurt just to look, would it?

When Satan saw Eve walking toward the tree, spellbound by the forbidden fruit, he knew this was the opportunity he had been waiting for. The human race was young, innocent, and naive, and at this moment Eve was especially vulnerable. There might never be another occasion like this again. He needed to seize the opportunity.

Satan reached down into his big black bag of tricks and pulled out his most enticing lure. This would not be any old average temptation. In this most opportune of all moments Satan would unload the most potent weapon in his arsenal. The temptation may not be what you would think. In fact, it may seem downright juvenile, but therein lies the danger. Proverbs 1:17 says, "Surely in vain the net is spread in the sight of any bird" (KJV). The most treacherous traps of the enemy are the ones we do not immediately recognize as such. But because of God's Word "we are not ignorant of his devices" (2 Cor. 2:11, KJV). I pray that once you see this snare for what it is, you will never fall into it again, in Jesus' name.

Satan's secret weapon was a simple question of three words: "Hath God said?" It was these three words, a simple injection of unbelief into the heart of Eve, that brought about the fall of the human race. Every sin, every sickness, every broken heart, every destroyed life, every war, every genocide, every murder, every trace of hatred and suffering in the world can be traced back to that original temptation that began with these three words: Hath God said? And I submit to you that all temptation originates here. If you trace any transgression back to its origin, you eventually find this question, explicitly or implicitly, entertained in the mind of the transgressor: Hath God said?

- Eve entertained the question, "Hath God said?" She ate the forbidden fruit, and the entire human race was plunged into darkness. Her innocence was poisoned.

- Abraham entertained this question, and Ishmael was the result. Many generations of war, bloodshed, and hatred have been the consequence. His family's peace was poisoned.

- Moses entertained this question, struck the rock instead of speaking to it, and was unable to enter the Promised Land. His destiny was poisoned.

If you study the Scriptures, you will find that every time the enemy was able to win the victory over God's people, it can be traced back to this simple injection of unbelief: Hath God said?

It may surprise you to learn that Satan even tried this temptation on Jesus! We read in Matthew two stories that flow together: the accounts of Jesus' baptism and His temptation. In our modern Bibles these stories are separated by chapter demarcations. The story of the baptism is in chapter 3, and the story of the temptation is in chapter 4. But in the original text there were no chapter or verse distinctions, and these two stories were intended to flow together as one. When we separate them, we don't see the full significance of either. But when we put them together, a wonderful revelation emerges. We will begin with the baptism.

> Then Jesus came from Galilee to the Jordan to be baptized by John. But John tried to deter him, saying, "I need to be baptized by you, and do you come to me?"
>
> Jesus replied, "Let it be so now; it is proper for us to do this to fulfill all righteousness." Then John consented.
>
> As soon as Jesus was baptized, he went up out of the water. At that moment heaven was opened, and he saw the Spirit of God descending like a dove and lighting on him. And a voice from heaven said, "This is my Son, whom I love; with him I am well pleased."
>
> —MATTHEW 3:13–17

At this point in Jesus' life His earthly ministry had not yet started. He had not yet performed a miracle, and He had not been revealed as the Son of God. This experience would have been the highlight of Jesus' earthly life thus far. It was the beginning of a new season when His power and glory would be manifested to the world. I want you to take special notice of what the Father says to Him in those baptismal waters: "This is my Son, whom I love; with him I am well pleased." This is a very important statement because it is the issue at hand in the next chapter when Jesus is tempted by the devil. Immediately after Jesus' baptism experience it says, "Then Jesus was led by the Spirit into the desert to be tempted by the devil" (Matt. 4:1).

Often the mountaintops of spiritual experience are followed by valleys. Many times great revelation is followed by great temptation. It was so in the life of Jesus, and it happens in our lives as well. But notice this was part of God's plan. The verse doesn't say Jesus was led by the devil into the wilderness. It says He was led by the Spirit into the wilderness to be tempted by the devil.

> After fasting forty days and forty nights, he was hungry. The tempter came to him and said, "If you are the Son of God, tell these stones to become bread."
>
> —MATTHEW 4:2–3

In the past I thought the devil was tempting Jesus to break His fast. If you have ever been on an extended fast, you know how strong the temptation to give in to the desire to eat can be. But this particular temptation had nothing to do with eating. In fact, the Scripture clearly says the temptation took place after the fast. The attack being leveled against the Son of God was far more significant than the temptation to break a fast. As we look closer, you will notice a surprising parallel between the temptation of Jesus and the temptation of Adam and Eve in the Garden of Eden.

Jesus has been called the second Adam, and we see many scriptural parallels between the life of Jesus and the life of Adam. What Adam got wrong, Jesus made right. Where Adam failed, Jesus succeeded. The fall of Adam passed curses down to his posterity, but the blood of Jesus was the seed of a new race that inherits blessings, salvation, and freedom from the curse! We find that as Satan tempted the first Adam and Eve in the garden, so he tempted Jesus.

Many times great revelation is followed by great temptation. It was so in the life of Jesus, and it happens in our lives as well.

If Satan saw the first Adam as a threat, Jesus was a million times more dangerous because Jesus was God and man—Satan's two nightmares combined! As a mortal, Jesus had the delegated authority over the physical realm, and as divine, in Him dwelt the fullness of the Godhead bodily!

But there was another side to the story. Never before in history had God made Himself so vulnerable. For the ageless eons of eternity the immortal, invisible, omnipotent, almighty God sat enthroned in absolute power and utter invincibility, surrounded by hosts of mighty angels. Satan was one of God's beautiful and powerful angels. He saw this glory firsthand and knew he had no chance of inflicting the slightest injury on Him. In fact, when the thought of mutiny entered Satan's mind, the omniscient God ejected him out of heaven with such force that he fell to the earth like lightning (Luke 10:18)!

But now God had condescended from the lofty throne of heaven to the lowest place on earth. He had clothed Himself with the weakness and vulnerability of human flesh. Satan watched Jesus as He walked the earth, and Satan waited for a golden opportunity like the one he found with Eve in the Garden of Eden. Now Jesus had gone into the wilderness and fasted for forty days. He was weary, He was tired, He was hungry, and He was weak and more vulnerable in that moment than He had ever been before. When Jesus was at His weakest, Satan recognized this as his golden opportunity. This was the moment he had been waiting for since the day pride arose in his heart, and he said, "I will ascend to the heavens; I will raise my throne above the stars of God; I will sit enthroned on the mount of assembly, on the utmost heights of Mount Zaphon. I will ascend above the tops of the clouds; I will make myself like the Most High" (Isa. 14:13–14). "Finally," he said to himself, "victory is within my grasp."

As he did in the Garden of Eden, Satan reached down into his big black bag of tricks and pulled out his most enticing lure. This would not be any old average temptation. In this most opportune of all moments, Satan would unload the most potent weapon in his arsenal—the same one he used on Eve as she stood before the forbidden fruit, the same weapon he had used successfully on humanity for thousands of years, his single most powerful and effective weapon.

I want you to remember that Jesus had just been baptized in the Jordan River, and do you remember what the Father said to Him? "This is my Son, whom I love; with him I am well pleased." Now Satan approaches Jesus, and the first seven words out of his mouth are these: "If you are the Son of God..."

Do you see it? It is essentially the same injection of unbelief Satan used on Eve in the Garden: Hath God said? Satan was saying, "Are You sure You're the Son of God? Let's see some proof. Do something supernatural. Do something miraculous." Looking around in the wilderness, rocks were in great abundance, while nourishment was scarce. Satan pointed to one of the rocks lying on the ground and told Jesus to perform a miracle and turn the stone into bread (Matt. 4:3). Satan was saying, "Let's see if You really are who God says You are."

We read about the first miracle Jesus performed at a wedding in Cana of Galilee a few days after this temptation. Interestingly the miracle bears a curious resemblance to this first temptation. At the wedding feast Jesus didn't transform stones into bread, but He transformed something else—water—into wine. And the Gospel of John tells us this miracle caused His disciples to believe He was the Messiah (John 2:11).

You know, many times our faith is anchored in the wrong foundation. For the disciples, at least initially, their faith in Jesus was anchored in His miracles. They believed He was the Messiah because He turned water into wine, multiplied the fish and the loaves, healed the sick, and raised the dead. Their faith was anchored in what they could see with their eyes. But if the foundation of your faith is sight, then your faith can be shaken by what you see. When Jesus was arrested and crucified, the faith of the disciples wavered—because it was based on what they could see rather than on God's Word!

The disciples needed the confirmation of a miracle to believe in Jesus. But for Jesus this miracle was not required to believe what His Father had spoken. Jesus replied to this first temptation by saying, "It is written: 'Man shall not live on bread alone, but on every word that comes from the mouth of God'" (Matt. 4:4). In other words, Jesus said, "Devil, I do not need a miracle to prove I am the Son of God. The only evidence I need is the fact that My Father has spoken. My faith is anchored not in miracles but on the Word that comes from the mouth of God. He said it, I believe it, and that settles it!"

The second temptation was like the first.

> Then the devil took him to the holy city and had him stand on the highest point of the temple. "If you are the Son of God," he said, "throw yourself down. For it is written: 'He will command his angels concerning you, and they will lift

you up in their hands, so that you will not strike your foot against a stone.'"

—MATTHEW 4:5–6

I used to think this temptation was a prohibition against extreme sports. As a little boy when doing something risky or dangerous, I would often hear the adults say, "Don't tempt the Lord." When someone was going skydiving or bungee jumping, we said they were "tempting the Lord" because we thought this is what the devil was tempting Jesus to do—BASE jump from the pinnacle of the temple, right?

Actually, this temptation had nothing to do with extreme sports, so feel free to go skydiving or bungee jumping if you're crazy enough! That is not "tempting the Lord." In reality, the temptation here was once again centered on those seven words of unbelief: "If you are the Son of God..." Here it is again: the age-old injection of unbelief from the mouth of Satan, the same temptation he used on Eve in the Garden: Hath God said?

The essence of this temptation was once again to doubt God's Word, but this time it was presented in a slightly different way. "If You are the Son of God," Satan said, "prove it. Throw Yourself down from this pinnacle of the temple, and put God's promise to the test." Jesus' reply was amazingly simple but utterly profound: "It is also written: 'Do not put the Lord your God to the test'" (Matt. 4:7).

Whenever you see the phrase "It is written," it means the following quote is a reference to the Old Testament. If we want to understand the full meaning of what Jesus was trying to say, we need to go and see where it was written.

If the foundation of your faith is sight, then your faith can be shaken by what you see.

We find the verse Jesus was referencing in Deuteronomy 6:16: "Do not put the LORD your God to the test as you did at Massah." This verse clearly refers to an event in Massah that took place while the children of Israel were wandering in the wilderness. The Lord had delivered them from Egypt with a mighty hand and an outstretched arm. He parted the

Red Sea for them and caused them to walk across on dry land. He led them with a pillar of fire by night and a pillar of cloud by day. He provided manna for them to eat. He caused the clothes on their backs not to wear out.

He delivered them from hostile neighboring nations and met their every need year after year. Then one day they encountered a challenge. In this place called Massah, the children of Israel ran out of water and began to grumble and complain to Moses. They allowed unbelief into their hearts and even began to accuse Moses of trying to kill them.

> And the people thirsted there for water; and the people mur-
> mured against Moses, and said, Wherefore is this that thou
> hast brought us up out of Egypt, to kill us and our children
> and our cattle with thirst?
> —Exodus 17:3, kjv

After all God had done for them, after all the miraculous provision and all the undeserved faithfulness, at the first sign of trouble they immediately began to doubt and even accuse God of setting them up to die of thirst. But notice what it says a few verses later. This is where this story links to the temptation of Jesus.

> And he called the name of the place Massah, and Meribah,
> because of the chiding of the children of Israel, and because
> they tempted the LORD, saying, Is the LORD among us, or not?
> —Exodus 17:7, kjv

When Jesus said, "It is also written: 'Do not put the Lord your God to the test,'" He was saying, "Devil, I am not going to tempt the Lord like the children of Israel tempted Him in Massah. God doesn't need to prove to Me that He has good intentions for Me. I trust Him completely, and I believe He is faithful. I believe He is good. He has never failed Me yet, and I believe His Word is true, not because He passes My test, but because He said it, I believe it, and that settles it!"

My friend, Jesus was demonstrating what true faith looks like. This faith is unadulterated, uncontaminated, and unpoisoned by any hint of unbelief. Faith is absolute, unconditional trust. True faith trusts God no matter what is being experienced in the natural realm. True faith does not say, "I will trust You as long as You're doing things the way I want them to be done." True faith says like Job, "Though he slay me, yet will I trust in him" (Job 13:15, KJV).

The third and final temptation is the only one in which Satan does not explicitly use the words "If You are the Son of God." But as you will soon see, the temptation is the same as the other two.

> Again, the devil took him to a very high mountain and showed him all the kingdoms of the world and their splendor. "All this I will give you," he said, "if you will bow down and worship me."
> —MATTHEW 4:8–9

I always wondered what made the devil think he had any chance of getting Jesus to bow down and worship him. Why would he even waste his time with such a foolish temptation? But there is much more going on here than meets the eye, and to understand this temptation, we have to once again go to the Old Testament, this time to the Book of Psalms.

Psalm 2 is considered a Messianic psalm because it contains references to Jesus, the Messiah. In fact, in Hebrews 1:5 we have definitive New Testament corroboration that the following passage is indeed referring to Jesus. In Psalm 2:7 God the Father says to Jesus the Son, "Thou art my Son; this day have I begotten thee" (KJV).

Does this sound familiar to you? Does it remind you of the words the Father spoke to Jesus in the baptismal waters of the Jordan River? Now look at the next verse. The Father continues by saying, "Ask of me, and I shall give thee the heathen for thine inheritance, and the uttermost parts of the earth for thy possession" (v. 8, KJV).

Essentially the Father is saying to Jesus, "You are My Son, and as My Son You are going to receive an inheritance—the nations, the kingdoms of the world, the heathen, and the uttermost parts of the earth. I'm going to give them to You."

Now Satan comes to Jesus in the wilderness and essentially says, "Jesus, I know what God said to You in the Jordan River. He said You are His Son. But don't forget, Jesus, He said the same thing in Psalm 2:7. And when He said You were His Son through that prophetic psalm, with the same breath He said He would give You the nations.

But look, Jesus, instead of giving those kingdoms to You, He gave them to me!" (Second Corinthians 4:4 identifies Satan as the "god of this world" [ESV].) "Now," Satan was saying, "if God didn't keep His promise then, how can You believe Him now? How can You be sure You really are who He says You are?"

Do you see it? Discreetly tucked into these sinister words, there is the same temptation, "If You are the Son of God…" Satan's words contain the same injection of unbelief he used on Eve in the Garden: Hath God said? With this temptation Satan moved in for the kill. "Jesus," he said, "it seems God can't be trusted. It seems He has not been totally honest with You. I'll tell You what—let's make a deal. You bow down and worship me, and I will give You the nations."

True faith trusts God no matter what is being experienced in the natural realm.

I want you to attempt to put yourself in Jesus' shoes as He stood there in the wilderness, tired, hungry, weak, and lonely. He had endured forty days without food, the scorching heat of the desert sun, and now the most insidious temptations the devil could throw at Him. He was as much a human as you are. He had emotions. He felt pain and frustration. But I want you to notice what Jesus did in this moment. He didn't go into an eschatological Bible study with the devil, explaining how God's promise would ultimately be fulfilled. In fact, in that moment, having limited Himself as a finite being, perhaps He did not even know those details. But look how He responded.

> Jesus said to him, "Away from me, Satan! For it is written: 'Worship the Lord your God, and serve him only.'"
> —MATTHEW 4:10

What should you do when you are at your lowest, when you don't understand, and when nothing seems to make any sense? Do you begin to question God, doubting His plan and His Word? My friend, follow the example of Jesus. Turn your back to the devil, turn your eyes toward heaven, and begin to worship!

WHOM ARE YOU IN AGREEMENT WITH?

It's worth mentioning the circumstances through which all I have just mentioned became real to me. I am the successor to a famous evangelist by the name of Reinhard Bonnke. His ministry has been one of the most powerful and fruitful ministries in history. He founded the ministry of Christ for all Nations, which I lead today. As of this writing, our ministry has seen over seventy-eight million people come to Christ since 1987. I am talking about documented conversions, not estimations. When I became the president and CEO of this ministry, I was just twenty-eight years old. We had ten offices on five continents, were conducting multiple massive crusades each year, each costing almost one million dollars. Budgets, boards, crusades, conferences, fund-raising, and more were suddenly my responsibility. I was out of my depth. I knew it, and everyone else knew it too.

I often took courage in the fact that I had not asked for this assignment. I had never manipulated anything to make it happen. I don't have time to tell the whole story here, but I was sure God had called me to this task. There had been supernatural confirmations along the way, and I knew God's hand was on me. This was a great comfort. When faced with issues beyond my depth, I would often say, "Well, Lord, You put me here. This is Your idea, so I'm sure You'll give me the grace to make it through." Time and time again I was astounded by the way He would give wisdom and guidance just when I needed it.

One man who was close to me in those days was less than encouraging. He was my friend, but he wanted to make sure that I kept my head out of the clouds. He would often say to me, "You know this can't work, right?" He would describe to me the impossibility of the situation. How could an inexperienced, twenty-eight-year-old guy like me fill the shoes of a legend like Reinhard Bonnke? "It's OK," my friend would assure me. "It will never work, but at least you'll get some good experience." In the beginning I didn't appreciate his negativity. But over time I realized that he was just trying to prepare me for inevitable disappointment. I saw his good motives and didn't take what he was saying personally. Then over time I found myself agreeing with him and even repeating his words. "It will never work, but at least I'll get some good experience." I had completely internalized those words in my heart.

One day as we discussed things over dinner, he once again explained to me why it could never work, and I agreed with him. Afterward I went back to my hotel room, and suddenly the Lord spoke. "Don't *ever* question My word again," He said. It was a rebuke, but it did not crush me. Instead it carried with it a power and a grace that set my bones on fire. In one instant that entire revelation on the temptation of Christ in the wilderness—how it all tied into the words of the Father in the Jordan, how it connected to Satan's temptation in the garden—dropped into my spirit like an instantaneous download. I was overwhelmed. I repented. I said, "I'm sorry, Lord. From now on I will choose to agree only with Your word." A few days later that man was removed from my life. I realized that even though he was a good Christian person, he was being used by the enemy to plant seeds of unbelief in my heart that would have destroyed me had I not been intercepted by the Lord's rebuke.

This reminds me of the story of Peter we discussed in the last chapter. In Matthew 16 Jesus asked His disciples, "Who do people say the Son of Man is?" He then asked His disciples, "Who do you say I am?" (vv. 13, 15).

It was Peter alone who had the revelation: "You are the Messiah, the Son of the living God" (v. 16).

"Blessed are you, Simon son of Jonah," Jesus said, "for this was not revealed to you by flesh and blood, but by my Father in heaven" (v. 17).

Later in that same chapter Jesus explained to His disciples that He was going to be killed and raised to life. When Peter heard this, he took Jesus aside and said, "Never, Lord!...This shall never happen to you!" (v. 22).

Then Jesus rebuked him, saying, "Get behind me, Satan! You are a hindrance to me. For you are not setting your mind on the things of God, but on the things of man" (v. 23, esv).

Jesus called Peter, one of His closest disciples and friends, "Satan" and proceeded to tell Peter he was being used as a stumbling block. Yes, even sincere friends—and Christian ones at that—can be used by Satan to bring thoughts into your mind that exalt themselves against the knowledge of God!

But there's more. You see, Jesus says something we ought to pay careful attention to here. I have already mentioned this, but I reiterate it here for the sake of emphasis. This issue will come up again and again throughout this book. After calling Peter "Satan," He says, "For you are not setting your mind on the things of God, but on the things of man." Do you realize that the way man thinks is demonic in nature? The carnal mind is set against God because it is satanically inspired.

We must be diligent to guard our minds and our souls, keeping them aligned with God's Word and resisting the earthly, sensual, demonic way of thinking that governs this world.

IT IS WRITTEN

At this point it's important for me to emphasize something about this story. Jesus never responded to the devil's temptations by telling him what He had experienced in the Jordan River. You know, when you are on the spiritual mountaintop and you hear God's voice clearly, it is a thrilling experience. But when you come down to the valley, it is easy to begin to question what you experienced on the mountaintop.

When you are in a powerful church service on Sunday, the preacher is preaching, and the worship band is playing, you feel the anointing and you hear God speaking. But on Monday when the enemy begins to attack you at your job or in your family, he will try to make you question your Sunday morning experience. And if you allow your faith to be rooted in your experience, Satan will easily sift you like wheat. But the good news is that God has given us a solid rock for our faith that cannot be shaken—it is the written Word of God! When Jesus responded to the devil, every time He said, "It is written..."

THE SWORD OF THE SPIRIT

The devil hates God's Word because it is a two-edged weapon of warfare that can cut him to ribbons! It is unmovable and unchangeable. It is a solid foundation for your faith and an anchor for your soul. You can trust it, you can stand on it, and you can believe it with your whole heart because God honors His Word! No matter what you are experiencing in the natural, agree with the Word and confess it over your health, your finances, your family, your business, your ministry, and every area of your life!

> IT IS WRITTEN: "And my God will meet all your needs according to the riches of his glory in Christ Jesus" (Phil. 4:19).

> IT IS WRITTEN: "He will call on me, and I will answer him" (Ps. 91:15).

> IT IS WRITTEN: "The one who sows righteousness reaps a sure reward" (Prov. 11:18).

> IT IS WRITTEN: "If that is how God clothes the grass of the field, which is here today and tomorrow is thrown into the fire, will he not much more clothe you—you of little faith?" (Matt. 6:30).

> IT IS WRITTEN: "I have given you authority to trample on snakes and scorpions and to overcome all the power of the enemy; nothing will harm you" (Luke 10:19).

> IT IS WRITTEN: "No harm will overtake you, no disaster will come near your tent" (Ps. 91:10).

> IT IS WRITTEN: "The righteous person may have many troubles, but the LORD delivers him from them all" (Ps. 34:19).

> IT IS WRITTEN: "And the prayer offered in faith will make the sick person well; the Lord will raise them up" (Jas. 5:15).

> IT IS WRITTEN: "Cast your cares on the LORD, and he will sustain you; he will never let the righteous be shaken" (Ps. 55:22).

> IT IS WRITTEN: "The angel of the LORD encamps around those who fear him, and he delivers them" (Ps. 34:7).

> IT IS WRITTEN: "Commit your way to the LORD; trust in him and he will do this" (Ps. 37:5).

IT IS WRITTEN: "He settles the childless woman in her home as a happy mother of children" (Ps. 113:9).

IT IS WRITTEN: "His mercy endures forever" (Ps. 136:1, NKJV).

IT IS WRITTEN: "We are hard pressed on every side, but not crushed; perplexed, but not in despair; persecuted, but not abandoned; struck down, but not destroyed" (2 Cor. 4:8–9).

QUESTIONS FOR DISCUSSION

- Have you experienced the temptation to question something God has promised you?

- How was the temptation of Jesus in the wilderness similar to the temptation of Adam and Eve in the garden?

- Why do you think unbelief is so dangerous?

- How can we transform our minds to align with God's Word more?

CHAPTER 4

THE ZEITGEIST

An invasion of armies can be resisted; an invasion of ideas cannot be resisted.

—VICTOR HUGO, *THE HISTORY OF A CRIME*

The cross stands high above the opinions of men and to that cross all opinions must come at last for judgment.

—A. W. TOZER, *THE RADICAL CROSS*

ZEITGEIST IS A German word that literally means time spirit. It refers to the spirit of the times, or the spirit of the age. In other words, it is the attitude or mood of a culture during a particular time period that gives rise to its unique values and beliefs. We all understand the idea on a gut level, even if we never actually articulate it. We seem to know instinctively that many trends typify the passions or angst of certain eras in certain places. For example, the countercultural zeitgeist of the 1960s was expressed through distinct styles of music, literature, religious experience, antiauthoritarianism, and drug experimentation.

When cultural eras shift in the world, it can feel as if an invisible hand is pushing things along. This is both figuratively and literally the spirit of the age. People of wisdom have always sensed it. But today it is impossible to be denied, even by the most oblivious. The world is changing so quickly now that each new generation seems to have its own distinct culture, almost foreign to the previous generation. Ideas battle one another on multiple fronts, sometimes contending just below the surface of our collective consciousness. We see them in movies, music, and other works of art. We hear the conflicting opinions of preachers, politicians, pundits, athletes, actors, and artists. Soon public opinion begins to shift, laws are written, and society seems to embrace one set of ideas and reject another.

Things once considered taboo are now *en vogue*. How does this happen? How do entire countries become communist or fascist? How do homosexuality and transgenderism go from being socially unacceptable to fashionable in just a few short years? How do you explain the many radical shifts in culture, especially in the West, that have taken place over the last few hundred years, such as the Renaissance, the Reformation, the Scientific Revolution, and the Enlightenment? It seems we are living in an epoch of revolutions! How do you account for philosophies that originate in some classroom among stuffy intellectuals but soon become guiding principles in society, finding their ways into the language and thinking of ordinary people with no idea where their ideas come from? Working-class people unwittingly regurgitate ideas of postmodernism, Marxism, and relativism. Children's stories reflect the ideas of Freud, Maslow, Kant, Jung, and Piaget. All of it seems to work together in some strange way, as if orchestrated by a cosmic marketing company that has been working over many centuries, shaping the minds of men into what they are.

Merriam-Webster has this to say about the word *zeitgeist*: "Scholars have long maintained that each era has a unique spirit, a nature or climate that sets it apart from all other epochs. In German, such a spirit is known as 'Zeitgeist,' from the German words *Zeit*, meaning 'time,' and *Geist*, meaning 'spirit' or 'ghost.' Some writers and artists assert that the true zeitgeist of an era cannot be known until it is over, and several have declared that only artists or philosophers can adequately explain it. We don't know if that's true, but we do know

From the biblical perspective the zeitgeist is not an abstraction. Literal spirits—powerful, demonic spirits—are actively pushing an agenda from their high places.

that 'zeitgeist' has been a useful addition to the English language since at least 1835."[1]

Obviously it would be impossible to paint any epoch in history with one broad stroke. Surely a more nuanced and high-resolution analysis would show many different zeitgeists in many different locations. For example, the zeitgeist in Germany in World War II must have been different than that in Russia, the United Kingdom, and the United States. The zeitgeist in one era and in one place might be better or worse than that of another time and location. Yet there is an interesting way in which the zeitgeist of each era most often seems to find itself in opposition to the Christian worldview. There is a consistent theme of antipathy for Christ and all that He stands for. This hatred is both implicit and explicit. This is what John meant when he talked about "the spirit of the antichrist, which…is already in the world" (1 John 4:3).

This is also what Paul was talking about when he said, "For we do not wrestle against flesh and blood, but against principalities, against powers, against the rulers of the darkness of this age, against spiritual hosts of wickedness in the heavenly places" (Eph. 6:12, NKJV). In other words, from the biblical perspective the zeitgeist is not an abstraction. Literal spirits—powerful, demonic spirits—are actively pushing an agenda from their high places.

We often think of spiritual warfare as a personal issue. And that's true. Spiritual attacks come against individuals on a personal level. We must be on the alert. But it is crucial for us to understand that at its heart the demonic agenda is not merely about making individual Christians miserable. The demonic agenda does not exist to make your car break down or give you a bad day at work. Satan and his angels constitute that age-old mass-marketing company that works through every means available to influence the minds of human beings. They want to impose the demonic way of thinking on humanity, as we discussed in the last two chapters. This is what the real war is about.

This issue of the zeitgeist goes all the way back to the Garden of Eden. When the serpent tempted Eve, he successfully transmitted his way of thinking to her. That demonic thought pattern is what has become natural for humans ever since the fall. Today the collective human consciousness—the global zeitgeist, the spirit of the age—is still under the enchantment of that demonic spell. In fact, John makes a quite obvious allusion to the temptation in the garden when he says, "For all that is in the world, the lust of the flesh, and the lust of the eyes, and the pride of life, is not of the Father, but is of the world" (1 John 2:16, KJV). Remember, Genesis 3:6 says Eve "saw that the fruit of the tree was good for food" (the lust of the flesh). It was "pleasing to the eye" (lust of the eyes). And it was "also desirable for gaining wisdom" (the pride of life). According to John, this way of thinking that Eve adopted from Satan is now "all that is in the world." This pattern of thinking, which is "of the world," directly contradicts what is "of the Father."

Today Satan holds the whole world under his dominion through enslaved minds. "The god of this world has blinded the minds of the unbelieving" (2 Cor. 4:4, NASB). But this way of thinking does not seem obviously demonic on the surface. In fact, it feels quite natural. Yet as we have already seen from what Jesus said to Peter,

If you aren't being persecuted, perhaps you are so in line with the spirit of the age that you are no threat to it.

Satan has passed his way of thinking on to humans (Matt. 16:23). Today the natural, carnal way of thinking is actually demonic. As Paul said, "The carnal mind is enmity against God; for it is not subject to the law of God, nor indeed can be" (Rom. 8:7, NKJV).

The spirit of antichrist sets itself against Christ. Everything Jesus taught and represented is its enemy. And this is how Christians end up in the cross fire. As we have already discussed, the great dragon has no teeth. He has only a silver tongue. His weapon is deception. He works through the minds of men to influence the world. Those of us with the mind of Christ are set in opposition to that demonic movement. This is the reason the enemy targets us.

Jesus said, "If the world hates you, you know that it hated Me before it hated you" (John 15:18, NKJV). The world hates us for the same reason it hated Jesus. His life was in direct contradiction to the spirit of the age, and He had the power to conquer the spirit of the age. When we have His mind and live like Him, we become the enemy of the antichrist zeitgeist. This is why Paul said, "Everyone who wants to live a godly life in Christ Jesus will be persecuted" (2 Tim. 3:12). If you aren't being persecuted, perhaps you are so in line with the spirit of the age that you are no threat to it.

Jesus embodied God's way of thinking in the world. He was the Word become flesh (John 1:14). His whole life was an assault on the demonic spirit of the age. This had never happened before with such intensity and thoroughness. Yes, God had given the Law to Moses. But it was an incomplete revelation—a tutor until Christ came in the fullness of time (Gal. 3:24–25; 4:1–5). After the epoch of Moses, "grace and truth came through Jesus Christ" (John 1:17). Jesus said of Himself, "I am the light of the world. Whoever follows me will never walk in darkness, but will have the light of life" (John 8:12). Before Him and without Him, there is no light—the whole world walks in the darkness of demonic shadows. But when Jesus came, there was suddenly a light in the darkness. Think about how powerful the influence of Jesus Christ has been. A man who died at thirty-three years of age has more than two billion followers two thousand years later! His teachings and the story of His life are known and loved by billions. Amidst the backdrop of darkness that is the horror show of human history, there is one man whose life shines out in stark contrast like a diamond among coals. No wonder John says that His "life was the light of men" (John 1:4, KJV).

The evangelist Billy Sunday said:

> When the bright cloud hid Him from the gaze of those who loved Him with a devotion that took them to martyrdom, the only record of His sayings was graven upon their hearts, but now libraries are devoted to the consideration of them. No words were ever so weighty or so weighed as those of Him who was so poor that He had not where to lay His head. The scholarship of the world has sat at His feet with bared head, and has been compelled to say again and again, 'Never man spake as He spake.' His utterances have been translated into every known tongue, and have carried healing on their wings wherever they have gone. No other book has ever had a tithe of the circulation of that which contains His words, and not only that, but His thoughts and the story of His life are so

interwoven in all literature that if a man should never read a
line in the Bible, and yet be a reader at all he could not remain
ignorant of the Christ.[2]

Jesus directly and powerfully influenced the zeitgeist of the world
not only in His own day but also ever since. Consider how remarkable this is. No other man has ever had such influence. But the fascinating thing is not just that Jesus was so influential. What is even
more remarkable is the improbability that such ideas would prevail
in the minds of so many people throughout history in a world satu-
rated with a totally contrary zeitgeist. God's thoughts are just not our
thoughts. They go against everything in human nature.

Jesus waged spiritual warfare every day of His life. He did not do
it by waving banners, blowing shofars, and boxing the air. He did it
through His way of life, His teaching, and His demonstration of God's
kingdom on the earth through His works, death, and resurrection.

With this in mind, spiritual warfare in Jesus' ministry is not always
what you might expect. Consider, for example, the Sermon on the
Mount (Matt. 5–7). Most Christians know and love its message. Yet
we have become so familiar with it that we often miss its significance.
This teaching of Jesus opens our eyes to an entirely new way of thinking.
It's hard to convey how utterly revolutionary and even scandalous this
would have been to its first recipients. Remember, Jesus taught this
to people who lived in the Roman Empire of the ancient world. At
that time in Roman society, power was the ultimate virtue. Mercy was
weakness, and weakness was despised. Immorality, debauchery, hedo-
nism, and violence were celebrated.

Then Jesus came along and said the blessed ones are the poor in
spirit, the mournful, the meek, the merciful, the pure, the persecuted,
the peacemaking, and the righteous.

The meek will inherit the earth? How unthinkable. Don't the powerful and violent ones conquer nations and rule the world? Lust is
adultery? Hatred is murder? Persecution is cause for joy? We should
forgive our enemies—and even love them? Care for the needy? Give,
pray, and fast in private so no one on earth will know and give us
credit? Invest our treasures in heaven instead of earth? Reject anxiety?

Love God more than our own lives? Refuse to judge others? Walk the narrow and least popular road?

Again, it's hard for us to understand how revolutionary these ideas would have been in Jesus' time. We live during an era when two thousand years of Christian influence has deeply and positively influenced the zeitgeist of the world in ways of which we are not always conscious. For example, we have a tendency to show mercy to the poor, weak, sick, orphans, and widows. But this is not the way it used to be. The heathen cultures into which Christianity was introduced valued the strong and the proud. The idea of human rights is a Christian idea. The idea of individual freedom to choose is a Christian idea. The idea of natural law is a Christian idea. Freedom of speech, separation of church and state, and even the scientific method are products of Christianity.

Western culture has been so influenced by the teachings of Jesus and the Bible that its people are often familiar with biblical themes and stories even if they have never read the Bible. And if they aren't aware of the stories themselves, they have still been influenced by their morals. Even the famous and outspoken atheist Richard Dawkins writes about the importance of the Bible as it pertains to the English language. He lists 129 biblical phrases that every educated English speaker uses and understands, even if they never read the Bible. These include "the salt of the earth," "go the extra mile," "I wash my hands of it," "filthy lucre," "through a glass darkly," "wolf in sheep's clothing," "hide your light under a bushel," "no peace for the wicked," "how are the mighty fallen," and many others.[3] Dawkins says, "A native speaker of English who has never read a word of the King James Bible is verging on the barbarian."[4] Think about what it has done to a society when stories such as the parable of the good Samaritan and the parable of the prodigal son have had two thousand years to work their way into the public consciousness. Even the Old Testament has become part of Western thought because of the pervasive influence of Christianity (think David and Goliath or the Ten Commandments).

In many ways, much more than our secular detractors would like to admit, the peaceful, sophisticated, and tame society we Westerners enjoy today owes its existence to Christian influence. Yet it has been under assault for hundreds of years. The greatest society man has ever built has been under attack by the very people who benefit from it.

And they attack with the most vehemence the very thing that made it great. Why? As Dostoevsky says, "Man is stupid, you know, phenomenally stupid; or rather he is not at all stupid, but he is so ungrateful that you could not find another like him in all creation."[5] Or maybe there is another explanation still. Perhaps this pervasive hostility toward Christ and all He stands for comes from the satanic, antichrist spirit already in the world.

THE CROSS—DIVINE WISDOM

The divine way of thinking is so contrary to the satanic way that when God made His most brilliant move, Satan never saw it coming. Neither did those who think like Satan. Paul says of the divine wisdom, "None of the rulers of this age understood it, for if they had, they would not have crucified the Lord of glory" (1 Cor. 2:8). So not only does Satan deceive people, but he is also deceived himself! His evil way of thinking saw the cross as weakness and failure when it was actually the power and the wisdom of God.

This is what we must recognize. God's wisdom looks nothing like human wisdom. It exists in a category entirely by itself, utterly separate from the world's way of thinking and accessible to humans only by faith in Christ Jesus. If we try to fight spiritual battles with techniques familiar to us in the flesh, we will fail to defeat Satan and even find ourselves fighting on his side. For example, in a physical fight anger, rage, and hatred are your friends. They light a fire inside you that will hurl you at your enemy like a deadly weapon. But spiritual battles are not fought this way. Hate, anger, and vengeance are the enemy's methods of gaining justice. How can we use the enemy's methods to overcome the enemy? The moment we take them up, we lose the battle and align ourselves with the enemy. James and John wanted to call down fire upon the Samaritans when they disrespected Jesus. But Jesus rebuked them, saying, "You do not know what kind of spirit you are of" (Luke 9:55, NASB). Their carnal response aligned them with a spirit completely contrary to Christ. Jesus doesn't hate His human enemies. He loves them. He doesn't die as a suicide bomber, blowing Himself up to hurt His enemies. Instead He lays down His life on behalf of His enemies, giving His life to save theirs. It's almost impossible to comprehend this way of thinking. In fact, we cannot understand it without the mind of Christ. But according to the gospel, *that* is the divine wisdom—the way of Christlike, sacrificial love—that overthrows the forces of darkness.

Jesus said to His disciples, "I am sending you out like sheep among wolves" (Matt. 10:16). I have to admit that this sounds incredibly unappealing. I don't want to be a sheep. I'm a man. I'm strong. I'm capable of defending myself. I'd rather He said, "I'm sending you out as *lions* among wolves." I want to prey on the predators, not become their lunch. But that is the fallen, carnal mind speaking. From a natural standpoint, wolves are predators and sheep are prey. But in God's wisdom, the sheep ultimately conquer the wolves. In Revelation, when the Lion of the tribe of Judah was introduced as the One who conquered, John turned and saw a *Lamb*—a Lamb as if it had been slain (Rev. 5:6). The Lion gained victory over His spiritual enemies as a sacrificial Lamb.

"The meek...will inherit the earth" (Matt. 5:5). True, we don't always win in the short term, and sometimes we suffer in this demonically controlled world. Even Jesus was surrounded by the "strong bulls of Bashan" as He hung on the cross. They tore His flesh with their teeth like lions (Ps. 22:12–13). Yet at that moment, He was overcoming those bulls. Only by dying could He conquer the power of death. He rose from the dead with complete victory over His enemies forever!

Christ's life conflicted so starkly with the demonic spirit of the age that they clashed in mortal combat. This was no mere rhetorical argument between two ideologies. Jesus didn't battle  How can we use the enemy's methods to overcome the enemy? The moment we take them up, we lose the battle and align ourselves with the enemy.

the satanic way of thinking through a moderated debate. It was war—the ultimate spiritual war that would define eternity. Other rabbis had taught things similar to what Jesus taught, but no one had ever embodied the wisdom and modeled it perfectly. Jesus physically walked out the wisdom of God to the very end, when a bloody corpse and ribbons of mangled flesh lay cold and still in a borrowed tomb. And to all who watched with natural eyes, it must have seemed obvious who won. Roman soldiers stood triumphantly over the dead body of love.

But three days later the earth shook as God's wisdom broke through the crust of thousands of years of demonic thinking that had covered the planet like a thick shell.

YOU ARE THE LIGHT OF THE WORLD

Earlier I mentioned that Jesus declared Himself to be the Light of the world. But that was not the end of the story. Jesus then turned to His disciples (and us) and said, "*You* are the light of the world" (Matt. 5:14, emphasis added). When we are filled with the Holy Spirit and therefore receive the mind of Christ, we become reflections of His light! His way of thinking and living becomes ours. When this happens, we pierce the darkness everywhere we go. We are walking extensions of God's kingdom! This is true spiritual warfare!

Our job as Christians is not merely to fight spiritual battles through prayer and intercession. We combat darkness by living like Jesus—by walking out His radical, kingdom way of thinking. Our daily behavior must embody God's thoughts and ways. This may not sound like the most exciting way to fight the demonic spirit, but it is extremely powerful. Think of it like this. How can we combat the demonic zeitgeist if we are thinking and living in alignment with it?

Paul declares how the demonic zeitgeist will manifest in the last days. "But know this, that in the last days perilous times will come: For men will be lovers of themselves, lovers of money, boasters, proud, blasphemers, disobedient to parents, unthankful, unholy, unloving, unforgiving, slanderers, without self-control, brutal, despisers of good, traitors, headstrong, haughty, lovers of pleasure rather than lovers of God, having a form of godliness but denying its power. And from such people turn away!" (2 Tim. 3:1–5, NKJV).

You can be sure this description of people in the last days opposes everything that is of the Father. And we who are children of the light are expected to walk contrary to all that is in the world.

In a world where most people live under a demonic spell, Jesus' followers have a totally different way of thinking and living. People of the world love themselves; we love not our lives. They love money; we love sacrifice. They are proud and boastful; we are meek and humble. They blaspheme; we worship. They are lawless; we are obedient. They are unthankful, unholy, and unloving; we are grateful, pure, and full of Christlike charity. They are bitter; we forgive. They slander; we praise. They are brutal; we are gentle. They despise good; we contend for it. They love pleasure; we love God.

Paul repeatedly contrasts this new way of thinking and living with our old way under the dominion of that demonic zeitgeist. "As for you, you were dead in your transgressions and sins, in which you used to live when you followed the ways of this world and of the ruler of the kingdom of the air, the spirit who is now at work in those who are disobedient" (Eph.

Our job as Christians is not merely to fight spiritual battles through prayer and intercession. We combat darkness by living like Jesus— by walking out His radical, kingdom way of thinking.

2:1–2). "What we have received is not the spirit of the world, but the Spirit who is from God, so that we may understand what God has freely given us" (1 Cor. 2:12).

I would venture you never saw the fruit of the Spirit as spiritual weapons. But these virtues, developed through the work of the Holy Spirit in our lives, are supernatural. They are heavenly. They come from above, reflecting God's wisdom and exerting divine influence. That means they directly contradict the demonic zeitgeist at work in the world. For example, faith operates not by what is seen but by the Word of God. Faith is a Christlike way of thinking, not a carnal one. It aligns us with God's mind, through which His power flows into the earth.

I've heard songs from Christian rock and rap groups that talk about assassinating demons or blowing up Satan's kingdom. These ideas have always seemed quite silly to me. Satan is not worried about bullets or bombs. What is extremely dangerous to the satanic system is the cornucopia of virtues that emerges from the Spirit's unique way of thinking: love, sacrifice, humility, patience, faith, consecration, self-discipline, holiness, joy, meekness, and many more.

BATTLES AND BUILDERS

Earlier I referred to the Sermon on the Mount as spiritual warfare. It represents the divine thought pattern that directly contradicts and therefore attacks the demonic zeitgeist. This clash of kingdoms is what the cosmic war is about. If we want to fight on the side of the Lamb, there is only one way to do it. We must have what Paul calls "the mind of Christ" (1 Cor. 2:16). Our thoughts, beliefs, actions, and lifestyle must fully align with Christ. This is exactly what Paul means when he says, "Do not conform to the pattern of this world, but be transformed by the renewing of your mind. Then you will be able to test and approve what God's will is—his good, pleasing and perfect will" (Rom. 12:2). To conform to the pattern of this world is to come under the influence of the antichrist spirit—whether we realize it or not. With the wrong mindset, even God's children can fight on the wrong side. Remember, Jesus called Peter, His disciple and good friend, "Satan," because "you are not *setting your mind* on God's interests, but man's" (Matt. 16:23, NASB, emphasis added). When we adopt the world's way of thinking, we give its zeitgeist admission into our minds, mouths, and atmosphere. Thus we promote and advance a satanic system. This is why Jesus is so extreme in His call to follow Him.

Jesus is black and white in His teaching. There isn't much nuance in His positions. "He who is not with Me is against Me; and he who does not gather with Me scatters" (Matt. 12:30, NASB). Jesus' imagery here refers to the gathering and scattering of sheep. Who gathers the sheep? The shepherd. What scatters the sheep? A predator. You are either a shepherd or a wolf. There is no in-between. He explicitly says, "If you're not with Me, you're against Me!" There are no neutral souls and no neutral zones. There is no Switzerland in the spiritual world. There are only two teams. You can fight for God, or you can fight for the devil. Those are your only two choices. And it's easy to know which team you are on. If you have not made a conscious decision to serve God, then by default you fight for the other side—against God!

Many other passages express the same sentiment. For example: "No one can serve two masters. Either you will hate the one and love the other, or you will be devoted to the one and despise the other" (Matt. 6:24). Notice, there is no option to love one and just be OK with the other. The choice is not between which one you like more and which you like less. The choice is between love and hate.

The choice Jesus gives us is so stark, He doesn't limit His love-hate choice to two masters. He takes it even further. "If anyone comes to me and does not hate his own father and mother and wife and children and brothers and sisters, yes, and even his own life, he cannot be my disciple. Whoever does not bear his own cross and come after me cannot be my disciple" (Luke 14:26–27, esv). This is radical by any standard. But I am not cherry-picking these passages to make my point. This sheer radicalism comprises the majority of Jesus' teaching. He is unambiguous about the requirements to follow Him. His kingdom cannot afford people who serve Jesus without full surrender. Not only are they unhelpful, but they are also actively harmful.

Jesus told a story about a fig tree that did not produce any fruit, so the master demanded it be cut down. He said it was wasting the soil (Luke 13:7). In other words, this was no harmless tree. It was taking up space, nutrients, and sunlight. It weakened the soil and brought harm to the other trees in the garden. There was no neutrality. The tree was a categorical liability. The master wanted to cut it down for the good of the vineyard, not just out of spite. Again, we are either helpful or harmful—there is no middle ground.

If someone claims to be a Christian but continues to live under the spell of the demonic zeitgeist, on a practical level he does not represent Christ. He represents Satan. There are only two main spirits in the world. There is the spirit of Christ and the spirit of antichrist. To align with one is to reject the other. The way Jesus sees it, if we are not actively connected to Him and bearing the fruit of the Spirit, then we are destructive—whether we realize it or not. We are being used by the devil whether we know it or not.

Jesus told another parable:

> For which one of you, when he wants to build a watchtower [for his guards], does not first sit down and calculate the cost, to see if he has enough to finish it? Otherwise, when he has laid a foundation and is unable to finish [the building], all who see it will begin to ridicule him, saying, "This man began to build and was not able to finish!"
>
> —Luke 14:28–30, amp

I have seen this often in Africa. A man who grew up in a poor village has a stroke of good fortune and ends up a rich businessman or politician. As a sign of his wealth he commissions a mansion to be built in his hometown. Sometimes it's the biggest and most impressive building ever constructed in that town. But for some reason, before the building is finished, he runs out of money. It is not normal to build houses with loans in Africa (just as it was not normal in Jesus' time). If you want to build something, you build with cash. But if you run out of cash, the building stops. It's as simple as that.

I saw many half-finished mansions in Africa that had apparently lain dormant for thirty years. Weeds and even trees had grown up inside of them. Vagrants had moved in, had put up a few extra boards, and were living inside. What was meant to be a monument becomes an eyesore, and that "big man" becomes the mockery of the whole town. Jesus takes up this honor-versus-shame imagery and uses it to make a point about full surrender. With Him it's all or nothing. Anything in between becomes both a failure and a shame.

When you claim Christ, you are claiming the loftiest name there is. As if you are constructing a huge tower or a mansion, people will take notice of your enormous claim. If you take on the name of Christ but are not able to finish what you started, you will bring shame on your name and His. "Thou shalt not take the name of the LORD thy God in vain" (Exod. 20:7, KJV). This is not just about using "God" as a swear word. It is about bringing reproach upon the name of the Lord by taking it, or using it, in vain. If you call yourself a Christian, you have taken upon yourself the name of Jesus—the name above every other name. That means His reputation is attached to yours. You had better take that seriously.

Lukewarm Christian, you are one of the devil's most powerful weapons against the gospel. When people look at you and see the life you live and realize your life is no different than theirs, they become convinced they don't need Jesus. Remember the famous quote attributed to Gandhi: "I like your Christ, but I dislike your Christians." In other words, the lives of Christians were incongruous with the Christ they claimed to serve. This lack of Christlikeness among *Christ*ians is one of the biggest deterrents to people accepting the gospel. We are at war. We cannot merely don the uniform of God's kingdom while fighting half-heartedly for both sides. This is dishonorable, dangerous, and treasonous.

In light of these things, what should we do?

Let's look at Jesus' next parable after His story about the unfinished tower. The two stories seem to form bookends to the case for following Christ. On the one hand, the illustration of the tower tells us to count the cost of following Jesus and tells us not to make that decision lightly. But on the other hand, the next story tells us to count the cost of *not* following Him and then tells us exactly what to do.

> Or what king, when he sets out to meet another king in battle, will not first sit down and consider whether he is strong enough with ten thousand men to encounter the one coming against him with twenty thousand? Or else, while the other is still far away, he sends a delegation and asks for terms of peace. So then, none of you can be My disciple who does not give up all his own possessions.
>
> —Luke 14:31–33, NASB

In this story the warring king is severely outnumbered two to one. He has no chance of winning against a much more powerful king. Therefore he will quickly send a delegation to surrender. In the ancient world, when a king surrendered, he was usually treated with kindness and often allowed to remain in power as a deputy of the conquering empire. But if he resisted, there would be no mercy.

The kingdom of God is greater than any earthly kingdom and infinitely greater than any personal ambition. A wise person will realize it is futile and dangerous to "kick against the goads," as God said to Saul on the road to Damascus (Acts 26:14). A quick surrender is the most reasonable thing to do.

This book is about spiritual warfare. We are talking about being part of God's army. Indeed, the Christian life is a warring life in the spirit. But here Jesus gives us a much more precise metaphor. Joining the army of the Lord is not simply a matter of going down to a recruitment office and enlisting. We are not by nature citizens of this kingdom. We are natural enemies of God. We cannot begin merely by joining Christ. We must first surrender!

All of us also lived among them at one time, gratifying the cravings of our flesh and following its desires and thoughts. Like the rest, we were by nature deserving of wrath.

—EPHESIANS 2:3

Once you were alienated from God and were enemies in your minds because of your evil behavior.

—COLOSSIANS 1:21

Listen to Paul's language. He is talking about the "cravings of the flesh," "its desires and thoughts," and how we were "enemies in [our] minds." He is referring to the demonic zeitgeist I have been describing. In order to be a part of God's army, we have to surrender this old way of thinking and living. This is why repentance is necessary for salvation. To repent is to revolutionize the way we think and therefore live!

TAKE UP YOUR CROSS

I have used a number of metaphors in this chapter. Allow me to call on one more. This is not my metaphor but one used by Jesus Himself. He said that if we want to follow Him, we must deny ourselves, take up our cross, and follow Him (Matt. 16:24). Earlier we talked about the wisdom of the cross—how it contradicted all worldly wisdom and dealt a fatal blow to the demonic zeitgeist. Here Jesus instructs us that if we want to be His disciples, we carry that same cross. But what does it mean to take up the cross?

The cross is a symbol of suffering and death. A person who carries a cross is on his way to be crucified. He is a dead man walking. The old, carnal, demonic way of thinking cannot simply be changed. It must be killed.

Jesus requires us to lay aside the person we used to be and to take up a new identity, a new pattern of thinking, and a new way of living. We may live in the same physical body, but our old self is dead. We have been transformed by the renewing of our minds. This is precisely what is required for effective spiritual warfare. Any soldier without a cross on his back is fighting for Satan. The battle rages not only in the world but also within us. We are where the change must begin.

QUESTIONS FOR DISCUSSION

- What are some things that characterize the current zeitgeist of your world/culture?

- How are the trends of culture and society in opposition to the spirit of Christ?

- What are some philosophies or systems of belief you have adopted that might be contrary to the teachings of Jesus?

- How do we guard our hearts against the pervasive influence of the spirit of the age?

CHAPTER 5

THE COSMIC BATTLE

Every single soldier must know, before he goes into battle, how the little battle he is to fight fits into the larger picture, and how the success of his fighting will influence the battle as a whole.
—FIELD MARSHAL BERNARD MONTGOMERY

A dead thing can go with the stream, but only a living thing can go against it.
—G. K. CHESTERTON, *THE EVERLASTING MAN*

IN THE PREVIOUS chapter I wrote about the demonic zeitgeist, the spirit of the age that controls the thinking of the natural man. It is the same demonic way of thinking that Satan passed to Eve in the Garden of Eden. Jesus came as the Light of the world. He broke through the darkness of that demonic deception with the wisdom of God. This wisdom is completely contrary to the world's wisdom, and its ultimate expression was the cross. Now Jesus says to us, "*You* are the light of the world" (Matt. 5:14, emphasis added). When we are saved, we are born again, transformed from the inside out with a new heart and a new mind. We now reflect His light through a new way of thinking and living in the world—we think and live like Christ. "As He is, so also are we in this world" (1 John 4:17, NASB).

I've presented this view because we often have a narcissistic view of spiritual warfare. We think that when our car breaks down or we get in a fight with a family member before church, it's because all of hell wants to ruin our day. We do face spiritual resistance in our everyday lives; I am not downplaying that reality whatsoever. But there is a big picture we need to be aware of. Satan's goal is to control the world through the minds of men who have been bewitched by his way of thinking. When we combat his agenda by carrying our cross, following Christ, and representing His wisdom to the world, it is spiritual warfare at its finest.

But all of this might seem a little mundane. Are we just supposed to be good little Christians until Jesus returns? Is that all there is to spiritual warfare? The answer is no! We have yet to discuss other aspects to it, but this foundational big picture is necessary before we can put other issues in their proper context.

In this chapter we are going to zoom out a bit further to see an even bigger picture. We are going to put spiritual warfare into context not only in the Christian life but also in life generally. As we will see, this is no side issue. What we are about to discuss gets to the exact purpose for which man was created. We will see why Satan was so eager to deceive man in the Garden of Eden and how we are a part of God's plan to reverse it all.

THE MEANING OF LIFE

There was a brilliant seventeen-year-old girl who got perfect scores on the Scholastic Achievement Test and a perfect score on the University of California acceptance index—a feat never accomplished before. She was a true genius. But when a reporter asked her, "What is the meaning of life?" She replied, "I have no idea. I would like to know myself."[1]

The meaning of life stands as history's great existential question—the object of humanity's philosophical struggle since the beginning of time. The question has stumped the most brilliant thinkers, and it continues to intrigue both sinner and saint. Yes, even Christians can wrestle with the meaning of life. But they express the issue with far more precision, actually asking two questions: Why was I created? And why was I saved?

As we search the Scriptures, we find that the answer to both questions is the same. When you find the answer to one, you have found the answer to both—and thus to the meaning of life itself.

To answer the first question—Why was I created?—we go back once again to the very beginning. In the opening chapters of the Bible we find a theme that runs from Genesis to Revelation. As we have

Just as Eve was made as a helper suitable for Adam, so humankind was made as a helper suitable for God.

already seen, when God first created Adam and completed him with Eve, He gave the two of them a specific purpose as humans: subdue the earth and have dominion over it (Gen. 1:26–28). In other words, God made humanity not as another creature like the plants and animals but as His special assistant in ruling the world. Just as Eve was made as a helper suitable for Adam, so humankind was made as a helper suitable for God.

God's gifts and callings are irrevocable (Rom. 11:29), a principle that continues to apply to humanity's call to have dominion. Adam's fall in the garden has not changed that calling. God continues to honor it. In fact, this is God's eternal plan. We glorify God most when we fulfill the purpose for which He made us. That is why He has constrained Himself in such a way that He will not act in the earth without us. We are His agents, His representatives, His gatekeepers in this world.

God will not work without us. Likewise, Satan *cannot* work without us. Everything evil that happens in this world comes through evil people. Everything godly that happens in this world comes through godly people. This is why Satan tempts people to sin. He has no real power in this world except what we, the gatekeepers, give to him. This is also why in the Exodus saga God worked through Moses while Satan worked through Pharaoh. To natural eyes the showdown looked like a confrontation between two men. But it was a battle between God and Satan—each working through his man. And this is why, in the Book of Revelation, Satan needs the antichrist while God works through His servants the prophets (Rev. 1:1–3; 10:7; 11:10; cf. Amos 3:7).

I call this principle divine partnership. Once we notice it, we see it all throughout Scripture. When God wanted to display His righteousness and salvation during the judgment of the flood, He partnered with Noah, who built the ark. Later He partnered with Abraham to create a special nation, Israel, to bless all the other nations of the world. God partnered with Moses to deliver the children of Israel out of Egypt and with Joshua to bring them into the Promised Land. Whether God was using David, Solomon, Elijah, Isaiah, Jeremiah, or Ezekiel, we see divine partnership in action. There are so many examples of this principle at work that we can turn to virtually any page in the Bible and find one. In fact, Scripture itself is a product of divine partnership—men spoke and wrote "as they were moved by the Holy Spirit" (2 Pet. 1:21, NKJV).

JESUS: THE ULTIMATE EXPRESSION OF DIVINE PARTNERSHIP

But as it is with any great truth, we find the most powerful example of this principle in Christ Himself. When God wanted to display His greatest expression of glory and bring salvation to a lost humanity, He sent His own Son into the world (Heb. 1). But God's Son did not appear as an alien from a distant galaxy, a ghost from another dimension, or even as a shining angel from glory. He came as a human baby through a human mother. He was the ultimate human. And as the ultimate human Jesus became the ultimate example of divine partnership.

But this partnership with man relating to the advent of Christ did not begin at the moment the Holy Spirit overshadowed a virgin named Mary. In fact, God had been at work to bring about the incarnation of Christ ever since the beginning! The Book of Matthew starts with a long genealogy of Jesus going back to Abraham (Matt. 1). The Book of Luke traces His genealogy all the way back to Adam (Luke 3)! What these genealogies demonstrate is the lineage, the pedigree, the heritage of Christ—the legitimacy of Christ's claim as the rightful heir to the eternal throne of David and the Savior of the entire human race. He did not just materialize out of thin air and save us—He came through the proper channels. From the beginning God partnered with man to save humanity. Through the seed of Abraham, through the line of David, through the womb of Mary, the Redeemer was born as a man with flesh and blood.

We see that Jesus is the ultimate expression of God's partnership with man. But He is also the ultimate expression of man's intended partnership with God. The human comrade whom God desired from the beginning—the human Son He always wanted—He found in Jesus. From there Jesus walked this partnership out in the most profound and complete way. He shows us what true dominion looks like and what God's will has been all along: that His dominion would extend from heaven to earth through His people. And that is exactly what Scripture means when it refers to the kingdom of God.

Before Jesus appeared, we had an incomplete picture of this kingdom. Throughout the Old Testament, prophets, teachers, storytellers, and kings gave us bits, pieces, and glimpses of God's kingdom. They acted as signposts on the path, pointing the way to kingdom. But they were not the destination itself. Therefore they could not reveal the fullness of God's dominion on earth.

David ruled Israel as the most powerful type of Christ in the Old Testament. But sin proved his inadequacy and death proved his limits. Daniel saw visions of the coming kingdom. But the visions—though supernatural and overwhelming—were still like dots of light shining through tiny holes in a veil. The full light burned behind that veil, but the veil remained yet untorn. The ultimate kingdom still hid behind the shroud.

Moses, Elijah, and Elisha performed signs, wonders, and miracles. Surely God's dominion was breaking into the world through them. Even the dead were raised. They were men of whom the world was not worthy. But they still "did not receive what was promised" (Heb. 11:39, esv). The full kingdom stayed behind the veil. God's comprehensive, unrestricted kingdom had not yet been seen…until that young man from Nazareth came to the Jordan River for baptism.

THE KINGDOM

Jesus' teaching on the kingdom of God permeates the Gospels. His sermons, parables, and private teaching to the disciples are all about the kingdom. For years He continually taught about the kingdom right up to the day He was crucified. But even after He rose from the dead, the Scripture says that He spoke to them "of the things pertaining to the kingdom of God" for forty days before His ascension (Acts 1:3,

NKJV). The kingdom was the major theme of Christ's teaching from beginning to end. The kingdom is what He taught. And the kingdom is what He demonstrated. This is what spiritual warfare in the world is about—the advancement of the kingdom. We don't fight demonic spirits, principalities, powers, and the rulers of the darkness of this world in an arbitrary and subjective way. We fight for the advancement of God's kingdom! This is precisely what Jesus modeled for us in His earthly life.

In the Western world we often have teachers who teach subjects they understand only from an academic viewpoint. It reminds me of a professor I had in college who taught a class on entrepreneurship. He began the semester by announcing he had never started a business before, but he was going to teach us how to do it. This is not the kind of teacher Jesus was. In fact, for Jesus the demonstration did not follow the teaching; the demonstration actually came first![2]

Luke 24:19 says that Jesus was "a prophet mighty in deed and word" (KJV). To a Western ear it sounds strange to put those words in that order. We would use the phrase "word and deed." But Luke's Gospel clearly puts the actions before the words. In Acts 1:1 Luke talks about "all that Jesus began to do and to teach." Again the demonstration comes first and the explanation follows. Jesus taught His students in order to help them understand what they first saw Him do. But the sad truth is that most missed it—as they do today. Most looked right at Jesus and completely misinterpreted what He was doing and what He was saying.

And what exactly was He doing? Acts 10:38 declares it plainly: "God anointed Jesus of Nazareth with the Holy Ghost and with power: [he] went about doing good, and healing all that were oppressed of the devil; for God was with him" (KJV). This is perfect spiritual warfare.

Likewise, Jesus sent the disciples out with this commission in Matthew 10:7–8: "And as ye go, preach, saying, the kingdom of heaven is at hand. Heal the sick, cleanse the lepers, raise the dead, cast out devils: freely you have received, freely give" (KJV). We have been called to the same spiritual warfare that Jesus modeled. It is not just an arbitrary war against evil in general—it is the advancement of the kingdom of God on earth!

We must not overlook this crystal clear truth. When God's kingdom comes, it must look like something. It must have tangible demonstration. God's dominion is no ethereal, theoretical doctrine without real-world consequences. When the kingdom of heaven collides with the natural world, there is visible, demonstrable evidence of God's dominion. For example, sick people are healed, the lepers are cleansed, the dead are raised, the power of Satan is broken, and the oppressed are freed!

Jesus' miracles demonstrated His dominion. By demonstrating God's kingdom through the power of the Holy Spirit, Jesus showed us what it looks like when a human being fulfills his destiny as an extension of God's kingdom into the fallen world. Jesus demonstrated what a human can do under the power of the Holy Spirit. He showed us

The kingdom was the major theme of Christ's teaching from beginning to end. The kingdom is what He taught. And the kingdom is what He demonstrated.

what a real warrior, a dragon slayer, looks like. Now we get to follow His example.

Some mistakenly think that Jesus' miracles simply proved that He was the Messiah. How convenient that would be for us! If the miracles of Jesus were merely proof of His Messianic claims, we are off the hook. But this simply is not the case. Jesus' miracles were more than evidence about His role; they were actually demonstrations that imply our role.

For example, Jesus performed mighty miracles in Matthew 12. He healed a man with a withered hand (v. 13). Then He healed a demonized, blind, and mute man so that he spoke and saw (v. 22). In fact, verse 15 tells us that "great multitudes followed Him, and *He healed them all*" (NKJV, emphasis added). Yet in that same chapter, just a few verses later, the scribes and Pharisees still insisted, "We want to see a sign from you" (v. 38)! Can you imagine such nerve? They had just seen how every sickness, every disease, and every infirmity among a great multitude of people were healed! I don't know of a greater demonstration of the miraculous in history. But the critics were not impressed or convinced.

These miracles were not the kind of signs the doubters sought. They wanted something more spectacular, more grandiose. They wanted Jesus to part the sea like Moses or call down fire from heaven like

Elijah. Jesus would eventually give them that kind of sign—His resurrection from the dead—and they still would not believe (Matt. 12:39–40). But in the meantime His healings and miracles were not attempts to prove anything to the skeptics. Rather they were demonstrations of what it looks like when a human being walks in kingdom dominion. In other words, Jesus did not perform miracles to prove that He could. He performed miracles to prove that *we* could! He was saying, "Look! This is the kingdom I have been telling you about! This is what it looks like when it comes to earth! This is what I want you to do!"

But there is a problem. Fallen humans cannot walk in kingdom dominion. We are dead in trespasses and sins. We are under the curse and controlled by the powers of the air. We are hypnotized by the demonic zeitgeist with which Satan controls the world. That is why Jesus not only demonstrated and taught the kingdom—He also died to give the kingdom to those who believe (Luke 12:32). His death on the cross was not simply to rescue us from hell; it was to restore the dominion we lost in the garden—and so much more. Remember, Jesus said, "For the Son of Man has come to save *that which* was lost" (Matt. 18:11, NKJV, emphasis added). Most people quote that verse incorrectly, saying Jesus came "to save *those who* were lost," but He came "to save *that which* was lost."

Jesus died to restore humanity to our divine destiny, to restore the purpose and calling God placed on the human race since the beginning of time. He died to make us kings and priests to God. He calls us once again to subdue the earth and take dominion—not simply over plants and animals, but over "serpents and scorpions, and over all the power of the enemy" (Luke 10:19, NKJV). Jesus died so we could live the same way He lived. He died so we could be dragon slayers just as He was. Jesus did not die just to get us into heaven. He died to get heaven into us and into the world through us!

THE PURPOSE FOR SALVATION

So here we find the answer to our second question, Why was I saved? We were saved so that God's kingdom could come through us, and His will could be done on earth as it is in heaven!

But God's redemptive work did not end at the cross. Jesus told the disciples to go to the Upper Room and wait until they had received power from on high. Ten days later the Holy Spirit came to abide with us forever. It was a new kind of incarnation. When Jesus came into the world, God wrapped Himself in the flesh of one man, who became "the firstborn among many brethren" (Rom. 8:29, NKJV). Now, through the Holy Spirit, God has wrapped Himself in the flesh of a new race, born again not by "the will of man, but of God" (John 1:13, NKJV).

Jesus did not perform miracles to prove that He could. He performed miracles to prove that *we* could!

The *Westminster Shorter Catechism* says, "Man's chief end is to glorify God, and to enjoy him forever."[3] I agree with this statement completely, but I have an issue with the way it is often interpreted. To some people it means they plan to spend eternity in an endless praise and worship service. They even imagine singing along with an angelic worship band forever and ever. For them, to *glorify God* means merely to sing words and melodies. This is the only way they understand worship. But bringing glory to God involves far more than our words or music. We glorify God through obedient lives that conform to the image of Jesus Christ. That means we represent Him as ambassadors by partnering with Him for His purposes, walking in dominion, and becoming an extension of His kingdom. That is why we were created. That is why we were saved. And that is the meaning of life!

Ultimately the spiritual war was already won on the cross. Yet we live in a world where people are still slaves to sin and the devil. Their minds are still under that demonic spirit of the age. We are called to set them free. We proclaim the good news, and then we demonstrate the kingdom of God by bringing its power to bear. Where there are demons, we cast them out. Where there is sickness, we heal it. Where there is bondage, we break it. Where there are strongholds, we pull them down. We do this with all the tools God has given us—preaching, prayer, faith, prophetic words, signs, wonders, miracles, love, sacrifice, acts of service, and so on.

I emphasize these things because often when people think of spiritual warfare, they think of a one-dimensional aspect of it—usually praying loudly. But spiritual warfare is not confined to prayer. Jesus modeled how we wage our war against darkness. Jesus is the dragon slayer we should seek to imitate.

QUESTIONS FOR DISCUSSION

- Based on this chapter, how would you explain the meaning of your life?

- How would you explain the concept of *divine partnership* discussed above?

- How can you use your talents, your job, and your influence to further God's kingdom?

- What are some ways we can worship God that do not involve singing or music?

CHAPTER 6

SPIRITUAL WARFARE DEMYSTIFIED

Nothing in this world can take the place of persistence. Talent will not; nothing is more common than unsuccessful men with talent. Genius will not; unrewarded genius is almost a proverb. Education will not; the world is full of educated derelicts. Persistence and determination are omnipotent.[1]

—UNKNOWN

The very first feature in tactics is, to know how to stand well, and many things will depend upon that.

—CHRYSOSTOM, *HOMILIES ON EPHESIANS*

I F YOU'VE EVER ridden a bicycle, you probably already know that you can *feel* a hill, even if you can't see it. Some grades are too subtle to be observed, especially if there are a lot of distractions along the path—trees, random passersby, barking dogs—all vying for your attention. But your legs don't lie. They know when progress is hard and when it is easy. They can feel even the slightest elevation that resists their effort.

Just as there is physical resistance, there is also spiritual resistance. The apostle Paul told the Ephesians, "Our struggle is not against flesh and blood, but against the rulers, against the authorities, against the powers of this dark world and against the spiritual forces of evil in the heavenly realms" (Eph. 6:12). One obvious takeaway from the above verse is that though it may be unseen, the struggle is real. Like riding that bike up a subtle but definite slope, we do not usually see the actual forces pushing back on our progress. But we sense them nonetheless. Our spiritual legs do not lie. At that point, we must choose to dig in, push back, and endure until we finish the course.

This sense of unseen resistance is what Christians often identify as spiritual warfare. Maybe they are getting ready for a mission trip and one thing after another goes wrong. It feels as if someone is actually *trying* to sabotage their plans. Or maybe they are experiencing unusual challenges with their children or marriage that seem sinister. The people involved are not acting like themselves. They seem to have come under a kind of spiritual funk. Or perhaps odd sicknesses keep popping up in someone's body or in the bodies of loved ones. Or a business or their finances seem to be under unrelenting assault. All of this resistance feels as if it is coming out of nowhere, and there is the distinct impression it comes from beyond the natural realm. It is not always obvious what to do during such times in life. In this chapter we will discuss what spiritual warfare really is and get some wisdom on how to prepare for it.

THE TERMINOLOGY

Like many useful terms the phrase *spiritual warfare* does not appear in Scripture as such. The wording is instead rooted in the use of scriptural military analogies to describe the manner in which Christ followers are to prepare for and repel evil, in the form of both injustice and temptation. Perhaps the most famous example is found in the close of the apostle Paul's letter to the congregation of believers in Ephesus.

> A final word: Be strong in the Lord and in his mighty power. Put on all of God's armor so that you will be able to stand firm against all strategies of the devil. For we are not fighting against flesh-and-blood enemies, but against evil rulers and authorities of the unseen world, against mighty powers in this dark world, and against evil spirits in the heavenly places.
>
> Therefore, put on every piece of God's armor so you will be able to resist the enemy in the time of evil. Then after the

battle you will still be standing firm. Stand your ground, putting on the belt of truth and the body armor of God's righteousness. For shoes, put on the peace that comes from the Good News so that you will be fully prepared. In addition to all of these, hold up the shield of faith to stop the fiery arrows of the devil. Put on salvation as your helmet, and take the sword of the Spirit, which is the word of God.

Pray in the Spirit at all times and on every occasion. Stay alert and be persistent in your prayers for all believers everywhere.

—Ephesians 6:10–18, nlt

A soldier in the ancient Roman Empire would put on his complete battle gear before engaging the enemy. Likewise, says Paul, we should also be fully dressed in *spiritual* armor—with both the defensive and offensive components—designed to protect and advance our spiritual lives. An experienced combatant understands that every inch of a warrior's outfit provides specific protection. To forget so much as one sock could prove a fatal mistake. Since we face an enemy who is serious about our demise, we should take the battle against evil as an issue of life and death—and dress accordingly.

GET DRESSED

At this point you may expect me to do a point-by-point commentary on God's armor to show how each piece functions spiritually. For example, people often say that righteousness is a breastplate because it guards our hearts. Or salvation is a helmet because it protects our minds, etc. However, I don't think this is what Paul is trying to say. He is rather using the whole armor as a metaphor to help us understand the way spiritual battles are fought in general. Just as physical battles are fought with physical weapons, spiritual battles involve spiritual implements. That is Paul's main point. It is not that righteousness protects only our hearts while salvation protects only our minds. That kind of interpretation takes the metaphor too far.

We know this because Paul uses similar metaphors in different ways elsewhere. For example, although faith is a shield in Ephesians, it takes on other images in other contexts. It is a door in Acts 14:27 and a breastplate in 1 Thessalonians 5:8. Also, Scripture uses shields as metaphors for virtues other than faith. David uses the image of a shield to symbolize salvation (2 Sam. 22:36), favor (Ps. 5:12), and the Lord Himself (Ps. 33:20). The language is flexible. We must not over-interpret with a strictness that distracts us from its main point.

Paul means that these are the kinds of provisions God has made available for our protection in the Spirit. Spiritual warfare requires us to cultivate the Spirit's life into our actual characters. That means truth, righteousness, peace, faith, and salvation are more than godly virtues. *They are spiritual battle gear.* We need these virtues in order to be good witnesses but also to be effective soldiers. We must therefore wrap ourselves in these spiritual defenses, so to speak, in order to be prepared to combat all kinds of evil.

What's more, Paul's meta-phor must be understood in its broader scriptural context. Though he adapted the met-aphor for his own purposes,

We are God's children in peace; we are likewise His children in war.

Paul did not invent it. A Jewish audience would have immediately rec-ognized the armor of God passage as a reference to Isaiah's descrip-tion of Yahweh, girding himself for battle against His spiritual foes.

> Yes, truth is gone, and anyone who renounces evil is attacked. The LORD looked and was displeased to find there was no jus-tice. He was amazed to see that no one intervened to help the oppressed. So he himself stepped in to save them with his strong arm, and his justice sustained him. He put on righ-teousness as his body armor and placed the helmet of salvation on his head. He clothed himself with a robe of vengeance and wrapped himself in a cloak of divine passion. He will repay his enemies for their evil deeds. His fury will fall on his foes. He will pay them back even to the ends of the earth.
> —ISAIAH 59:15–18, NLT

Again, if the helmet of salvation means that salvation is meant to protect the mind of the Christian, then why does *God* put it on in this passage? He does not need salvation, nor does His mind need protection. These virtues refer rather to attributes of God's character that take on a whole new meaning in the context of spiritual warfare. This is why we must not interpret the armor pieces too strictly. However—and this is the main point—the armor metaphor does speak of its wearer's intent to vanquish evil and injustice, with a passion fitting to all-out war. By borrowing Isaiah's divine imagery and applying it to Christians, Paul is communicating to his readers that they should treat evil the same way the Lord does: as an enemy to be completely vanquished. We are God's children in peace; we are likewise His children in war. We put on salvation, righteousness, and faith so we can stand firm against the strategies of the devil as we fight against evil rulers and authorities in the unseen world.

THE RADICAL NORMALITY OF SPIRITUAL WARFARE

Throughout this book I have taken time to place spiritual warfare within its cosmic context. We have talked about how Satan, the prince of the power of the air, has tried to poison the human way of thinking. The demonic zeitgeist, the antichrist spirit already in the world, positions itself completely against God and His ways. In reality, then, spiritual warfare is anything that undercuts Satan's stranglehold on this world. We can and should be waging warfare in our everyday lives, not just at special prayer meetings or conferences. Our efforts might not always seem heroic or earth-shattering. But imagine what would happen if every Christian took one chip out of the wall of Satan's kingdom every day.

For many Christians—especially Charismatics and Pentecostals—the idea of spiritual warfare is often acted out in physical ways. You will sometimes see prayer meetings with intercessors waving flags, blowing shofars, dancing prophetically, or even making physical gestures that resemble a physical fight with an invisible opponent. It is crucial for us to understand, however, that most spiritual warfare is not fought this way at all. Spiritual warfare often takes on the most mundane of appearances. Some of the most destructive things a Christian can do to Satan's dark kingdom occur through a life of purity, acts of kindness, Christlike forgiveness, humility, and self-sacrifice.

Even when spiritual warfare does become outwardly dramatic and physical, it often looks like anything but an impressive victory. Consider for example the ultimate spiritual weapon: *the blood of Jesus* is the thermonuclear bomb of spiritual warfare that has forever changed the game and has already rendered Satan a defeated foe. The cross of Christ was the ultimate act of spiritual warfare. Yet it hardly looked like a dramatic display of eternal military might. On the contrary, it looked like utter weakness, total loss, and complete failure. What seems powerful and effective in the flesh is often completely impotent in the spiritual realm. Likewise, what seems weak and small to the human eye can make the realms of darkness tremble. The most effective spiritual warfare occurs below the surface, in the depths of our character, godliness, and sacrifice.

None of this is to say there are no outward expressions in spiritual warfare. Later in this chapter I will defend those who practice spiritual warfare in more physical and demonstrative ways, especially in intercession. But for now I want to stress this more fundamental point. Shofars and banners are not listed anywhere in Scripture as weapons for spiritual warfare. In fact, to emphasize how practical spiritual warfare is, consider the armor listed for us in Ephesians: truth, salvation, righteousness, the gospel of peace, faith, and God's Word. These are all invisible attributes made visible only by a Christian lifestyle. Further, every item mentioned here directly contradicts the spirit of the age—the demonic antichrist spirit we discussed earlier. This should reinforce the truth that our internal alignment with God and the behavior that proceeds from that alignment are vitally important to spiritual warfare. Indeed, they are the very root of victory in any spiritual battle. If Paul's message in Ephesians is not clear enough about this point, consider the way he frames spiritual armor in Romans.

This is all the more urgent, for you know how late it is; time is running out. Wake up, for our salvation is nearer now than when we first believed. The night is almost gone; the day of salvation will soon be here. So remove your dark deeds like dirty clothes, and put on the shining armor of right living. Because we belong to the day, we must live decent lives for all to see. Don't participate in the darkness of wild parties and drunkenness, or in sexual promiscuity and immoral living, or in quarreling and jealousy. Instead, clothe yourself with the presence of the Lord Jesus Christ. And don't let yourself think about ways to indulge your evil desires.

—ROMANS 13:11–14, NLT

Notice this military terminology is being used to address our own personal war against sin. I stress this because some readers may feel I am taking license with this *spiritual warfare* terminology and downplaying its significance by applying it to our internal struggle. I want this to be clear—biblical spiritual warfare begins in us. Here Paul specifically emphasizes that our spiritual armor does not merely protect against outside evil powers but also against the internal, personal practice of sin. Paul admonishes his readers in both passages to protect themselves against evil and sin by wearing, so to speak, right thinking, pure actions, and the actual presence of God.

Paul uses strong military language out of a deep concern for the personal holiness of his audience (which includes us). He does not want to see the churches—the precious people for whom he has poured out his life—taken down by a flippant attitude toward evil in all its forms. He encourages them to prepare for battle against temptation. And once they have done everything possible to get ready, he encourages them to rise up and actually *fight* the battle.

GET READY; STAY READY

Getting dressed for battle is no small task. Modern American soldiers carry more than sixty pounds of gear, and longer patrols can more than double that amount! Rations, medical equipment, weapons, ammunition, communication technology, and miscellaneous gadgets fill every pouch and pocket. Needless to say, people don't go through the effort to prepare like that unless they are going to war. That is true today, and it was true two thousand years ago when Paul wrote Ephesians. Nobody prepares like this to go shopping. To be clothed for war signals the intention to fight. This is the way Isaiah used the armor metaphor in the passage above, and it is the way Paul communicates it to Christians now. We gear up because we understand we are in a spiritual battle. Therefore we don't naively walk around unarmed and oblivious like private citizens. The mindset of a warrior is different than the mindset of a civilian. Paul refers to this warrior mentality when he tells Timothy, "Join with me in suffering, like a good soldier of Christ Jesus. No one serving as a soldier gets entangled in civilian affairs, but rather tries to please his commanding officer" (2 Tim. 2:3–4).

The theme of military readiness saturates the warfare passage in Ephesians 6. Paul talks about being able to stand firm against the strategies of the devil (v. 11). He talks about being able to resist the enemy in the time of evil (v. 13). He talks about putting on our shoes so that we will be fully prepared (v. 15). Then he talks about praying in the Spirit at all times and on every occasion. "Stay alert and be persistent in your prayers for all believers everywhere" (v. 18, NLT). In fact, within its context all of the armor seems to be a matter of preparation and readiness.

You will notice that Paul does not specify the exact methods of fighting a spiritual battle in this passage. He rather emphasizes that we should be equipped and ready. Paul doesn't even tell us what to do with the sword; he just tells us to have one. Nor does Paul provide particular strategies for fighting. In fact, he doesn't talk much about the fight at all. His basic instruction is to get dressed and stay dressed in God's armor, then stand and fight.

To be clothed for war signals the intention to fight.

One of the worst things that could happen to a soldier is to be caught off guard, undressed and sleeping, in the middle of the night. In a war we never know when the attack will come. The enemy always prefers to take us by surprise. But there are often signs that something is not right. Sometimes we can feel it in our gut. It often feels like what I described earlier. We are pedaling along on what seems like a normal path, but then an unseen force seems to resist us. When we sense that resistance, it is time to make sure we are dressed. Indeed, we should already be dressed and ready at all times.

It is essential to be ready at all times because we just don't always know when a spiritual attack is coming. Other times we may not initially be able to tell the difference between a spiritual attack and the normal difficulties of life. But a person who is ready for battle is able to handle everything that comes his way. "Be alert and of sober mind. Your enemy the devil prowls around like a roaring lion looking for someone to devour. Resist him, standing firm in the faith, because you know that the family of believers throughout the world is undergoing the same kind of sufferings" (1 Pet. 5:8–9).

Without becoming superstitious or fearful, we stay ready for battle by keeping our hearts and minds aligned with Christ. Sometimes we will be under demonic assault, and other times we will simply be handling the volatilities of life. We will not always know which is which, but our preparation will assure that in every situation we are more than conquerors.

STAND AND FIGHT

Paul makes an interesting statement in the Ephesians 6 warfare passage. After "having done all, to stand," he then says, "Stand" (vv. 13–14, NKJV). Once we put on the armor of God and make all the preparations for the fight, there is still one thing we must do—resolve to stand and fight the battle when it comes.

We have everything we need to gain victory in spiritual warfare. Through Christ we have God's own battle gear—the finest in the universe. No spiritual weapons compare to those forged in heaven and wielded by the Holy Spirit through us. The armor is actually a gift to us. All we need to do is put it on. But the resolve to fight must come from within. Even the most well-equipped soldier will be defeated if he doesn't fight.

This might sound obvious and perhaps even unnecessary to say, but it is amazing how many people encounter spiritual resistance and give up. Overwhelmed with frustration and fear, they sit down and cry. They watch through the tears as the enemy ravages their lives and they ask, "Why, God?"

You have to get some fight in you! You have to be resolved that you are not going to let the devil have your life, your children, and your marriage. You have to determine that the enemy is not going to destroy you with sickness, financial problems, fear, addiction, lust, and lies. You need to make sure you are dressed in the armor of God—and then fight!

When God puts on His armor in the Isaiah 59 passage, it's like a scene out of an action movie. You can almost hear the film score, building to a crescendo. In slow motion He tightens His belt and sheathes His sword. You can almost envision God's eyes burning with a fearsome gaze as He steps out to vanquish His enemies. This is what Isaiah wants you to see, and this is also what I believe Paul is trying to convey in his passage about the armor of the Lord. It's not so much about the individual implements as much as the heart of the warrior, girding himself for battle and stepping out to conquer his enemies. In spiritual warfare you have to have a burning heart and the eye of the tiger—that fierce determination to win and never back down.

As I mentioned in the second chapter, it must have been a pitiful sight when Eve was tempted in the garden. For some inexplicable reason Adam just stood there and watched the whole scene unfold. He should have grabbed that serpent by the head, put it under his heel, and applied all his weight. Instead he allowed his wife to put that fruit in her mouth, knowing full well what God said.

Like Adam did, many men today stand idly by as Satan destroys their families. They are too busy sitting on the couch with a beer and watching football or playing video games to notice there's a snake in the house. In Jesus' name, get out of your recliner, put down the remote control, grab your sword, and fight! Maybe you need to pull your family together and have family devotions, read the Bible and pray together. Maybe you need to take your son, daughter, or spouse on a date, talk to them, listen to them, pray with them, and be a leader in your home. Maybe you need to lock yourself away in the closet and pray with all the grace God gives you until He shows you where that snake is hiding. Maybe you need to fast. There are a thousand ways you might feel led to fight back against the enemy—far too many to mention here. But we can say this for sure: get ready for battle by getting dressed in the armor of God. Then when the battle comes, stand and fight! This is spiritual war!

THE NATURAL AFFECTS THE SPIRITUAL

In this chapter I have emphasized the importance of internal, personal preparation and the less dramatic aspects of spiritual warfare. Throughout this book I do the same, dealing far more with our personal lives than our outward demonstrations. I would, however, like to say something for those who intercede demonstratively and physically in spiritual warfare. It is a mistake to think that we can punch the air and knock demons out (not that anyone actually believes this; it's just the way it looks sometimes). We cannot fight spiritual battles with physical weapons. That much is self-evident. But this does not negate the fact that natural actions do affect the spiritual world. We see many examples in Scripture of outward acts that carry tremendous spiritual significance.

Before I mention some biblical examples, I think it is worthwhile to say this is also a matter of simple common sense. Everything in the spiritual realm interacts with the physical realm, and vice versa. We live in the natural world. So even though *spiritual* warfare is *spiritual*,

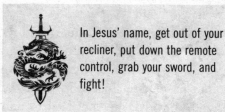

In Jesus' name, get out of your recliner, put down the remote control, grab your sword, and fight!

it still always intersects with the physical realm. The two spheres are connected when people are involved. Each of us is a body, soul, and spirit. The natural and the spiritual come together in us. And while these realities (the physical and the spiritual) are distinct from one another, and even sometimes contrary to one another, in us they collide in a way that often makes it hard to tell where one ends and the other begins. Prayer, for example, involves our brains, our voices, and our bodies. These are physical things that have spiritual efficacy. Fasting, as we will discuss in more depth later, is also a physical discipline that has bearing on the spiritual realm.

A peculiar story illustrates my point. Jehoash, the king of Israel, went to see Elisha the prophet before the prophet died (2 Kings 13:14–19). Elisha told Jehoash to take arrows and strike the ground but gave him no explanation or additional instructions. Jehoash struck the ground three times and stopped. Elisha got angry with him and said, "You should have struck the ground five or six times; then you would have defeated Aram and completely destroyed it. But now you will defeat it only three times" (v. 19).

It is not obvious on the surface what is happening in this passage. But the prophet Elisha understood there would be some very real spiritual ramifications to the physical actions of the king. Jehoash's corporeal response would reverberate in the spiritual realm and directly affect Israel's military campaigns against Aram. God apparently saw the zeal with which Jehoash struck the earth as an indication of his heart. Maybe Jehoash's lack of enthusiasm exposed his heart and showed where his deepest motivations lay. Perhaps it was a sign he did not trust in the Lord. Whatever the case, Elisha knew that Jehoash had to act something out physically. Without the outward actions there would be no spiritual effects. Whether many strokes or few, Jehoash's physical performance would have serious, real-world consequences.

In a similar story the Israelites battled the Amalekites. As long as Moses held up his hands—with God's staff—on the hilltop, Israel prevailed against Amalek in the valley below. But as soon as Moses lowered his hands, Amalek prevailed (Exod. 17:9–13). Again we see an outward action directly affected God's supernatural intervention. The same thing happened in Jericho. Somehow the Israelites' march around the city walls directly affected the supernatural collapse of those walls (Josh. 6). Elijah told Naaman to dip in the Jordan River seven times (2 Kings 5:1–14). Jesus put mud in a blind man's eye (John 9:6), and He told the disciples to cast their nets on the other side of the boat (John 21:6).

There are many examples such as these throughout Scripture. Of course, the greatest example is the cross of Christ. Nothing could have been more physical than the way Jesus died. He bled physical blood on a physical cross. He suffered in a human body pierced and marred beyond recognition. Then He experienced a physical death. All of this, though completely within the natural world, shook the spiritual realm from the top of heaven to the bottom of hell. Never before or since has there been such a significant spiritual event. And yet it was accomplished entirely in the physical world.

THE GNOSTIC HERESY

This exact issue lies at the heart of the Gnostic heresy John addressed in 1 John. The Gnostics taught among other things that the physical world is inherently evil. Only the realm of the spirit is good. Thus "salvation" occurred when a person's spirit was released from the world of flesh through knowledge, or *gnōsis*. This philosophical system led the heretics to deny Jesus' humanity and reject His literal, physical death and resurrection. But this heresy still finds its way into our modern way of thinking in the church. Sometimes in explicit ways but other times in subtle ways, we try to separate the physical and spiritual worlds. One is bad and the other is good.

Because the word *flesh* is often used to refer to the sinful nature (cf. Rom. 7:18, ESV, NLT), we think everything in the physical, human world is evil. Yes, *flesh* can refer to the carnal (sensual, demonic) nature as well as a way of thinking that is contrary to Christ (as I have discussed at length in this book). But God made the physical world, including our flesh, in the beginning. And then "the Word became flesh" (John 1:14). "The earth is the LORD's and all it contains" (Ps. 24:1, NASB). There is simply no biblical justification for a way of thinking that sees the physical world as inherently evil. On the contrary, the New Testament emphasizes with great force that our spiritual faith must be incarnated in our physical bodies or it is not legitimate faith. (See, for example, 1 Corinthians 6:12–20.) The physical world is the exact place the spiritual kingdom is meant to come. "Your kingdom come, your will be done, *on earth* as it is in heaven" (Matt. 6:10, emphasis added). This is why physical actions can also have such profound effect on the spiritual realm.

Because of this powerful truth, the Bible contains many examples of physical actions affecting spiritual realities. It's a mystery how physical gestures can actually make a difference in the spirit. But that is part of my point. We do not always know what God is doing or why or how He is leading people, and we certainly do not understand how the spiritual world operates in great detail. If someone is interceding and doing something outwardly that looks strange, don't be quick to judge. They are in good company, as we have seen from these biblical examples. It is highly possible that someone might see tremendous breakthrough spiritually as a result of something that looks foolish to a casual observer—particularly when such activity comes out of obedience to the Holy Spirit.

QUESTIONS FOR DISCUSSION

- How can virtues like faith, hope, and love be weapons against Satan's dark kingdom?

- How did Jesus wage spiritual warfare throughout His earthly life?

- Have you sensed that some area of your life has been under attack recently?

- How would you describe your current state of mind? Are you ready for spiritual battle, or are you in civilian mode?

CHAPTER 7

DISCIPLINE, CONSECRATION, AND SPIRITUAL AUTHORITY

Self-control is the chief element in self-respect, and respect of self, in turn, is the chief element in courage.

—THUCYDIDES, *HISTORY OF THE PELOPONNESIAN WAR*

Why is discipline important? Discipline teaches us to operate by principle rather than desire. Saying no to our impulses (even the ones that are not inherently sinful) puts us in control of our appetites rather than vice versa. It deposes our lust and permits truth, virtue, and integrity to rule our minds instead.

—JOHN F. MACARTHUR, *MOMENTS OF TRUTH*

OD SENT PAUL and Silas to Macedonia through a dream. On their way to prayer one day, they met "a certain female slave who had a spirit of divination" (Acts 16:16, LEB). She began to stalk them, following them everywhere and shouting over and over, "These men are servants of the Most High God, who are telling you the way to be saved" (v. 17). After several days of this, Paul had enough. "He turned around and said to the spirit, 'In the name of Jesus Christ I command you to come out of her!' At that moment the spirit left her" (v. 18).

This passage contains many interesting takeaways, but here is the one I want to emphasize: any demon you tolerate will stay with you. Too many people are tormented by spirits that would in fact leave if they were no longer welcome. Jesus rebuked the church in Thyatira for tolerating a Jezebel spirit (Rev. 2:20–21). As a result they had been deceived into sexual immorality and other sins. This spirit was misleading and deceiving them, not because it was too powerful for them, but because they were allowing it to reign unchallenged in their midst.

SPIRITUAL AUTHORITY

We have already established that Satan's only power is the power we give him. But how can we exercise authority over spirits that we tolerate or, even worse, that we submit to? If a person is bound by lust, he will have no authority over that spirit. If a person is bound by addictions, he will not have authority to break them off of others. If a person is full of jealousy or pride, these spirits will reign unchallenged in his presence.

Jesus said, "Hereafter I will not talk much with you: for the prince of this world cometh, and hath nothing in me" (John 14:30, KJV). Nothing of demonic origin dwelled in Jesus. He had not yielded to that demonic pattern of thinking. He had not yielded to temptation. Satan had nothing in Him. This is why the devil had no power over Him. Even death itself could not hold Him. It is no wonder, then, that Jesus had such complete authority over demons. Those dramatic instances of exorcism were just a visible demonstration of the way Jesus walked in complete authority over the dragon every moment of every day.

We may not always walk in perfect victory over sin, self, and the devil, as Jesus did. But as God's children we are called to grow consistently under Christ's authority. There must be "no end to the increase of His government" in our daily lives (Isa. 9:7, AMP). Jesus' victory over the forces of darkness cannot merely remain a theological or positional truth. It must become practical. It must become a lifestyle. We must actually walk in authority over sin and the devil as our Christian characters grow into Christ's image. The bottom line: we are called to live lives of discipline and holiness.

Then this authority over darkness in our own practical lives will extend into the world around us. When we are confronted with demons in others, we have authority over them as well. But when we yield to Satan in our lives, we will find it extremely difficult to take authority over his influence on someone else's life. This is both a spiritual and practical matter. If we yield to something, we agree with it. This agreement then manifests in our actions, even if our words declare God's truth. Such disparity between our words and lives will carry no weight against satanic forces.

But it's important to understand the distinction I am making. I am not saying we have authority over demons in our own strength—when we are good enough or disciplined enough. Our authority does not come from an adequate amount of religious works or random acts of self-discipline. Our authority comes from our submission to God's authority. In fact, submission to God contradicts human pride, self-confidence, and religious works. Submission to God recognizes our deep and desperate need for His grace. But such humble surrender to God must still occur practically. Therefore, if we do *not* submit to God in our lifestyle, we actually *resist* His authority. How can we possess God's authority while simultaneously resisting it? Without submission we have no authority to confront satanic forces. When we submit to God, we receive His authority, which therefore enables us to release it to others.

Just as the centurion's authority over his men came from his submission to the authority of his superiors, so too our spiritual authority over sin and demons comes from our submission to Christ.

"Submit yourselves therefore to God. Resist the devil, and he will flee from you" (Jas. 4:7, ESV). Our ability to resist Satan is contingent on our submission to God, and for good reason: all spiritual authority comes from God. We have no authority over Satan in ourselves. In order to release *God's* authority, we must submit to it. In fact, Jude tells us that even Michael, the great archangel, said in a dispute with Satan, "The Lord rebuke you!" (v. 9). Not even mighty warrior angels possess authority within themselves over demonic forces. It comes from God alone. Likewise, our authority comes from being under His authority.

The centurion of Capernaum understood this crucial dynamic well. "The centurion replied, 'Lord, I do not deserve to have you come under my roof. But just say the word, and my servant will be healed. For I myself am a man under authority, with soldiers under me. I tell this one, 'Go,' and he goes; and that one, 'Come,' and he comes. I say to my servant, 'Do this,' and he does it" (Matt. 8:8–9). Just as the centurion's authority over his men came from his submission to the authority of his superiors, so too our spiritual authority over sin and demons comes from our submission to Christ. No wonder Paul calls himself Christ's slave (Rom. 1:1, LEB). Then elsewhere he says that he makes his body *his* slave (1 Cor. 9:27). Paul's body was a slave to Paul, who was a slave to Christ. This is what it means to be under authority. Jesus made it clear that we cannot serve two masters. We must choose one or the other (Matt. 6:24). If we are not submitted to Christ, then we are enslaved to sin (Rom. 6:16–23). The picture is clear: without submission to God in holiness and consecration, we possess no spiritual authority.

DISCIPLINE

One of the often-overlooked secrets for a victorious spiritual life is simple obedience to Christ and discipline. Some see Christianity as something that just happens after you pray the sinner's prayer. They think that *works* is a dirty word and that anything that demands resolve and effort is opposed to grace. But this is not what the Bible teaches.

"For it is by grace you have been saved, through faith—and this is not from yourselves, it is the gift of God—not by works, so that no one can boast" (Eph. 2:8–9). This verse is well known and widely quoted. But few people quote the next verse: "For we are God's handiwork, created in Christ Jesus to do good works, which God prepared in advance for us to do" (v. 10). In other words, though we were not saved *by* good works, we were saved *for* good works. We cannot negate the importance of works. Regarding salvation, works are meaningless. But once we are saved and filled with the Holy Spirit, God expects us to bear good fruit.

Many Christians have missed this revolutionary idea. You have the ability to do what is right! You do not have to sin. You do not have to fall. You can be disciplined. You can say no to sin and yes to righteousness. In fact, God expects you to do that. If you think that is legalistic or in some way opposed to grace, remember what Paul tells Titus about grace: "For the grace of God has appeared that offers salvation to all people. It teaches us to say 'No' to ungodliness and worldly passions, and to live self-controlled, upright and godly lives in this present age, while we wait for the blessed hope—the appearing of the glory of our great God and Savior, Jesus Christ" (Titus 2:11–13).

Susanna Wesley gave this word of wisdom to young John Wesley: "Would you judge of the lawfulness or unlawfulness of pleasure, of the innocence or malignity of actions? Take this rule,—Whatever weakens your reason, impairs the tenderness of your conscience, obscures your sense of God, or takes off the relish of spiritual things; in short, whatever increases the strength and authority of your *body* over your *mind*, that thing is a sin to *you*, however innocent it may be in itself."[1]

This is a good time for a little diagnostic test. What is it that weakens your reason? What is it that impairs the tenderness of your conscience? What is it that obscures your sense of God? What is it that takes the relish off spiritual things? Maybe it's video games. Maybe it's pornography. Maybe it's just wasting time or neglecting your responsibilities to your family. Maybe it's not being faithful to the church. Maybe it's neglecting your time with Jesus in prayer and in the Scriptures. By saying these things, I am not trying to create extrabiblical rules. What I am asking you to do is allow the Holy Spirit to show you the areas of your life where there is compromise. When He shows you what you're doing that displeases Him, STOP! If you want to fight the devil and bring his kingdom down, start by getting your own house in order.

FASTING

Many important spiritual disciplines should be part of the Christian's arsenal. Later in this chapter I will briefly describe a number of them. But first I will address in greater detail one of the most powerful spiritual disciplines—fasting. Fasting is the intentional choice to abstain from food and/or drink for a period of time. Today many use the term to describe abstention from any number of things—from chocolate to video games. Whether applied exclusively to food or drink, or more broadly to less-necessary activities, fasting means self-sacrifice. When we fast, we give up something we want or even need to make more space for God in our lives. And seen through that lens, it is the perfect complement to spiritual warfare. When we fast, we deny ourselves. That in and of itself turns the devil on his head. His goal, after all, is to dupe us into obeying him by putting our desires, our advancement, and our very selves above God. Remember his original temptation in the garden: "You will be like God" (Gen. 3:5). When we put our basic needs temporarily on hold in order to know and serve God better, it directly thwarts Satan's agenda to put ourselves first. It also signals that he will make little headway with us.

Fasting and prayer combine as an incredibly effective spiritual recalibration technique. If you sense your heart is starting to harden, pride is seeping in, or your soul is starting to align with the flesh, then fasting and prayer will cause a quick realignment like few other things could. As you deny yourself and become intimate with your own weakness, you will become aware of how far you have drifted, like awakening out of a dream. After just a couple of days of fasting, often you will not understand why you did not do it sooner. You will find your prior way of thinking to be strange and foreign. Fasting and prayer are spiritual disciplines that should be close at hand for every believer.

Fasting plays an interesting role in several key Bible stories. Moses fasts for forty days when he ascends Mount Sinai to receive the Law from God (Exod. 34:28). David fasts when he prays for his sick newborn son to survive (2 Sam. 12:16, 21–22). Esther fasts before approaching the king about the death sentence he decreed for the Jewish people (Est. 4:16). And one story about the prophet Daniel is particularly fascinating and relevant.

Daniel was a prophet with extraordinary insight into dreams, visions, and even natural matters. He was taken captive from Judea, along with many of his fellow Jews, by an invading army from Babylon. Despite his captive status, Daniel's gifts opened a place for him as an adviser to the king. He was so favored in fact that even after Babylon was taken over by yet another empire, Persia, the new king chose to keep Daniel on staff.

About three years into Daniel's tenure under the king of Persia, God gave Daniel a vision that troubled him deeply. Daniel knew that its message was true and that it concerned a great war. But he could neither distill its meaning nor shake its ominous tone. Daniel sought God for an understanding of the vision (Dan. 10:1–12). In addition to his prayers, Daniel tells us, "I ate no choice food; no meat or wine touched my lips; and I used no lotions at all until the three weeks were over" (v. 3).

As a courtier of the Persian Empire and a highly ranked personal adviser to the king, Daniel had access to the best of the best. He did not need to bring his own peanut butter and jelly sandwich to work every day. One of the perks of this gig was access to the most extraordinary delicacies available anywhere. The wealth of the nations poured into Persia; they owned the known world. The palace was the epicenter of wealth, and Daniel was at the epicenter of the palace. It is safe to say he usually ate well.

Yet despite all of this he recognized that he could not get the answers he needed in his own strength. He stopped paying attention to himself. He did not pamper his vanity with exquisite, perfumed lotions. He did not satisfy his cravings for fancy foods. The king still made demands on his time, but Daniel did only what was needed to perform his duties. Otherwise his attention was focused on God. His priority was the breakthrough of God's word into his situation. After twenty-one days of self-denial Daniel received an extraordinary message from heaven. Daniel was standing by a river when it all took place.

> I looked up and saw a man dressed in linen clothing, with a belt of pure gold around his waist. His body looked like a precious gem. His face flashed like lightning, and his eyes flamed like torches. His arms and feet shone like polished bronze, and his voice roared like a vast multitude of people....
>
> And the man said to me, "Daniel, you are very precious to God, so listen carefully to what I have to say to you.... Since the first day you began to pray for understanding and to humble yourself before your God, your request has been heard in heaven. I have come in answer to your prayer. But for twenty-one days the spirit prince of the kingdom of Persia blocked my way. Then Michael, one of the archangels, came to help me, and I left him there with the spirit prince of the kingdom of Persia. Now I am here to explain what will

happen to your people in the future, for this vision concerns a
time yet to come.

—DANIEL 10:5–6, 11–14, NLT

God dispatched a messenger the moment Daniel made his request.
But along the way the angel encountered "the spirit prince of the
kingdom of Persia." The spirit prince of Persia was the power behind
the throne, the demonic attaché who set the tone of the empire's culture and influenced the human king's decisions. The prince blocked
God's angelic messenger from his destination, which was with Daniel.
God dispatched one of His own warring angels—"Michael, one of the
archangels"—to combat the spirit prince of Persia and free up the messenger to deliver his missive.

Daniel 10 is dense with meaningful details that give us wonderful
insights.

First, God's concern for His friends is paramount. The moment
Daniel prayed, God answered. Though the arrival of the answer was
delayed because of spiritual resistance, the answer itself was immediate.
God does not hold back from us.

Second, when factors we do not fully comprehend get in the way,
we can rest assured that our Father has already seen to everything we
need. Fasting is not our way to coerce God to act on our behalf. It is
rather an expression of patient confidence that God has already acted.
It is an expressed trust in God. It reminds us that God's strength is
at work and breakthrough is imminent, and it compels our physical
bodies to accept this truth.

Third, one person's actions can influence the much larger picture.
Daniel's choices assert God's eternal plan over an entire empire—many
nations and peoples are represented under the spirit of the prince of
Persia. In other words, in this case Daniel's fast was an act of spiritual
warfare that had significant influence on a conflict in the heavens and
a breakthrough on the earth. The far-reaching, cosmic effects of our
thoughts and actions are not always obvious from street level. Daily
life doesn't usually afford us so complete a view. Nonetheless, no matter
how obscure our lives may feel on earth, the ramifications of our relationship with God are enormous. We should not underestimate the

import of our combat. The church doesn't have a junior varsity team; every Christ follower plays major-league ball.

Fourth, a benefit of fasting is the involvement our physical bodies in our quest for spiritual answers. The involvement of our physical bodies is important because we are not only spiritual beings but also physical. We experience our lives on the material plane, that is, in the realm of existence that can be perceived and interpreted by our five physical senses. However, our physical bodies are animated by a spirit, breathed into us by God Himself (Gen. 2:7). The body and spirit are in turn bridged by a soul comprised of our intellect, emotions, and will. The apostle Paul confirms this human architecture when he prays that "the God of peace himself sanctify you wholly; and may your spirit and soul and body be preserved entire, without blame at the coming of our Lord Jesus Christ" (1 Thess. 5:23, ASV).[2]

We are part dirt, part spirit. Each element of our construction makes unique contributions to our experience as humans, but we most certainly interact with the world with God through our bodies. "Don't you realize that your body is the temple of the Holy Spirit, who lives in you and was given to you by God? You do not belong to yourself, for God bought you with a high price. So you must honor God with your body" (1 Cor. 6:19–20, NLT). God did not just redeem our spirits or command us to renew our minds. He also purchased our bodies to give habitation and expression to the Spirit of God within us.

C. S. Lewis describes the value of involving the body in spiritual warfare in his classic fictional presentation *The Screwtape Letters*. In this brief book Lewis imagines a correspondence from an experienced demon named Screwtape to his nephew and apprentice, Wormwood. Screwtape instructs the trainee on methods for securing the soul of a recent convert to Christianity. In one such note Screwtape presents Wormwood with a paradox.

> At the very least, they can be persuaded that the bodily position makes no difference to their prayers; for they constantly forget, what you must always remember, that they are animals and that whatever their bodies do affects their souls.[3]

Starving the body for a short season strengthens the spirit the same way pruning a tree produces more fruit. When we posture ourselves in a position of hunger, God will satisfy us. Daniel was hungry for spiritual answers—answers he could not manufacture on his own. So he positioned his body with hunger until the answers came. But God did not answer Daniel because he fasted. God released His answer the moment Daniel prayed. God isn't moved by hunger strikes. Rather, Daniel's fast physically expressed his need for God. Daniel's closeness with God had taught him that he could not be satisfied by his own strength. His fast gave that lesson form—it brought the truth into the real world. We are wise when we do the same.

In case there is any confusion on this point, I would like to clarify something. We do not fast for power. This is the way witch doctors fast, attempting to manipulate the spirit world to their own advantage. I do not encourage this kind of fasting. I do not think it is right or even effective. Also, there is a story told in the Gospels in which Jesus seems to indicate that fasting is needed for casting out certain kinds of demons. I will address this in more depth in chapter 10. But for now suffice it to say this interpretation is not necessarily accurate.

Fasting is an extreme embodiment of submission. The flesh is brought under radical subjection by the soul (the will), and the soul submits to God.

So how does fasting relate to spiritual warfare? We have talked at length in this book about the importance of internal alignment with God's heart and will for spiritual warfare. It is the principle taught in James 4:7: "Submit yourselves, then, to God. Resist the devil, and he will flee from you." As mentioned earlier, this submission to God (being under authority) gives us authority over the demonic realm. This is why all spiritual disciplines are important issues. Fasting is an extreme embodiment of submission. The flesh is brought under radical subjection by the soul (the will), and the soul submits to God. At this point it is almost effortless to bring one's entire being in alignment. It is a strange irony that as the flesh weakens, we begin to sense a greater strength and authority in the spirit.

OTHER SPIRITUAL DISCIPLINES

Fasting is one example of a spiritual discipline. These are behaviors that when put into practice, bring the self to heel and God to the fore in our lives. The Bible mentions many such activities. But to get us started, I will list twelve commonly recognized disciplines that you can weave into the patterns of your life. Each one targets a specific aspect of the self. As we get out of our own way, we make it easier to see God. We can understand the specific disciplines as ways to better illuminate specific aspects of God. As we learn of His character in that area, we find ourselves freer from temptations that trouble us in that domain.

The spiritual disciplines break neatly into two groups: disciplines of self-denial and disciplines of engagement.[4] Here are lists of some of the disciplines included in each group.

Disciplines of self-denial

> **Solitude**—the practice of taking time away from others with the specific intent of being alone with God. Through solitude we cut off distractions that prevent us from hearing from the Lord. Through solitude we deny ourselves any company save God's.

> **Silence**—the natural partner of solitude. When we are quiet in both our environment and our minds, we more clearly hear the "still, small voice" through which the Spirit often chooses to speak. (See 1 Kings 19:11–13.) Through silence we deny ourselves any voice except for God's.

> **Fasting**—the intentional refusal of food and/or drink for a period of time. It may also be abstention from an activity such as sex (see 1 Cor. 7:5), various media, or some other recreation. When we fast, we deny ourselves any nourishment (physical or mental) save that which God provides by His presence and Word to us.

> **Sacrifice**—the practice of giving of our time, talent, or treasure whereby we ourselves no longer have what we

need to meet our basic requirements. Sacrifice, financial or otherwise, requires us to trust God to make up the difference. And it is a challenge He is ready and waiting to take.

Secrecy—the practice of withholding from others information about our spiritual lives or generosity. (See Matthew 6:3.) It is connected to solitude (praying privately or giving anonymously). Through secrecy we enhance intimacy with God in that there is a (righteous) part of our lives that only He is allowed into. In secrecy we deny ourselves any credit for an activity except that which God bestows on us.

Submission—the voluntary surrender of our own will with the specific intent of fulfilling God's will. Through submission we deny ourselves the satisfaction of any desires except God's.

Disciplines of engagement

Study of Scripture—reading the Bible with an eye toward understanding the contexts of specific passages, learning the author's intent, revealing the overall themes, and memorizing various verses. By studying Scripture, we engage in God's inspired Word and renew our minds to be like Christ's.

Worship—offering God thanks and adoration for His divine attributes (loving-kindness, goodness, beauty, etc.) Worship can take the form of song, liturgy, or even silence, and it can be done alone or by a group. Worship often involves physical expressions of surrender such as lifting the hands, kneeling, or lying facedown on the floor. By worshipping, we engage God's presence.

Prayer—conversing with God, especially with an awareness of our dependence on Him to satisfy our spiritual, mental, physical, social, and financial needs. By praying, we engage God's personhood, His will, and His capacity.

Meditation—Paul described this as setting our minds on things above. Probably the most common way is dwelling on the Scriptures—pondering and thinking deeply about God's Word and allowing God to speak to you through it.

Community—meeting with other believers for fellowship, worship, prayer, prophecy, and the Lord's Supper (Acts 2:42; 1 Cor. 11:17–14:40). We need family-level connections with other believers both for encouragement and accountability. The Bible commands us to pursue hospitality (Rom. 12:13), submit to one another (Eph. 5:21), and confess our sins to one another (Jas. 5:16; see also 1 John 1:9). The practice of true community is one of the greatest needs in the church's spiritual life today and one of the most effective weapons in spiritual warfare (Rom. 16:20; Eph. 4:7–16).

Reflection—contemplating our inner selves to recognize and appreciate the work of the Holy Spirit in our lives. We may consider a passage of Scripture that had a surprisingly immediate application, an anecdote from a fellow believer, or an impression that led us to share our faith. Any number of experiences could be relevant to what God is doing in us. By reflecting, we engage with God's ongoing process of personal redemption.

Service—giving of our time, talents, and treasure to meet the needs of others. Service could include volunteer efforts to feed the poor, help with the homeless, or set up and break down for church services; tithing; or simply sharing your lunch with a colleague. By serving, we engage God's humble, selfless nature and His way of interacting with the world.

As with physical discipline, spiritual discipline can be exhausting at first. It makes sense to start slowly and build up. Five minutes of prayer is much better than no minutes of prayer. Reading one verse of Scripture is much better than reading no Scripture. Sitting in the back of a church service after arriving twenty minutes late is much better than sitting in no church service! You have to start somewhere. As legendary New York Yankees' catcher Yogi Berra was mistakenly reported to have said, "In theory there is no difference between theory and practice; in practice there is."[5]

In other words, the most important step is the one that converts the discipline from a mere idea into a real-world action. Get started! Once you have seen the fruit of fasting one or two meals or reading a few passages of Scripture each day, you will find yourself wanting more. God will meet your small effort with His massive grace, and you will be floored by the results.[6]

QUESTIONS FOR DISCUSSION

- If fasting doesn't make God answer our prayers, what does it do?

- Self-discipline doesn't always seem like fun. How would you encourage others to keep it up?

- From what temptations might the various disciplines listed in this chapter bring freedom? (Example: Sacrifice is an antidote for greed.)

- What is the role of our physical bodies in spiritual warfare?

CHAPTER 8

HOW TO KILL YOUR
PET DRAGON

*The full purpose of our salvation is that we might enjoy the
manifest, conscious presence of God as well as He enjoys
our presence. When we are enjoying the conscious presence
of God, we are fulfilling the tenets of our salvation.*

—A. W. TOZER, *EXPERIENCING THE PRESENCE OF GOD*

Only the enjoyment of Christ can keep us in right relationship with God.

—ERIC GILMOUR

JACK KENT WROTE a children's book called *There's No Such Thing as
a Dragon*. The story is about a little boy named Billy Bixbee, who
was surprised one morning when he woke up to discover a dragon
in his room. It was a nice little dragon—about the size of a kitten. It
was friendly and even allowed Billy to pat its head. Of course, Billy
couldn't wait to tell someone about his new little friend, but when he
told his mother, she said as if she meant it, "There's no such thing as a
dragon!" Soon the dragon was downstairs, even sitting on the kitchen
table. But Billy's mother ignored it. She had already said there was no
such thing as a dragon. How could she now tell a dragon to get off the
table? The story goes on to relate how the dragon became a nuisance
and grew so large it eventually filled the house. But everyone ignored

it. Billy's mother continued to say, "There's no such thing as a dragon." Soon the dragon's head was sticking out the front door and his tail out the back. He was so large that when a bread truck drove by, the hungry dragon chased it down the road, carrying the Bixbee house on his back like a snail shell.[1]

In January 2018 an article in *National Geographic* was published with the following headline: "Why an 8-Foot Pet Python May Have Killed Its Owner." It goes on to tell of how a man in England was killed by his yellow African rock python named Tiny.[2] At one point this deadly serpent had been a cute little snake. Its coils could have easily been broken even by a child. But as it grew, fed and nurtured by the man it would eventually kill, no one realized the tragedy the man was inviting.

People create their own monsters every day. Most often these things that destroy people start small. By the time they are taken seriously, they have grown into formidable predators that tear apart lives and families. This is why Solomon warned us that it is "the little foxes that spoil the vines" (Song of Sol. 2:15, NKJV). Jesus also warned us about the small seeds of sin when He taught us that monsters such as murder and adultery begin their journey as little pets of anger and lust. Ultimately these things that destroy us begin within us. We give birth to them, feed them, and nurture them, and they become the dragons we battle.

James tells us exactly how this process goes: "When tempted, no one should say, 'God is tempting me.' For God cannot be tempted by evil, nor does he tempt anyone; but each person is tempted when they are dragged away by their own evil desire and enticed. Then, after desire has conceived, it gives birth to sin; and sin, when it is full-grown, gives birth to death" (Jas. 1:13–15).

These evil desires become dragons of death because their owners often coddle them (like Tiny's owner) or ignore and deny them (like Billy Bixbee's mom). The battle against the dragons in this world begins with the human heart and mind. This is where the battle starts, and this is where the battle must be won. We can be very passionate about changing the world, but unless our own hearts are changed, we are just fooling ourselves.

In Matthew 6 we read what is known as the Lord's Prayer. Here we find the account of Jesus teaching His disciples to pray by modeling for them the perfect prayer. I love the way verse 10 is rendered in the King James Version. It says, "Thy kingdom come, Thy will be done in earth, as it is in heaven." Notice it says "in earth" instead of "on earth." Now maybe I am drawing more out of this than the original language warrants, but I think my point is valid. Genesis 2:7 says that God formed man from the dust of the ground. God told Adam in Genesis 3:19 that he was made from earth and would return to the earth. We are earth. We all want God's kingdom to come *on* earth. We all want God's will to be done *on* earth. But how much do we agonize of His kingdom coming *in* earth and His will being done *in* earth—that is, in us! After all, we are the earth God desires. Jesus didn't die for mountains and fields. He died to redeem human beings and fill their jars of clay with His Spirit.

When I was a child, I worried about monsters under the bed. When I became a man, I realized the monster is me.

If this is the case, and it most certainly is, it is no wonder that the battle rages primarily within the human heart. When I was a child, I worried about monsters under the bed. When I became a man, I realized the monster is me. There are no literal, physical dragons in the world. But there are many monsters in men. Jeremiah 17:9 says, "The human heart is the most deceitful of all things, and desperately wicked. Who really knows how bad it is?" (NLT). Every evil in this world comes through the hearts of men. Yes, unexplainable natural disasters, diseases, and tragedies occur. But these are not intentional, malevolent acts. Those acts of true evil come only through human agents. As Aleksandr Solzhenitsyn wrote in *The Gulag Archipelago*, "The line dividing good and evil cuts through the heart of every human being. And who is willing to destroy a piece of his own heart?"[3]

Everyone battles a dragon at some point in life, and some people battle many. Sometimes the demonic zeitgeist produces great evils that take millions of lives. Abortion, racism, perversion, false religion, persecution, corruption, and terrorism are a few of the dragons my generation is battling. But in reality most of the dragons we face are not the type that exist outside of us. Most of the dragons that threaten us are ones we have incubated, nurtured, and raised in our own hearts. Lust, pride, greed, selfishness in all its forms, hatred, the abandonment of responsibility, lack of self-discipline—these are the kind of dragons that usually destroy us. And in fact it is these "small" internal dragons that become the huge external ones mentioned earlier. Take abortion, for example—a dragon of genocide that has claimed hundreds of millions of innocent human lives.[4] At its core this boils down to a decision to worship at the altar of convenience. It is part of the zeitgeist of a generation that has little value for life and a supreme love of pleasure.

Or take, for example, a true monster, such as Adolf Hitler, who killed millions of innocent people, destroyed countless lives, and changed the world through his senseless barbarity. Never has a more hideous, fire-breathing dragon haunted this world. Yet at one time he was an innocent child. Somewhere along the way a thought came into his mind that began to change him. Perhaps it was an offense that brought with it a root of bitterness. Maybe he heard someone eloquently spewing hatred. Whatever it was, his murderous rage had some origin. From that seed sprouted a hateful dragon that ravaged the world and cost millions of lives.

But just as the evil that produced the Nazi nightmare began in someone's mind, so did the courageous deeds that vanquished it. Imagine what went on inside the minds of those young men who stormed the beach in Normandy on D-Day, June 6, 1944. As the ramps of amphibious transport vehicles came down on the blood-soaked sand, the men looked ahead and could see nothing but carnage. Thousands of their brothers were already dead or wounded on the beach. Against every survival instinct and all the desire to live, they ran headlong into danger to combat the great evil. World War II is usually seen as one big war, but in reality it was millions of wars fought in millions of minds. Millions of men and women determined to vanquish evil had to start by battling their own dragons of fear and cowardice.

Let's return to the question at hand. How do you kill your pet dragon? Whether it has grown into a murderous man-eating serpent like Tiny, or it is still the size of a kitten, the way Billy Bixbee's dragon started, here are a few words of wisdom that can give you victory over your pet dragons.

GET IT YOUNG

The easiest way to kill a dragon is obviously to smash it while it is still inside its egg. If you can kill it in its gestation period, you will never have to battle a monster—and you might enjoy some scrambled eggs as a bonus. Big things start small. Big addictions come from simple curiosity. Big sins grow from small seeds, as we discussed earlier. If you can be honest with yourself, you will often realize what is going on. When you realize you are coddling a monster in the making, kill it quickly!

I have always hated haircuts. Whenever I have to get one, I just want it over with. I don't like the itchy hairs that fall into my shirt. I am an introvert by nature, which means I don't like having to make small talk for forty minutes. Nothing about getting a haircut is pleasant to me. But years ago I started going to a salon where things changed. In this particular salon the lady I was assigned to was very attractive. She was interesting to talk to and seemed very interested in me. When she cut my hair, the time flew by. I went to that salon for about two months and enjoyed my interaction with this young lady each time.

So many disasters could have been avoided painlessly if someone had just dealt with little temptations ruthlessly.

One day I woke up and saw that I had a haircut scheduled for that day. I felt a little flutter of excitement inside. It surprised me. I always hated getting a haircut, but now I was looking forward to it. Why? Obviously I was excited at the thought of seeing that attractive young woman. Now, I should mention that I was married at that time with two or three children already. The fact that I was looking forward to spending time with another woman alarmed me. I realized what was happening. Something was growing. It was still very innocent, but if I continued down that road, I shuddered at the thought of what it might become.

I called the salon, canceled my appointment, and never went back. Most likely that situation would never have developed into anything serious. I am fully aware of that. I am also aware that every affair could be traced back to a little, innocent flutter of excitement. So many disasters could have been avoided painlessly if someone had just dealt with little temptations ruthlessly.

Now, I'm sure some people might see this as a ridiculous overreaction. But remember how Jesus told us to deal with temptation—if your hand offends you, cut it off. If your eye offends you, gouge it out (Matt. 5:29–30). I was honest with myself. I know I am not invincible. I recognized the latent potential for a little dragon egg to begin growing in my life, and I dealt with it quickly and thoroughly. If you think you are beyond such temptation, remember that greater men and women than you and I have been destroyed by sin. First Corinthians 10:12 says, "Wherefore let him that thinketh he standeth take heed lest he fall" (KJV). Those who think too highly of themselves and their immunity to temptation are setting themselves up for failure. This is why Paul said, "Do not think of yourself more highly than you ought, but rather think of yourself with sober judgment, in accordance with the faith God has distributed to each of you" (Rom. 12:3).

SHOW NO MERCY; TAKE NO PRISONERS

We tolerate sin and compromise in our lives because we do not see these things for the destructive enemies that they are. I recently read in the newspaper about a pastor who had been caught in a moral scandal. He was forced to step down from the leadership of his church, losing everything in the process—his family, his ministry, his job, and all his credibility. He stood before his congregation on his last Sunday as the pastor and in tears read a statement about how sorry he was for the way he had disappointed and failed everyone, including those he loved the most. As I read his statement, transcribed in the newspaper, I wondered where this dragon that destroyed his life was born.

Things like this don't grow overnight. They are often the product of many years of feeding and coddling. I wondered how he would have responded all those years ago, when this sin was still in its infancy, if he could have seen the monster it would become and the way it would destroy his life. Imagine if after that first lustful thought or fleeting fantasy he could have suddenly had a vision of his future and witnessed how he would read that heartbreaking speech with tears and regret. I think he would have become vicious with that little sin. He would have become violent and brutal with it.

This is the reason Jesus was so radical when He said, "If your hand or your foot causes you to stumble, cut it off and throw it away. It is better for you to enter life maimed or crippled than to have two hands or two feet and be thrown into eternal fire. And if your eye causes you to stumble, gouge it out and throw it away. It is better for you to enter life with one eye than to have two eyes and be thrown into the fire of hell" (Matt. 18:8–9). Jesus was trying to express how brutal our attitude toward sin ought to be. It is not a side issue. It is not insignificant. Sin can destroy our lives, both in this world and in eternity. Not only that but it can also destroy the lives of those around us. If we could get the right perspective on sin, I believe we would become absolutely ruthless in our intolerance of it.

God hates sin because He sees the beginning from the end. He sees the damage and destruction sin causes in our lives and in the world. If we can get God's perspective on those little dragons in our lives, if we can see them as they really are—fire-breathing monsters in the making—we will become ruthless with them, just as God is. If we find ourselves coddling sins or tolerating compromise in our own lives, something is dangerously wrong. We have to get serious about sin.

ADMIT IT EXISTS

What if my dragon is already out of control? What if it has been growing for years and is a full-blown monster with three heads and a zip code of its own? For Billy Bixbee the key was admitting there was a dragon. Each time he acknowledged the dragon's existence, it got smaller and smaller. Put simply, this is just the principle of admitting you have a problem. Even secular psychologists and twelve-step programs such as Alcoholics Anonymous require people who want help to admit they have a problem. Unless they become honest about their problems, there can never be solutions.

This is actually a biblical principle. James 5:16 says, "Therefore confess your sins to each other and pray for each other so that you may be healed. The prayer of a righteous person is powerful and effective." Why should we confess our sins to one another? Because when we walk in accountability, we are able to receive help and grace from other people. Without this transparency, our sin stays in the dark. This is where little dragons grow into big ones. But when we bring these monsters out into the light, they begin to die. First John 1:7 says, "But if we walk in the light, as he is in the light, we have fellowship with one another, and the blood of Jesus, his Son, purifies us from all sin."

USE A SECRET WEAPON

Dragons in various mythologies the world over are typically characterized as being impervious to ordinary weapons. Often a special or even magical weapon had to be used to bring them low. Thankfully, for the Christian, God has provided supernatural weapons, capable of slaying even the fiercest serpent. In the next chapter we will talk about the mighty weapons of our warfare, but in this chapter I would like to give you a powerful secret weapon against temptation that most Christians do not seem to understand.

In the previous chapter we discussed the importance of discipline in spiritual warfare. The inescapable reality is that dragons, especially big ones, don't die willingly or easily. Temptation has to be resisted, and sometimes it's a fight. Without holiness and consecration a Christian will soon be in the coils of temptation, suffocating to death. But your question might be, How do we reach this lofty place of submission to God? Is it simply a matter of trying harder? Should we develop complicated legalistic regulations for life like the

Without this transparency, our sin stays in the dark. This is where little dragons grow into big ones. But when we bring these monsters out into the light, they begin to die.

Pharisees had? Should we join a convent or a monastery? How do we actually become holy and consecrated unto God?

The monastic lifestyle emerged in the third and fourth centuries out of a disdain for the abuses many saw within the church. Some very sincere monks went to exceptionally extreme lengths to deny their flesh and consecrate themselves. Some monks bathed in ice to ward off temptation. Others would hold their fingers over a candle's flame until some literally burned off their fingers! Some were known to have castrated themselves, and the practice of self-flagellation was common.

One monk, Simeon Stylites, lived atop a platform on a pillar that reached as high as sixty feet for thirty-six years with an iron collar around his neck.[5] One of his disciples was known to have spent sixty-eight years upon a similar pillar! Francis of Assisi took as his wife "Lady Poverty."[6] He denied himself even the simple pleasure of enjoying the food he ate. "He rarely or hardly ever ate cooked foods, but if he did, he would sprinkle them with ashes or dampen the flavor of the spices with cold water."[7] Another monk, Anthony, lived in solitude in the desert for eighty-five years.[8]

These are only a few examples of the extremes to which some men have gone in an attempt to consecrate themselves unto God. Yet is this what God expects from us? Is this what consecration requires—isolating ourselves from the rest of humanity and living atop a tower, or punishing our bodies to the point of utter misery and despair? My friend, when God asks us to be wholly His, I believe He has something else in mind—something wonderful, beautiful, and fulfilling.

In Deuteronomy 6:5 God commanded the children of Israel, saying, "You shall love the LORD your God with all your heart and mind and with all your soul and with all your strength [your entire being]" (AMP). Notice that God places the emphasis on love because He knows true consecration can be a consequence only of love. This kind of love results in a supernatural satisfaction with God alone that makes the counterfeit pleasures of sin pale in comparison. God knows consecration will not come about as a result of self-mutilation and legalistic bondage. The key to consecration is love—and not just any love, but a love so fervent that it thoroughly consumes the heart, soul, mind, and strength.

As a bride longs for her groom and separates herself from all others for the sake of his love, so those who love Christ most are those who are more committed to Him. God knew we could never be truly separated, or consecrated, apart from radical love. This is why when Jesus was asked what the greatest commandment is, He reiterated God's command: "Love the Lord your God with all your heart and with all your soul and with all your mind and with all your strength" (Mark 12:30).

Even today this command is a central part of Judaism and quoted by religious Jews every day as part of the Shema liturgy, which begins, "Hear, O Israel, the Lord is our God, the Lord is One. Blessed be the name of the glory of His kingdom forever and ever. You shall love the Lord your God with all your heart, with all your soul, and with all your might."[9]

Yet there is a problem. Despite the command to love God, authentic love is not something that can be called up on demand. Nor can love be conjured by repetitious confessions. We love someone we can relate to and identify with, someone we can see and feel and know. How could we ever truly love a cosmic, ethereal, invisible Being who is so different from us, so elusive, so untouchable? The command to love God with all our heart, soul, mind, and strength was actually impossible to fulfill in its deepest sense—until Jesus came. When we saw Jesus, we fell in love with God. Suddenly we could relate to Him. When we saw His eyes so full of love, when we saw His compassion for the sick, when we heard His words of mercy and forgiveness, when we saw Him beaten and bloody, hanging on a Roman cross, dying for us, and declaring, "Father, forgive them," in response to this cruciform love we could truly begin to love God with all our heart, soul, mind, and strength.

We don't love God simply because we were commanded to, but "we love Him because He first loved us" (1 John 4:19, NKJV). Nineteenth-century preacher Charles Spurgeon said, "How great the wonder that such as we should ever have been brought to love Jesus at all! How marvellous that when we had rebelled against Him, He should, by a display of such amazing love, seek to draw us back. No! never should we have had a grain of love towards God unless it had been sown in us by the sweet seed of His love to us."[10]

God has every right to demand our love and devotion because He knows He is the only One who can truly satisfy us. He created us in such a way that we are unable to find true fulfillment outside of Him. Real satisfaction and delight are found in Christ alone!

Basilea Schlink once wrote:

> Jesus can only be our true love, our first love, if our love for
> Him takes priority and, when having to choose between Jesus

or people and things, we choose Him. Jesus has every right to make such a claim upon our love, because He has no equal. No one is so glorious, so majestic and yet so winsome as Jesus. His love is so compelling, so tender and intimate, so fervent and strong that no human love could ever compare with it. No one loves us so faithfully, loves us as if we were the only one. No one is so caring. No one is so available so exclusively for us as is Jesus. Jesus knows what He can give with His love. He knows how deeply happy He can make a person. That is why He has the right, a thousand times more than any bridegroom on earth, to say, "Give me everything—your whole love. Make me your first love, for which you would leave all else behind, just as an earthly bride would give up her home and native land, indeed all her desires."[11]

And consider the words of seventeenth-century minister Thomas Doolittle: "If Christ has our love—then he has our all. Christ never has our all from us—until he has our love. Love withholds nothing from Christ, when it is sincerely set upon him. Then he shall have our time, and he shall have our service, and he shall have the use of all our abilities, and gifts, and graces! Yes, then he shall have our estates, liberty, and our very lives, when he calls for them."[12]

HOW TO BE HOLY

When a man has come to the place where his love for Christ has surpassed his desire for all else, only the presence of God will satisfy him, and the will of God becomes his delight. It is in this place of satisfaction that true consecration is born. If a person's longings are satisfied in Christ, he no longer desires the bitter taste of sin. But without this divine fulfillment there is an endless search for satisfaction for which the pleasures of sin provide a temporary but attractive solution.

Have you ever noticed that things taste so much better when you're hungry? But after you have eaten and you're full, you could walk right past a buffet of delicious delicacies and not have the slightest desire for them. Proverbs 27:7 says it this way: "A satisfied soul loathes the honeycomb, but to a hungry soul every bitter thing is sweet" (NKJV).

Perhaps you have heard the cliché that we were created with a

God-shaped hole inside of us that only He can fill. Augustine said it this way: "Thou hast made us for Thyself and our hearts are restless till they rest in Thee."[13] But if that hunger is not satisfied with God, then even the bitter taste of sin becomes appetizing. If a person strives to be holy by desperately trying to avoid the buffet of worldly indulgences without having satisfied his soul in God, that person will remain hungry, and the temptation to sin will become greater and gain more and more power over him. Without love you just might

God has every right to demand our love and devotion because He knows He is the only One who can truly satisfy us.

need to live atop a pillar for sixty-eight years to avoid temptation. But when you get full of God, sin will lose its appeal. If you become satisfied by the ultimate delight of God's presence, you will not want to waste your time with anything less.

Holiness is not a miserable discipline; it is the natural consequence of the discovery of ultimate delight! The psalmist said, "They are abundantly satisfied with the fullness of Your house, and You give them drink from the river of Your pleasures" (Ps. 36:8, NKJV). God is not against pleasure—in fact, He wants to satisfy us with pleasure as we have never known. Psalm 16:11 says, "In Your presence is fullness of joy; at Your right hand are pleasures forevermore" (NKJV). A person who has found complete satisfaction need not look anywhere else for fulfillment, and there are no longer any rivals for the throne of his heart because he knows that no one else can compare to Christ. Can you see it? This is how a person becomes consecrated, separated, and holy—not through self-flagellation, mutilation, and penance, but through complete satisfaction in Christ alone!

Take for example an accomplished concert pianist who has spent many years of his life refining and honing his extraordinary skill. How many times did he deny himself the pleasures his peers were enjoying? During childhood, while his friends were outside playing football, he was sitting at the piano. While they were playing video games, he was practicing tedious scales and repeatedly rehearsing the same piece. Why was he willing to deprive himself of what others enjoyed? Did he have to strive to avoid football and video games? No! His motivation came from a greater desire, and his energy was directed toward the pursuit of that greater longing. He desired a pleasure far greater than what was being offered on the sandlot or in front of the television. Maybe he longed for the applause of the crowd and the warmth of the limelight, or maybe he simply loved music and found in it a freedom for his soul. Whatever the motivation, one thing is certain: he forfeited a lesser amusement for a greater delight.

CULTIVATING INTIMACY

I believe that if we are cultivating a life of intimacy with God in prayer, enjoying His presence, and listening to His voice, He will always show us where those dragon eggs in our lives are. I find it implausible that a person who is intimate with God and obedient to His promptings will end up nurturing and raising a dragon while their Father looks on and says nothing. That will never happen. Christians who raise dragons are doing so for one of two reasons:

1. They aren't spending time with Jesus. They have no intimacy with the Lord and aren't hearing His voice. God would love to say many things to us, if we will only take the time to listen.

2. They aren't obeying. Hearing God's voice is one thing; obeying it is another.

Maybe you are reading this book hoping to find out the secret to routing demons. For most Christians what would be far more effective in your spiritual battle is simply learning to love Jesus more—sitting at His feet, drinking of His presence. Learning to trust Him and obey out of a place of love is even more powerful than the most articulate spiritual warfare prayer. In the next chapter I will say a bit about prayer and how to cultivate intimacy with God through it. There is nothing Satan fears more than your intimacy with Christ. In the midst of all your spiritual disciplines and prayers of intercession, don't forget the most important part: just be with Him. Chances are, many of the battles you are fighting will automatically lose significance and power as you become intimate with Jesus.

QUESTIONS FOR DISCUSSION

- What is our secret weapon against temptation?

- How do we know that God wants us to enjoy Him?

- What are some ways you can tell if you are deeply satisfied in God?

- If someone is not enjoying God, spending time in His presence, and finding satisfaction in Him, what would you suggest he do?

CHAPTER 9

THE WEAPONS OF OUR WARFARE

We are agents of omnipotence. This means that unlimited power is at our fingertips. It also means there are no great men working in God's Kingdom. Rather, there is a great God at work in human beings who have childlike faith.

—REINHARD BONNKE, *EVEN GREATER*

The Holy Spirit doesn't come just to help us speak in tongues or to make us fall to the ground. He doesn't come to us so we can dance in the Spirit or cry. He is a living manifestation of God's power in our lives, and He anoints us to do good works, heal those who are under the power of the devil, and proclaim the gospel of Jesus Christ; that is His purpose.

—CARLOS ANNACONDIA, *LISTEN TO ME, SATAN!*

W E HAVE SPENT a good deal of time in this book looking at spiritual warfare from an internal perspective—the war within us. This approach is intentional. The internal war is the one most people neglect, and it is also where most people fall. If you are defeated within, you will never have authority over the external world. Once you have brought your mind into the right way of thinking, submitted yourself to God, and clothed yourself in His armor, it is time to bring His kingdom into every corner of the world. That is our calling and purpose, as discussed in chapter 5.

Second Corinthians 10:4 contains this powerful parenthetical statement: "For the weapons of our warfare are not carnal, but mighty through God to the pulling down of strong holds" (KJV). What are these weapons? You might immediately think of the armor of God in Ephesians 6, which we have already discussed. But remember, this list contains only one offensive weapon—the sword of the Spirit, which is the Word of God. The rest of the gear is strictly defensive (i.e., they are not listed as weapons). Yet Paul says that we have mighty spiritual *weapons* (plural) for waging warfare and pulling down strongholds.

The question remains, What are these weapons? First, as I argued in chapter 6, it's important to keep in mind that Paul's teaching on the armor of God is not meant to be taken too strictly. Paul's metaphor approximates God's armor in Isaiah 59:15–18. It indicates a readiness for battle against evil and injustice. For us as well, clothing ourselves in spiritual armor is an indication we are on the warpath against evil. But obviously believers have many powerful weapons in our arsenal beyond those listed in Ephesians 6.

The Bible does not always use the military metaphor, but many of the virtues and gifts listed throughout Scripture are still mighty weapons for warfare. For example, in Galatians 5 fruit is used as a metaphor of the kind of virtues the Holy Spirit brings forth in our lives. Although fruit does not make a good cache of weapons in the nat-

The preaching of the gospel is the tip of the spear in spiritual warfare.

ural, when it comes to spiritual warfare, the devil fears few things more than a "drive-by fruiting." These virtues are powerful weapons against darkness. Remember that anything that contradicts a demonic pattern of thinking is a direct threat to Satan's dark kingdom. This means anytime we exalt the Christlike way of thinking and living, we are waging war. This means all the fruit of the Spirit are powerful weapons: love, joy, peace, long-suffering, kindness, goodness, faith, meekness, and self-control. In fact, there are too many weapons of our warfare to discuss them all in one chapter. But I would like to discuss three incredibly powerful tools God has given us that are extraordinarily "mighty through God to the pulling down of strongholds." And keep in mind, I am focusing now on spiritual warfare out in the world, not simply within ourselves. Having said that, these weapons work as well in our personal, internal battles as they work in the external world.

THE TIP OF THE SPEAR

One of the issues that might be confusing for some is this: If Jesus already won victory over sin, death, hell, and the grave through His death and resurrection, why are we still fighting? Usually, when a war is won, the fighting stops. This brings us to one of the most thrilling realizations of all. The war Jesus won in the spiritual world now has to be proclaimed and enforced in the earth. That is our job as sons and daughters of God. You will remember that earlier we talked about this as the meaning of human life and the specific purpose of our salvation. We were created as helpers for God the way Eve was created as a help-meet, or suitable helper, for Adam. We have been created with a physical body and a spirit so we can touch heaven with one hand and earth with the other. We are not like the angels who have spiritual bodies (similar to the way ours will be after the resurrection; see Matt. 22:30). We have bodies made of physical particles, the dust of the earth. Yet the Spirit who raised Christ from the dead dwells within God's children, who constitute His earthly temple. It is no wonder, then, that Adam was given authority over the earth. We are the ideal earthly instruments of divine omnipotence. Just as angels (spiritual beings) have been given authority in the air, or in spiritual realms, humans (spiritual and physical beings) have been given authority on earth, or the physical realm. We have been given the job of actualizing the victory Christ won on the cross in the realm of our responsibility—the earth. That is why Jesus said, "Go into all the world and preach the gospel to all creation" (Mark 16:15).

Notice that the last instruction Jesus gives us is to take His victory into the whole world. But He is also specific about how this ought to be done. It happens through the preaching of the gospel—that is the tip of the spear in spiritual warfare. For many people the word *preach* is a religious word. It is something people with white collars or elaborate vestments do in religious buildings on Sunday mornings. But the word for *preach* in Mark 16:15 (and thirty-one other times in the Gospels) is the Greek word *kēryssō*. The word means "to proclaim as a herald; to make an official, public announcement out loud."[1] It refers to a loud public announcement, which Jesus contrasts with quiet private conversation in Luke 12:3: "That which ye have spoken in the ear in closets shall be proclaimed [*kēryssō*] upon the housetops" (KJV). Another word used for the preaching of the gospel is *euangelizō*, which means, "to announce good news."[2] This word was used when an official messenger would announce something important, such as a victory in battle, liberation from enemies, or a king's accession to his throne.[3] In ancient times, when a nation won a battle, official heralds would announce the victory to its cities. This is the kind of picture these words carry—the public, joyful announcement of victory or liberation from enemies.

JUNETEENTH

One of the lesser-known American holidays is Juneteenth. It is the celebration of the June 19, 1865, proclamation of the abolition of slavery in the state of Texas. More commonly known, of course, is that the American Civil War assured the freedom of all slaves. The Emancipation Proclamation was signed on September 22, 1862, and went into effect on January 1, 1863. But news traveled slowly in those days. There was no radio, television, or internet. In many cases news had to be delivered in person.

The last state to officially hear the news was Texas, where an estimated 250,000 slaves lived. They were legally free, yet they were living in slavery. But more than two and a half years after the Emancipation Proclamation went into effect, Major General Gordon Granger arrived in Galveston, leading almost two thousand soldiers. They had been sent by the federal government to occupy Texas. On June 19, 1865, General Granger stood on the balcony of the Ashton Villa in Galveston and read General Orders, No. 3, which announced the emancipation of all slaves.[4]

This is a beautiful picture of what it means to preach or proclaim—*kēryssō* or *euangelizō*—the gospel. We are sent to proclaim freedom to all those who are slaves of sin and Satan. This is in fact what Jesus Himself did in His earthly ministry. He read those words from Isaiah and applied them to Himself:

> The Spirit of the Lord is on me, because he has anointed me to proclaim good news (*euangelizō*) to the poor. He has sent me to proclaim (*kēryssō*) freedom for the prisoners and recovery of sight for the blind, to set the oppressed free, to proclaim (*kēryssō*) the year of the Lord's favor.
>
> —LUKE 4:18–19

I have often had the privilege of preaching the gospel to people and on rare occasions even in places where the gospel has never been heard before. It is amazing to think that during the two thousand years since Jesus died on the cross, the demon spirits dominating these places have never once been confronted. They have reigned unchallenged since the beginning of time. The people, slaves to fear and darkness, have never heard victory was won on their behalf. They have never heard they can be free. When I arrive on the scene, I have an awareness that I am not simply there to teach the Bible or convert people to another religion. I am there as a herald, declaring the victory Jesus purchased on the cross and announcing to every listener, both human and demonic, that the satanic regime has been defeated. The war has been won. The price of their freedom has been paid in blood, and Jesus is Lord!

If this is not spiritual warfare, I don't know what is. This is what I mean when I say we fight from a place of victory. We bring the announcement of Satan's defeat into all the world. As the gospel is proclaimed, the power of heaven rides in on that proclamation, confirming the Word and setting captives free.

In the first chapter of this book I presented some of what the Bible has to say about angels and demons, as well as their roles and jurisdiction. I must admit, however, that although many interesting clues help us to paint a somewhat cohesive picture, there is much we still do not know or understand. Obviously God didn't think it was important that we know all the details of how the spirit world operates, or He would have told us more. I find that God has given us enough information that we can trust and obey Him. Beyond that, we ought not to speculate much. Part of faith is the willingness to live with the many mysteries in Scripture while obeying it without question.

In Acts 1, after Jesus had risen from the dead and appeared to His disciples over a period of forty days, the disciples asked Jesus if

He would "restore the kingdom to Israel" (v. 6). They were asking about the restoration of the physical kingdom in their lifetime. Jesus responded, "It is not for you to know the times or dates the Father has set by his own authority. But you will receive power when the Holy Spirit comes on you; and you will be my witnesses in Jerusalem, and in all Judea and Samaria, and to the ends of the earth" (vv. 7–8). In other words, Jesus told them the times and seasons the Father set by His own authority were none of their business. Jesus did not tell them what they did not need to know. Instead He told them to focus on their responsibility—to get the power of the Holy Spirit and take the gospel to the ends of the earth. I think this same principle applies to spiritual warfare. There are many things we do not know because they are none of our business. Our business is to proclaim the gospel with power.

I know some believers who are obsessed with the spirit world. Every time I talk to them, they tell me what is happening with the principalities over their region and how they are combating them with this prayer meeting and that prayer walk and through spiritual mapping and so on. I think if most of this is not joined with evangelism, it boils down to silly superstition. I am not saying principalities are not real. On the contrary, Scripture is clear that they do exist and we are fighting against them. But we do not necessarily understand much about what they do and how they operate, and I think that is because it is not really our business. Rather than getting caught up in something that ends up amounting to nothing more than conjecture and fantasy, let's wage the warfare we have been told to wage—preach the gospel, heal the sick, raise the dead, and cast out demons (Matt. 10:8).

I have seen the epic effects of the preached gospel enough to know Satan's dominion is trembling at the thought. I have seen people—not just in mass meetings but in restaurants and at gas stations and grocery stores—overcome by the power of the Holy Spirit, born again, delivered of demons, and miraculously healed. These are real results. We know the gospel works. When we wage spiritual warfare without taking the proclamation of the gospel into our world, we are indicating by our actions (or lack thereof) that we can do something more powerful than what Christ has already done. I love prayer and intercession, but without evangelism it will be limited in its effectiveness. On the other hand, if you connect prayer and intercession with evangelism, you will have a dynamic explosion that can change cities and regions!

DYNAMIS

One interesting detail in the Juneteenth story I mentioned earlier is that it was not just any messenger who issued General Orders, No. 3. It was a general—a military man. And he wasn't alone. He was accompanied by almost two thousand troops because the federal government knew those who owned the slaves might not be happy about being told to let them go. Although the war was won and the Emancipation Proclamation was already in effect, they had to be ready to enforce it with power if need be. Texas had not been a battleground state, yet the Emancipation Proclamation applied to it. General Granger brought the battle to the local level where those in slavery would be actually set free. This is where the liberation would move from a legal reality to a physical one. Those troops behind General Granger were there to ensure this liberation, by force if necessary.

When we take the gospel into the world, we are in the same situation as General Granger. We are there not only to proclaim Christ's victory on the cross but also to enforce it on a local level. Jesus said the violent take the kingdom by force, painting a picture of the way the gospel advances (Matt. 11:12). It requires not only words but also power. The apostle Paul said, "My message and my preaching were not with wise and persuasive words, but with a demonstration of the Spirit's power" (1 Cor. 2:4). And again, "For the kingdom of God is not a matter of talk but of power" (4:20). In both of these passages the word for *power* is *dynamis*. The word means "power, might, strength, force or capability."[5] It is especially used in reference to miracle-working power.[6] We are talking now about a power that accompanies the proclamation of the gospel, bringing supernatural results and even miracles! Where do we get this power?

Let's go back to Acts 1:8; Jesus said, "But you will receive power [*dynamis*] when the Holy Spirit comes on you; and you will be my witnesses in Jerusalem, and in all Judea and Samaria, and to the ends of the earth." Jesus promised them they would receive the power to spread the gospel when the Holy Spirit was poured out. The fulfillment of this promise happened a few days later on the day of Pentecost. We read about this outpouring in Acts 2. Throughout the rest of the Book of Acts we read over and over how those in the early church received this precious gift.

There are many debates about what Spirit baptism is or means. People argue about when it happens, if it is subsequent to salvation, if it comes with evidence, and what that evidence might be. I have written about this topic in depth elsewhere, but for our purposes in this chapter here is what I believe is important. Jesus said this outpouring would be accompanied by power (*dynamis*). Many Christians have reduced this power to something all believers have, whether or not they know it. It is more of a theoretical power than anything actual or tangible. It does not affect their lives in anything but the most ambiguous of ways. For those who see it as such, I would like to point out two things.

First, there is no example in Acts of anyone ever receiving the outpouring of the Holy Spirit without being aware of it. You can argue about what signs or gifts might be indicative of Spirit baptism, but you cannot deny that in every case they had a conscious Holy Spirit experience.

Second, some evidence of power always accompanied these Holy Spirit experiences. In some cases they spoke with tongues, prophesied, received boldness, etc. But in each case power was evident.

Without getting into a prolonged and detailed teaching on what Spirit baptism is, I would simply say that all Christians need an experience of empowerment in their lives. This should be something they are conscious of, not merely a theoretical and theological truth. This power is necessary for serving God and living for Him. It is a non-negotiable, mighty weapon of our warfare. It is also our inheritance as God's children.

EFFECTUAL PRAYER

You might find it curious that in a book about spiritual warfare I have waited so long to discuss prayer. And you may be surprised how little space I devote in this chapter to the subject. Most teaching on spiritual warfare is primarily about prayer, and I would never want to downplay its importance. In fact, I have written an entire book on prayer—specifically intercession—for those who want to go deeper on this subject.[7] On the other hand, whether you realize it or not, we have been building a foundation for effective prayer since the beginning of this book. We talked about the satanic strategy to bring humanity into agreement with a demonic way of thinking. This translates then into evil desires that bring temptation, sin, and death. If people pray under the influence of that way of thinking, their prayers will not be effective. John says, "This is the confidence we have in approaching God: that if we ask anything according to his will, he hears us" (1 John 5:14). Notice that alignment with God's will brings a confidence in prayer that God hears. On the other hand, David says, "If I regard iniquity in my heart, the Lord will not hear me" (Ps. 66:18, KJV). Do you see it? If the heart is aligned with iniquity, the heavens are brass.

You can be the most passionate prayer warrior—shouting to God, declaring and decreeing, binding and loosing, rebuking, naming, claiming, and calling forth—but if your heart is aligned with the satanic agenda, you are wasting your breath. God is ignoring you, and Satan is laughing at you. You cannot command Satan if you are in agreement with him. On the other hand, if your heart is aligned with God and submitted to His will, one hot tear can be enough to break the devil's back in prayer.

This is why James tells us that "the effectual fervent prayer of a righteous man availeth much" (Jas. 5:16, KJV). Notice that he refers to the prayer of a *righteous* man. Consider this biblical definition of *righteous*: "used of him whose way of thinking, feeling, and acting is wholly conformed to the will of God, and who therefore needs no rectification in the heart or life."[8] And in case you question whether James meant this, consider the fact that the first part of that verse says we should confess our faults to one another and be healed. Read the entire verse: "Confess your faults one to another, and pray one for another, that ye may be healed. The effectual fervent prayer of a righteous man availeth much." Proper alignment precedes effective prayer.

We see this clearly in one of the most famous spiritual warfare prayer passages in Scripture. Daniel fasted and prayed for revelation in Daniel 10. He was standing on the bank of the Tigris River when a beautiful and powerful messenger angel arrived with the answer to his prayers. Daniel had been fasting and praying for twenty-one days by this point, but the messenger told Daniel he had been dispatched with the answer immediately. However, while en route, the messenger was intercepted and detained by a powerful demon, identified as the prince of Persia. Michael the archangel came to the rescue and battled through the demonic resistance.

I would like to draw your attention to the way the angel described Daniel's prayer. He said, "Since the first day that you set your mind to gain understanding and to humble yourself before your God, your words were heard, and I have come in response to them" (Dan. 10:12). Notice the angel does not specifically comment on the content  If your heart is aligned with God and submitted to His will, one hot tear can be enough to break the devil's back in prayer.

of the words in Daniel's prayer or how loudly he prayed them. He rather comments on how Daniel's heart and mind had been postured before God. His mind was set to gain understanding from God, and his heart was humble. Daniel was a powerful man in the greatest nation on earth at the time. The demonic influence over that kingdom was profound. But Daniel—in the midst of a heathen, Gentile nation controlled by a pervasive demonic zeitgeist—was still able to align his heart and mind with God. This is the reason his words were heard and an answer was sent.

The Bible tells us even Jesus Himself needed this alignment with God in order to pray effectively. We know of course that He was always in alignment. He never yielded to temptation (Heb. 4:15), and He gave no place to the enemy (John 14:30). Jesus did only what pleased the Father (John 8:29). But still the author to the Hebrews felt it necessary to apply this truth explicitly to Jesus' prayer life: "During the days of Jesus' life on earth, he offered up prayers and petitions with fervent cries and tears to the one who could save him from death, *and he was heard because of his reverent submission*" (Heb. 5:7, emphasis added).

You may be surprised to read this. The author does not say Jesus was heard simply because He was the Son of God. Nor does the author say Jesus was heard because His cries were fervent. Yes, His cries were fervent, and that was good. But that is not why Jesus was *heard*.

Rather, the author tells us unequivocally the reason Jesus was heard: because He submitted fully and continually to His Father. He never let a demonic dart become a way of thinking, and He never veered from His Father's purpose. Jesus simply submitted like a good Son.

As we saw earlier, submission negates pride and self-confidence, and it releases God's authority. That is precisely why Jesus' prayers were so effective. He did not merely shout and pray "warfare prayers." He lived a life of submission and then offered prayers out of that life of submission. As a result every prayer was answered, and every prayer was invincible.

I quote James again: "Submit yourselves, then, to God. Resist the devil, and he will flee from you" (Jas. 4:7). Submission to God must come first. Then and only then our spiritual warfare is powerful. We cannot resist the devil when we are in agreement with him. But once we have submitted to God, we will have the mind of Christ and be able to pray in accordance with the will of God. Once we have gotten to this point, prayer is a pretty simple exercise—one that should be as intuitive and natural as all other kinds of communication.

INTUITIVE PRAYER

As a father of five kids I can tell you that humans are born to communicate. We arrive screaming. Then we graduate to words, sentences, and eventually the all-important rambling monologue. You haven't lived until a four-year-old has shared her in-depth take on a favorite movie you have actually seen with her more than ten times. Watching a child mature into a little communicator is a wonder and one of the true joys of parenting. We hear ourselves in them just as surely as we see ourselves in them.

Along the way we (hopefully) learn to listen as well as talk, and we pick up on any number of nonverbal signals—facial expressions, hand gestures, body postures, and subtle shifts in another's pupil dilation and breathing patterns. There is no end to the possibilities of human language. Linguists and psychologists refer to human language as "generative, which means that it can communicate an infinite number of ideas from a finite number of parts." It is also "recursive, which means that it can build upon itself without limits."[9] The faculty is hardwired into our species—it is built into our DNA.[10] We are psychologically and biologically attuned to take in, decipher, and relay language from its most general to its most nuanced forms, and we can do so with breathtaking speed and mental dexterity. In short, language is a defining element of our humanity.

I believe this capacity is one of the facets of the image of God in us. If this is so, and we are born to communicate, nothing should come more naturally to us than prayer since prayer is simply communion with God. I think complicated and prolonged teachings about prayer often have the reverse of their intended effect. They are meant to illuminate prayer and inspire people to pray. Instead they sometimes convolute the issue so much that most people are daunted by the thought. Remember what Jesus Himself said. When the Gentiles pray, they "suppose that they will be heard for their many words" (Matt. 6:7, NASB). But He made it clear that is not why people are heard in prayer. We will not be heard because we have been to every seminar and can now offer long, complicated prayers that have more content than heart. Jesus said *not* to be like those who pray this way (v. 8).

He then taught a prayer—which is also a template—often called the Lord's Prayer (Matt. 6:9–13). I am not sure that is the right name for it since it includes the confession of sin and therefore cannot be a prayer Jesus prayed for Himself. On the other hand, He taught His disciples to pray it, so it is the perfect model prayer for us. It is also important in spiritual warfare for at least two reasons. First, Jesus teaches the prayer to His disciples in the middle of the Sermon on the Mount. We discussed earlier how this sermon reflects the Lord's entirely unique way of thinking and living, and it is therefore a foundation to spiritual warfare. Notice that Jesus did not teach about prayer by itself but about *life* in God's kingdom and *then* how to pray accordingly. In other words, Jesus taught us to pray in the context of a life submitted to God—the life of a disciple. Second, the prayer reflects the basic concerns that should emerge from every submitted disciple: petitions for God's glory, kingdom, and will, and then for our needs of provision, forgiveness, and victory. Follow Jesus' pattern of prayer. Don't complicate it. Just do it—naturally from a heart submitted to God.

In light of this important truth I will offer a few helpful words about prayer. They are not intended to complicate the issue but rather to simplify it.

INTIMACY WITH GOD

First and foremost, prayer should be thought of as communion with God. Prayer is more than words. In his book *Union*, my friend Eric Gilmour provides some wonderful quotes about the real character of prayer.

> Prayer is simply the soul's total fixation upon God.... Very simply, it is a posturing of your inner attention upon God. Madame Guyon said, "Prayer is the application of the heart to God." This is also a simplification, applying your affections to Him....
>
> So many people have no idea that communion with God can be a great delight. I submit to you that not only can prayer be a great delight, but it should be the very source of all our delight. John Ruusbroec wrote, "When God pleases us and we please God, therein is the practice of love and eternal life."[11]

In the last chapter I gave you a secret weapon for living holy and consecrated—delight yourself in the Lord. The kind of communion being described above is one of the great keys to that enjoyment of God. This kind of communion should be virtually effortless. It is not about how boisterous, articulate, or disciplined you are in prayer—it is simply about being with Him for no other purpose than Him alone. Sometimes you will use words. Other times you will simply set your heart upon Him with an internal gaze. This effortless enjoyment of God should be the foundation of your prayer life.

I am aware this description probably does not sound powerful to most people. When it comes to spiritual warfare, people are often looking for a weaponized version of prayer—prayers that sound and look dangerous. But as I have pointed out, just because something looks violent in the natural does not mean it carries an iota of authority in the spirit. Likewise, just because something looks quiet and gentle in the natural does not mean it will not terrify the enemy. I can assure you of one thing: there is no person so dangerous to Satan's kingdom as one who is intimate with God. But the reverse is also true. No amount of vocal volume in prayer can compensate for lack of intimacy.

Upon this foundation of intimacy in prayer other kinds of prayer will naturally emerge.

WARFARE PRAYER

Spiritual warfare prayer may contain a few basic forms. We may petition, simply asking God for needs such as healing, provision, or protection. We may decree or proclaim things in prayer, by faith, asserting forcefully what is needed in a given situation. Or we may intercede on behalf of others, crying out for the salvation or deliverance of a loved one. Regardless of what *form* prayers may take, two basic *characteristics* are indispensable to spiritual warfare: persistence and the leading of the Holy Spirit.

Persistence

Jesus Himself gives us some powerful keys to effective prayer. He says, "Ask and it will be given to you; seek and you will find; knock and the door will be opened to you" (Matt. 7:7). Jesus gives these verbal commands—ask, seek, and knock—in the present tense. He does not mean for them to be short-term, one-and-done prayer actions. They indicate continued action. This is why the Amplified Bible renders Matthew 7:7–8 this way: "Ask and keep on asking and it will be given to you; seek and keep on seeking and you will find; knock and keep on knocking and the door will be opened to you. For everyone who keeps on asking receives, and he who keeps on seeking finds, and to him who keeps on knocking, it will be opened."

But the passage doesn't stop there. It goes on to put this persistence within the context of a child asking his father for food.

> Or what man is there among you who, if his son asks for bread, will [instead] give him a stone? Or if he asks for a fish, will [instead] give him a snake? If you then, evil (sinful by nature) as you are, know how to give good and advantageous gifts to your children, how much more will your Father who is in heaven [perfect as He is] give what is good and advantageous to those who keep on asking Him.
>
> —Matthew 7:9–11, amp

As a father I can easily understand the persistence Jesus describes here. In another book I wrote about it like this.

> One day it suddenly occurred to me: children are persistent because they have to be. They are dependent creatures. The younger they are, the more needy they are, and as such, in order to survive, they must master the skill of persistence. My son asks incessantly because he sees me as his source. If I don't give him water, he'll go thirsty. If I don't give him food, he'll starve. I am his source of shelter, of clothing, of protection, of recreation—of everything. He is persistent because he must be so to survive, and he has every right to be.
>
> My son comes to me without hesitation or apprehension. He asks with a righteous audacity. He is not discouraged or put off in the least when I don't immediately meet his request; he simply asks again. Each time he asks, he expects to receive just as the time before. His seeking is incredibly simple and trusting. I would say it is a wonderful example of faith.
>
> But the older we become, the less willing people are to give us what we need simply for the asking. We must win our bread and climb the ladder of success. In order to survive, we must lose our dependency and master self-sufficiency. As we become self-reliant, we hate to ask for anything. We don't want to be pushy or presumptuous. If we must ask for something, we do so with timidity and are loath to ask a second time.
>
> So many people make the mistake of approaching God with this dignified, grown-up demeanor. They make cautious but eloquent requests that are logical and reasonable. If they don't see an answer right away, they either assume it was not God's will and leave it at that, or they become offended, frustrated, and discouraged.
>
> But the prize goes to the ones who are bold enough to take hold of heaven with reckless confidence. I am not talking about arrogant presumption but childlike assurance. Leave your incredible intellect, your proud rationale, and your deceptive self-reliance at the door. Come to terms with your utter and total dependency upon your Father. Understand that your sonship is the only grounds upon which you can

approach God in the first place. As a son or daughter of God it is your righteous privilege to ask, and it is God's divine pleasure to answer. Therefore, ask with audacity, confidence, and persistence.

Keep asking like a child asks a father for bread. Keep knocking as the widow before the unjust judge in Luke 18. Keep seeking as for a pearl of great price (Matt. 13:45–46). Push through resistance like the woman with the issue of blood (Mark 5:25–34). Lean into the Word like a man walking against the wind. Clamp down on His promises like a pit bull with a T-bone. Place a demand on what's yours. Give Him no rest day or night until His answer breaks through like a pent-up flood and makes your desert to blossom like a rose. If the answer doesn't come immediately, don't be discouraged or frustrated. With expectancy and trust just lift your eyes to the hills and ask and ask again. Keep on asking. Keep on seeking. Keep on knocking. Keep on keeping on until you receive—and you will in Jesus's name![12]

Leading of the Holy Spirit

Finally, we return to the Holy Spirit and our utter need for Him in spiritual warfare. I hope it is obvious how crucial the Holy Spirit is in the life of a Christian. We have seen we need Him for preaching the gospel, for power, and now for prayer. Every element of our spiritual warfare is dependent on Him. The Holy Spirit is so vital for our survival that Jesus even said it was better for us to have the Holy Spirit than for us to have Jesus in the flesh here on earth. It's an amazing statement—so astonishing in fact that I would find it unbelievable if Jesus had not said it Himself.

> It is best for you that I go away, because if I don't, the Advocate won't come. If I do go away, then I will send him to you.... There is so much more I want to tell you, but you can't bear it now. When the Spirit of truth comes, he will guide you into all truth. He will not speak on his own but will tell you what he has heard. He will tell you about the future. He will bring me glory by telling you whatever he receives from me.

> All that belongs to the Father is mine; this is why I said, "The
> Spirit will tell you whatever he receives from me."
> —JOHN 16:7, 12–15, NLT

The Holy Spirit is the one who brings awareness of both Jesus (the living Word) and Scripture (the written Word) to us in the midst of spiritual warfare. Jesus told us, "The Holy Spirit, whom the Father will send in my name, will teach you all things and will remind you of everything I have said to you" (John 14:26). If we will be faithful to put the Word in our hearts and minds, the Holy Spirit will be faithful to bring it to our remembrance at the right moment. He anoints and works with our diligence to deposit the Scriptures into our hearts. The more we store in our hearts, the more He has to work with. Then when we pray, He opens our hearts like a treasure chest to pull out the right passages at the right time.

This is one of the most effective ways to pray in spiritual warfare. As we worship or pray in the Spirit, certain texts will come to our mind. Once this happens, the Spirit will give us that inner sense on how to pray it through. We may have to labor intensely as we pray a passage line by line for a person. Or we may simply be directed to read a psalm out loud as a declaration. Perhaps the Spirit will take us to a story from the Gospels that gives us insight into a certain enemy attack. We then ponder the story prayerfully to discern what the Spirit is saying.

This may take some time. But over the days and weeks, as we continue to pray according to our growing insight based on the Word, we notice the situation getting more and more breakthrough until the victory comes. God's Word is the Spirit's touchstone. When we allow the Spirit to search for the treasures within us and allow the Spirit and Word to work in tandem inside our hearts and prayers, we will overcome many attacks and strongholds.

Further, sometimes the Holy Spirit Himself will pray the will of God through us. Paul reveals, "The Spirit helps us in our weakness. We do not know what we ought to pray for, but the Spirit himself intercedes for us through wordless groans. And he who searches our hearts knows the mind of the Spirit, because the Spirit intercedes for God's people in accordance with the will of God" (Rom. 8:26–27). Sometimes we do *not* have a passage of Scripture or any other known words we can pray. Rather, the Spirit heavily influences our emotions over a situation.

In times such as these we have far more feelings than words—yet the prayers must still come. We give ourselves fully to the Spirit's weighty, emotional presence on our hearts and can do nothing more than make sounds emanating from our inner person. "Deep calls to deep in the roar of your waterfalls; all your waves and breakers have swept over me" (Ps. 42:7). This is when the Spirit taps our deepest feelings while totally bypassing our minds. We feel the burden, but words cannot express it. When we align with the Spirit on such a deep, emotional, and inarticulate level, we carry tremendous power in prayer—a power that in the end will transform creation itself (Rom. 8:22–27). That means our shorter-term breakthrough will surely come.

The Holy Spirit ensures that the believer always fights Satan from a position of advantage. He provides us with the Word and at times our very prayers. The Holy Spirit gives altogether the armor, sword, and shield—power beyond our own means—and allows us to communicate our greatest needs and desires directly to God. With Him even the most terrifying dragon seems like a mere garden snake.

QUESTIONS FOR DISCUSSION

- Prayer is a request to God. Why is it correct—i.e., not selfish—to ask God for things?

- Why do you think some prayers are not answered?

- What does prayer in the Holy Spirit look like? Have you experienced examples of this power-infused prayer?

- Can we pray together to experience more of this dynamic expression of being a Christ follower?

Father God, we ask for a fresh touch from Your Spirit. Come and fill us again. In the name of Jesus, amen.

CHAPTER 10

CASTING OUT DEMONS

When Jesus cast out demons, He went beyond the precedents of the Old Testament. From the time of Moses onward, God's prophets had performed many miracles that foreshadowed the ministry of Jesus. They had healed the sick, raised the dead, made miraculous provision for multitudes and demonstrated God's power to control the forces of nature. But there is no record that any of them had ever cast out a demon. That was reserved for Jesus. It was a unique demonstration that the Kingdom of God had come upon the people of His day.

—DEREK PRINCE, *THEY SHALL EXPEL DEMONS*

Demons are spiritual enemies and it is the responsibility of each Christian to deal with them directly in spiritual warfare.

—FRANK HAMMOND, *PIGS IN THE PARLOR*

I T WAS THE summer of 2003. I was a twenty-two-year-old worship pastor on staff at an Assembly of God church in central Florida. The senior pastor asked me to come to the church at 7:00 p.m. to assist in a deliverance. The church did not normally do deliverance ministry, but a need had suddenly arisen. A terrified young woman had shown up at the church office around noon, asking to see the pastor. She told him her boyfriend was demon-possessed. Her grandmother had encouraged her to seek help from a Pentecostal church, and she had found ours in the phone book. The pastor asked her to come back that evening and she agreed. In the meantime he asked several church members—some elders and me—to be a makeshift deliverance team. I'm pretty sure I was the only one on the team who had any experience with deliverance before. I had worked on a deliverance team for Carlos Annacondia once in the 1990s, and I had some experiences with deliverance in my high school and college years. What we were about to encounter, however, was beyond anything I—or anyone else in this group—had ever seen.

When the man arrived with his girlfriend that evening, we were all immediately taken aback from the first sight of him. His name was C. J. He was under obvious distress. He stumbled through the door, helped along by his girlfriend, Nikki. He was hunched over, walking with a slow and lumbering gait, as if he were carrying a heavy burden. His face was gaunt, and his eyes were dark. The small group that had gathered was in the front of the auditorium praying when he arrived. He sat on the back row of the church, unwilling—or perhaps unable—to come forward.

Nikki briefly told us about some of the problems C. J. was having. She was obviously shaken up, and he was clearly demonized. He was conscious and able to respond to those around him, but he was distant, and communication was difficult. Later I would find out the remarkable backstory. Honestly, if I had known how serious the case was at the time, I might have been less enthusiastic.

C. J. was raised in what he describes as a "crazy house," full of hatred and fear. His family was known for dealing drugs. He started smoking marijuana at five or six years old, was a regular user by seven years old, and was a full-blown drug addict by his early teens. The laundry list of drugs he was using is not worth naming. It was essentially everything illegal—including hard-core street drugs, especially amphetamines, hallucinogens, and cocaine.

A defining moment happened when C. J. was fifteen years old. His mother, sick of his dogs barking, forced him to shoot them and bury them in the yard. The dogs had been his best friends. That experience made him a bitter, hateful, and angry young man. He believes that was the point when demons began to possess him. He started having violent psychotic episodes, sometimes using deadly weapons. He would be arrested, Baker Acted, or committed to psychiatric hospitals. He eventually ran away from home and became a vagabond, sleeping in the woods and under bridges, always moving from place to place. He said he was unable to rest. Anytime he would start to feel comfortable somewhere, an internal restlessness would drive him to wander again.

He was arrested more than two dozen times and often sent to mental institutions. He was diagnosed as schizophrenic and then later with dissociative disorder. He was put on dozens of different psychiatric drugs, up to eight different drugs at once, including Thorazine, Zyprexa, and phenobarbital. Nikki said his regimen was a handful of prescription drugs three times per day!

All this time C. J. had been dealing illegal drugs as well as using them. As he got older, his life of crime became more and more serious. Things went from bad to worse. During this time different "personalities" began to take control of him from time to time. He had encounters in his home with demons he could physically see. He was so tormented by fear that at times he would barricade his bedroom door with furniture.

One personality, which called itself Frankie, seemed to be in charge. It would often take control of C. J.'s mind and take him into psychotic episodes in which he saw absolutely horrifying scenes. Frankie would give him a tour of a terrible place that C. J. believes was hell. His descriptions of this place are too terrible for me to put into writing. Frankie assured C. J. that he would not suffer the fate of those being tormented there. Instead C. J. was told he would be given special status in hell after he died.

In case you are wondering, these experiences were not drug induced. They happened when he was sober. During this time he also began to have what was diagnosed as grand mal seizures up to eight times per day, and he was prescribed huge doses of an antiseizure medication called Dilantin to control them.

He became extremely suicidal, attempting to kill himself more than twenty times. Each attempt failed, sometimes in bizarre ways. For example, he tried to hang himself from a rafter in his attic, but the beam broke. He took unbelievable amounts of drugs in dangerous combinations hoping to overdose, but somehow it never worked. He was also self-harming, cutting and burning himself.

As he lost regard for his own life and safety, his criminal activity became more and more serious. He was arrested for participation in an organized crime ring and sent to state prison for more than four years. Because he was racist, he associated with the Aryan Brotherhood and white supremacists both in and after prison. After he was released from prison, he became connected with the mob, working as an enforcer and using a baseball bat to beat and maim people who would not pay their debts. He lost the ability to feel remorse and empathy, fully accepting the reality that he was a monster—even reveling in it.

C. J.'s girlfriend, Nikki, did not grow up in a Christian home either. She was not allowed to go to church because her father was an atheist and hated the church. But her grandmother was a Christian and went to an Assembly of God church. Her grandmother told her stories of seeing healing and deliverance on mission trips in the third world. Her grandmother was the only person Nikki could think of to call.

She called her grandmother and told her she thought her boyfriend was demon-possessed. Her grandmother asked why she had come to that conclusion. When her grandma heard what was happening to C. J., her advice was (1) run for your life and (2) plead the blood of Jesus over yourself!

Of course, Nikki didn't know what it meant to plead the blood of Jesus, but whenever she felt afraid, she said the words, "I plead the blood of Jesus over myself." Even though she was still unsaved, as C. J. descended further into terrifying demonic darkness, she would often call on the name of Jesus the way her grandmother had said.

The demons would speak frequently to Nikki through C. J. with chilling words. At times when Nikki had privately spoken to her grandmother, the demons would be aware of it, asking her, "Who is praying?" At other times they would reveal their true feelings about humanity. They would sometimes speak in what she describes as "deep, dark poetry," telling her about their utter hatred and disdain for human beings. She said they consider us far inferior creatures and describe us as "monkeys." It was Nikki who sought the answer, and she was the one with the courage to bring C. J. to a church where he could find help.

When he stumbled into the church that day I met him, C. J. looked like death warmed over. For weeks the demons had been tormenting him to the extent that he was not able to get any rest whatsoever. He had become so psychotic that everyone around him was terrified. He had wandered into the national forest, thinking he was at his kids' school, talking to the guidance counselor. He went to the nuclear power plant and tried to order cheeseburgers.

His sister encouraged him to go into a bedroom and try to sleep. When he went inside, they padlocked the door so he could not escape. C. J. said the locks were actually unnecessary. He had no idea where he was, and he couldn't see any doors to escape, even if the door had been unlocked. He stayed confined to that room for two weeks.

C. J.'s sister was planning to take him to a mental institution where he had been committed before. But they had said if he was committed again, they would send him to a long-term facility. Not wanting him to be sent away indefinitely, Nikki asked them to bring C. J. to her house instead.

Nikki's Pentecostal grandmother encouraged her to look for a church that performs deliverance, so she went through the phone book and called more than twenty churches asking if they had a deliverance ministry before she found our little church.

At the time I met C. J., I was not aware he had not slept or eaten for more than twenty days. He now believes the demons were trying to kill him outright or get him to commit suicide. When he arrived on the doorstep of our church, it was his last hope.

After much encouragement C. J. slowly made his way to the front of the auditorium. Because I was the youngest, I stayed in the background, praying for the older and more mature believers who immediately began rebuking the devil, pleading the blood of Jesus, and commanding the demons to come out. He reacted violently at these commands, shaking, falling, blurting out obscenities, and mocking those trying to cast out the demons. This went on for a long time. Occasionally the demons would pretend to leave, and then when everyone relaxed, they would start laughing at us.

After more than an hour of failed attempts, the team was completely exhausted. I was still in the background interceding. They had been going in circles, being teased, taunted, mocked, and cursed by these demonic spirits. The person leading the deliverance exercise said it was enough, that we had done all we could do. We would pray for

C. J. and maybe invite him to come back another time when they could pull in some heavy hitters with more experience.

At this time, realizing C. J. was about to be sent home in this state and the demons would probably never let him live to see another day, I asked if I could try something before it was over. To make a long story short, within fifteen minutes C. J. was saved, filled with the Holy Spirit, and completely delivered from all demons, illegal drug addiction, anger, and mental illness.

Before I go on, I think it is important to understand this did not happen yesterday. This is a testimony that at the time of this writing has had nearly sixteen years to prove itself—which is one of the reasons I am telling it now. I am a skeptical person by nature, so it was many years before I asked C. J. to share this story publicly. I wanted to see the lasting fruit of his salvation and deliverance.

He experienced an instantaneous deliverance from demons, every psychotic illness, and all illegal and prescription drugs. Still, not everything was instantaneous. He continued to struggle with nicotine addiction for a while, and he was still living with his girlfriend out of wedlock.

Over the years I watched his progress. He stopped smoking. He attended church. I performed the wedding ceremony, marrying Nikki and him. I saw his consistency for more than a decade. Eventually he became the pastor of a church.

Today he is still free. He has never again taken illegal drugs. He has never again taken any of the medications for his mental issues. He has never had any more seizures or psychotic episodes. He has never again been arrested or committed to a mental hospital. He is still married to Nikki and living as a godly Christian husband and father, and he continues to pastor his church to this day. Again, this story carries credibility because it has stood the test of time. And that is what we are after—fruit that remains.

I'm sure you will be curious about how such dramatic results came so quickly, especially after so many failed attempts and in such a serious case. I will describe the simple process I used as we go through this chapter.

FIRST-WORLD DEMONS

Many of those who believe in demon possession seem to think it is something that happens only in faraway places, third-world countries, or heathen lands. I can assure you there are as many demons in Europe and America as in Africa and Asia. We may call them by different names or diagnose them as strange conditions. We might medicate them, institutionalize them, and pretend they don't exist. But demons are alive and well all over the world.

Several years ago I was invited to preach in a stadium in Germany. I preached an evangelistic message and gave an altar call to which hundreds of mostly young people responded. As I began to pray with them to received Christ, something unusual began to take place. All over the altar area demons started to manifest. The stadium workers, concerned these young people were having seizures, called the paramedics, who carried those manifesting out on stretchers. As I was leaving the stadium that night on my way back to the hotel, I passed the medical team on the front lawn, still working on several people. I knew they would not allow me to get close, but I advised them to get some of the pastors to help. I told the paramedics that what these young people were dealing with was beyond their medicine to cure.

I could tell many more stories similar to the one above—hundreds of cases of demon possession in other European countries, North and South America, and first-world Asian countries, as well as in the third world. Again, the problem of demonization is a real issue that the church is generally quite oblivious to and ill equipped to address. Somehow most Christians have forgotten that Jesus said to cast out demons as surely as He said to preach the gospel and heal the sick. Why is there so much neglect in this area? I tend to think it revolves mostly around fear. We fear what we do not understand and are unprepared for.

In this book we have already established much of the important theological basics regarding demons—what they do and what they are. We have also talked about the critical elements of spiritual warfare, both on the cosmic scale and within ourselves. As we draw near to the end of this book, I will briefly describe some important principles for casting out demons. These principles are drawn from Scripture and my own experience. This is not an exhaustive how-to manual—I have neither the space nor expertise to write such a thing. This is biblical and practical wisdom I hope will better prepare you for encountering demonization.

THE TERMINOLOGY

In this chapter I will refer to someone inhabited by demons, or heavily influenced by demons, as *demonized* rather than *demon possessed*. Most Bible translations use the latter term, and therefore so do most people. But technically the New Testament never says a person is "possessed" by a demon. The Greek word for *possess* or *possession* is not used in these contexts in reference to a demon. Rather, the authors of the New Testament say a person is either "demonized" (*daimonizomai*), "has" (*echō*) a demon, or is "with" (*en*) a demon (e.g., Matt. 4:24; 11:18; Mark 1:23). In other words, the Bible never comes out and says a demon possesses a person.

Demons never actually possess anything, so I don't want to give them the dignity of ownership—especially of a human being. Even if a person is so indwelled by demons that he is under their complete control, that person is not owned by the demons. In the end the demons will lose control of that person and go to their eternal judgment empty-handed. They will never own anything. They are thieves and robbers but never owners of anything in God's creation. Likewise, the person, even if he rejects God, will not stand before any demons on the day of judgment. He will stand before God. That means *God* is the One with the right of possession over that person. God is the One who owns, or possesses, that person, even if the person hates Him on earth. Therefore, when a person in this age is inhabited by demons, I stick with the New Testament terminology. This is not to say I am dogmatically against the use of the term *demon possession*—I understand what most people and translations mean when they use the term. I will occasionally use it myself if I think someone I am communicating with would understand that terminology better. On the other hand, it is important to point out the English word *possess* goes beyond the meaning of the text and gives demons more rights than they deserve.

BE READY

Throughout this book I have repeatedly emphasized the importance of being internally submitted to God in the heart and mind. I have also pointed out the need for personal holiness and consecration. Now this issue becomes quite serious. In deliverance ministry you will be confronting demons head-on. We know from the story of the seven sons of Sceva this is not the time to play games (Acts 19:13–16). If you know you are going to be ministering in deliverance, it would be good to recruit intercessors who will pray for you, as well as to make sure you have diligently sought the Lord in prayer yourself. You should practice the spiritual disciplines listed in chapter 7, such as fasting and prayer. The more submitted to God you are in body, soul, and spirit, the greater authority you will have in deliverance (Jas. 4:7). It is best to be ready at all times.

WORK WITH A PARTNER

Whenever it is possible, I suggest working with a friend in deliverance ministry. Even the disciples were sent out to minister in pairs (Mark 6:7). There are a number of good reasons we should use this same model today.

- There is a biblical principle that "two are better than one" (Eccles. 4:9).

- We can benefit from the gifts and grace in one another's lives (Phil. 1:7).

- We strengthen and encourage one another (1 Thess. 5:11).

- We can have an exponential impact when we work together (Lev. 26:8; Deut. 32:30).

- When two people work together, they are more accountable, and they also have a witness in case there is ever an accusation (2 Cor. 13:1).

KEEP ORDER, HONOR AUTHORITY

If you are working with a partner, or even in a group of people, I suggest that always one person leads and the other(s) back him or her up with intercession. It is not good to have several people shouting at the demon to come out. The devil loves confusion and thrives on it. The more restlessness and disorder, the more comfortable demons are. Since spiritual authority is a very important issue in deliverance ministry, we ought to demonstrate honor, order, and authority among ourselves first and foremost.

SALVATION FIRST

I will reiterate this point later. But as a basic truth, if someone comes to me for deliverance, I am going to lead him or her to Christ first. Salvation is the foundation of any spiritual benefit or blessing. When a person becomes a child of God, every legal claim demons have on his or her life is revoked. This goes even for church people. As an evangelist I can assure you that not everyone who goes to church is born again.

HONOR THE DEMONIZED PERSON'S SOVEREIGNTY

Christians have great authority through the name of Jesus. But one thing we do not have is the authority to make a decision on someone else's behalf. If someone does not want to be free, there is little, if anything, we can do to make things better for him. Even God honors individual sovereignty in making decisions.

In the earlier example about C. J., I first told the demon, which had been manifesting for an hour, to be quiet. I told it I wanted to speak to C. J., not to the demon. At that moment, everything became quiet and C. J. came to his right mind. I asked him if he actually wanted to be free. Keep in mind that for C. J. freedom meant leaving a whole way of living behind. In fact, he was still working for the mob at the time. I seem to remember it took him some time to make that decision; it seemed as if a war was going on inside.

C. J. was battling not only the demons influencing his body but also his will, his thought patterns, and the desires in his soul. This was something only he could do. I had to wait for that permission. Once he told me he wanted to be free, I told him there was only one way—he needed to repent and put his trust in Jesus. I briefly explained the gospel to him and asked him if he wanted to pray with me and surrender his life to Christ. He agreed. All of this happened as he was lying on his back on the floor.

I tried to lead him in a simple prayer. But whenever he would try to say the name of Jesus, demons would start to overwhelm him again. Each time I would take authority over them, and they would be quiet. Then I would get C. J.'s permission to continue, and we would start praying again. My authority as a believer needed the cooperation of C. J.'s authority as a sovereign individual. When he made the decision to surrender to Jesus, freedom came into his life.

DEMONIC SPIRITS IN DRY PLACES

Jesus told an instructive parable that teaches us a great deal about demonization and deliverance.

> When an impure spirit comes out of a person, it goes through arid places seeking rest and does not find it. Then it says, "I will return to the house I left." When it arrives, it finds the house unoccupied, swept clean and put in order. Then it goes and takes with it seven other spirits more wicked than itself, and they go in and live there. And the final condition of that person is worse than the first. That is how it will be with this wicked generation.
>
> —MATTHEW 12:43–45

Let's consider some important lessons from this passage.

Demons can return.

Someone might be wondering why in C. J.'s case I didn't just cast the demons out like Jesus—with a single word. This is a good question and a fair one. Given that I am not a member of the Trinity, I find myself often falling short of Jesus' example. If you are confronted with a demon, follow the Jesus method first. My story is not meant to be your ultimate example. It is just one of my experiences, though it turned out quite well.

Even if you are able to cast out a demon with one word, there is still the possibility the demon could return to the same host with other demons and actually make things worse. This is important because casting out a demon is not good enough. Jesus commanded His disciples to preach the gospel, heal the sick, cleanse the lepers, raise the dead, and cast out demons. These displays of power are remarkable. But don't forget: He also told them to "make disciples of all nations" (Matt. 28:19).

I would argue that casting out demons is the easy part. Once people get free, we have to be willing to walk with them. I discipled C. J. in the early years of his salvation. I encouraged him to marry Nikki, who was his live-in girlfriend and the mother of his children. I even officiated the wedding ceremony. I have stayed connected to C. J. even to this day. In fact, I interviewed him and Nikki in preparation for this chapter to confirm all the finer details of their story. We are still friends, and he calls me often. He has had his ups and downs, but he is still serving the Lord and is a pastor today. The deliverance happened in an instant. But he still had to walk out a Christian life. That takes time. In fact, that takes a lifetime.

Someone can end up worse after deliverance.

Jesus made a shocking statement. The final condition of that person was worse than the first! This directly relates to my point above. We all know someone who went on a diet, lost fifty pounds, then fell off the wagon and gained eighty pounds back! Deliverance is necessary, but it is not enough. With the deliverance there has to come a permanent change that prevents those demons from returning. Whatever allowed them to enter in the first place could give them access again if things do not change in the person's life. Certain behaviors and beliefs will give demons a right to access a person's life. One of them, as we will discuss, is unforgiveness and bitterness. Often you will discover that someone demonized has been involved in the occult. Sometimes substance abuse was the gateway to demons. If these doors are not shut, demons will return—with friends. The demonized person will be worse than before. This is why the next principle is so important.

You must fill the house.

Jesus said the returning spirits will take up residence in the old house if they return and find it unoccupied. In deliverance ministry it is imperative that the "house" is filled. Remember, we are talking about a spiritual principle now. The demons that took over the house previously were evil spirits. If the house needs to be occupied so those demons cannot return, there is one obvious solution. A delivered person needs to be filled with the Holy Spirit.

This is why when I encountered C. J. that day, I prayed with him to receive Jesus. I knew his deliverance would be complete and permanent only if the Holy Spirit came to dwell inside of him.

Deliverance is necessary, but it is not enough. With the deliverance there has to come a permanent change that prevents those demons from returning.

The Bible says that when we are born again, we receive the Spirit. Anyone who gets delivered from demons but is not born again is in a dangerous situation. He is an empty house with the front door standing wide open. As stated above, the demon problem he had will only become worse.

I also prayed with C. J. that day to be baptized in the Holy Spirit. When I laid my hands on him, the power of the Holy Spirit came upon him, and he was instantly and dramatically filled and began speaking in other tongues. I believe this is one of the most important aspects of deliverance. We need to make sure people are being baptized in the Spirit.

In Africa, each week during our gospel meetings, I take time one night to address demonic curses and bondage specifically. It is a night of mass deliverance. Later that same week, on one of the nights I focus on Spirit baptism. I pray over the vast crowd after thousands have received Christ, and I ask God to baptize them with His Holy Spirit. It always amazes me that on this night we cast out more demons than any other night—including the night I focus on deliverance. It seems the outpouring of the Holy Spirit is absolutely terrifying to demon spirits. As the Holy Spirit comes to take up residence, the demon spirits have to go.

RECOGNIZING DEMONIC INFLUENCE

It is not always obvious when you deal with someone who is demonized. It is usually a mistake to assume that just because something looks odd or even creepy, it is demonic. In many third-world countries people lack even the most basic medical care. What's more, institutions do not exist to remove the worst cases from the general population. As a result you will often encounter medical cases far more severe than anything you will see in public in the West. On one mission trip one of the young ladies on the team encountered a severely deformed person. The case was so tragic that she was sure it had to be demonic and wanted to know if deliverance was called for. In this case there was no reason to think this disability was demonic. She was simply going by the visceral reaction she had to the sight of a deformity more severe than anything she had ever seen. On the other hand, we know a physical sickness or ailment can sometimes be demonic in nature (e.g., Matt. 9:32; Luke 13:11). How can we recognize which is which? Here are a few tips. I could elaborate on each of these points with its own chapter. But for the sake of brevity I will simply state them plainly.

- Never assume someone is demonized unless there is something that overtly points to it.

- Every person should be treated with dignity and respect, even if you have good reason to think he or she is demonized. Don't embarrass or intimidate people unnecessarily. Do everything in love, and you will never go wrong.

- As already mentioned, always focus on leading people to Christ. If demons are involved in someone's life, it will become evident soon enough. Then you can deal with it.

- Pay attention to telltale clues that might indicate demonic activity. For example, when people are self-harming or having suicidal thoughts, it is often (but not always) an indication of demonic activity. In Scripture demons often caused people to harm themselves in ways such as throwing themselves in fire or water (e.g.,

Matt. 17:15; Mark 9:22). According to the Bible, these demons did this in an effort to kill their hosts.

SELF-HARM AND SUICIDAL TENDENCIES

The man in Mark 5 who was possessed by a legion of demons is an interesting case. The Bible gives us two important details about him. First, it mentions three times in the first five verses that he lived among the tombs. When the Bible repeats something so often, I pay attention to it. These demons were obsessed with death to the extent that they wanted to be close to the tombs even while their host was alive. Second, he was cutting himself with stones. In other words, he was self-harming. I see this a lot as I travel around the world, especially among young people. They are often called cutters. They are people who impulsively cut their bodies with knives and razor blades. They sometimes cut their wrists, and they have bodies full of scars from their cutting. This to me is one of the signs that demonic torment is going on. You will often find those who are cutting themselves are also having suicidal thoughts. In my opinion this points to something that is clearly demonic. Such a person needs deliverance. Demons love death and self-mutilation. When you see signs such as these, you should be aware you may be dealing with demonization.

Interestingly, at the end of the story these demons request that Jesus send them into a herd of pigs—a request He grants. Notice what happens. The pigs immediately run off a cliff and kill themselves. Demons love torment and death. It apparently brings them some sick satisfaction. No wonder Jesus said, "The thief comes only to steal and kill and destroy" (John 10:10).

As a side note, one of the most amazing miracles I have seen recently is the total healing of cutters. In some of our meetings I have seen how they were not only delivered, but the scars on their bodies literally disappeared! I have been in services where this happened multiple times in one instant. What an amazing moment when people all over the room begin to scream in utter amazement when they look at their arms and all the scars have miraculously vanished! The enemy's malevolence and tactics have not changed. But likewise Jesus is the same yesterday, today, and forever. He still sets the captives free.

SOME TELLTALE SIGNS

While it is not always obvious who is demonized and who is not, you should immediately recognize a few things:[1]

- mental blocks
- violent reactions
- blasphemies and cursing
- incoherent talk
- feeling of breathlessness
- looks full of hatred or glassy, unfocused eyes
- manifested oppression in some part of the body
- vomiting
- uncontrollable screaming

Discernment is always the most important tool in recognizing demonic influence.

BE AWARE OF ENTRY POINTS

When ministering to those who might be demonized, it is wise to keep your eyes, ears, and spiritual discernment attuned to what might have given those demonic spirits a right to enter their host. Demons don't attach themselves without some invitation. These invitations are not always intentional or conscious, but they are always part of the equation. When you know what you are dealing with, it can be helpful.

Past involvement in the occult, witchcraft, and idolatry might be the origin. Even things such as the oaths and covenants made by Freemasons or things such as Ouija boards and séances that seem like innocent games can give access to demonic spirits. I have often heard that one episode of uncontrolled rage or intense hatred can invite demonic activity. Violence can be an entry point—especially murder.

There is a video circulating of an abortion doctor in front of his clinic; he is wearing scrubs and clearly seems to be manifesting a demon. He hisses and proclaims he has a darkened heart and loves killing babies. It comes as no surprise to me that someone shedding so much blood is demonized.

Often those involved in genocide or mass murder report becoming obsessed with or even addicted to taking life. Sometimes in battle warriors are overcome with a desire to kill. There is even a word for this phenomenon—*bloodlust*. The dictionary defines *bloodlust* as "a desire for bloodshed and carnage, often aroused in the heat of battle and leading to uncontrolled slaughter and torture."[2] This makes a lot of sense to me. As we have already discussed, demons love death and destruction. It is only reasonable that bloodshed and violence would attract them.

It is also possible that certain drugs might unintentionally open doors to demonic spirits. For example, certain hallucinogenic drugs have been tied in with religious rituals for thousands of years. Today many people still go on hallucinogenic trips under the guidance of a witch doctor or shaman. I have heard of experiences where users of these drugs encounter and interact in bizarre ways with entities they describe as angels, demons, aliens, and even elves. Even more suspicious is that with certain drugs these experiences do not always seem to be merely subjective (as a hallucination would normally be), but users often report similar experiences. This happens often enough that scientists are now studying these experiences.[3]

We also live in a time when the New Age movement has become mainstream. As a result more and more people—even Christians—are inadvertently opening themselves up to dangerous demonic influences. For example, some Christians have given access to "spirit guides" without realizing they are actually demonic spirits. Roger Barrier, a Baptist pastor in Arizona, told the following story:

> One day, a man from the utility company finished his work at our home and said, "You're Roger Barrier, aren't you? I listen to your radio program every day. My wife and I are both Christians. She's having some problems; in fact, there are times when I wonder what's going on inside of her. Do you believe in demons?"
>
> "Yes," I replied. "Why don't we sit down in the kitchen and talk?"

"Several months ago," he began, "we went to a spiritualist church where we were encouraged to pray to receive spirit guides to help direct our lives. I didn't pray for any, but my wife did. She hasn't been the same since. Sometimes, it's as if there's a different person inside. Her voice changes; her face contorts; she has an aversion to the things of God. Our marriage is falling apart. She won't go back to our Christian church. It all came to a head last night! While we were arguing, she walked into the hallway, turned slowly, and said with a sneer, 'Don't you know who we are?' Her voice rose to a scream as she repeated, 'Don't you know who we are? Don't you know who we are?'"

He was shaking now. "I think," he said, "she is demon possessed like they talk about in the Bible. Can you help us?"[4]

When you know someone is demonized and you understand exactly what kind of spirits you are dealing with, you can take authority over them with great precision. However, this is not always necessary, and I have no desire to be dogmatic or create any extrabiblical doctrines around this idea. But this understanding is something that I and many who work in deliverance ministry have found helpful at times.

CAN CHRISTIANS BE DEMONIZED?

At this point you might be wondering if Christians can be demonized. This topic is a serious hot potato. I realize I am wading into dangerous territory by commenting on this. But since I am asked about it so frequently, I want to give my honest opinion. You may disagree with me, and you may be right to do so. I can give my take only as I see it at this writing.

I do not believe Christians can be demonized. When a person is saved, the Holy Spirit comes to dwell within him or her. So I don't see how a believer's "house," inhabited by the Holy Spirit, can be shared with demons. (See 2 Corinthians 6:14.) On the other hand, I have seen people who by every outward indication were in fact Christians. Yet they clearly manifested demons and received deliverance. This is something I have witnessed not once or twice but many times—even hundreds of times. I don't fully understand how this is possible, but I cannot deny what I have seen. Carlos Annacondia, who has one of the most powerful deliverance ministries I know of, said that according to his leaders, 30 to 40 percent of those receiving deliverance ministry in his crusades are members of a church.[5] Perhaps my position on this will evolve over time. But the following is how I have come to terms with this dilemma in my own mind.

First, there is much about the spiritual world we do not understand. There are many variables to consider, and all of them are invisible and mysterious. For example, I don't always know by outward appearance who is truly born again and who is not. However, I do believe even truly born-again Christians are sometimes physically attacked by the enemy in their bodies. I also know the enemy tries to influence the thinking of Christians. We already talked at length about this. Believers cannot embrace a demonic way of thinking—or have areas in their lives that are not under the Lord's control—and simultaneously take authority over the devil. When a Christian is in this state, is not the devil influencing him or her on some level?

Jesus rebuked Satan speaking through Peter, one of His disciples who was keeping His Word (Matt. 16:23; John 17:6). Paul warned believers not to give place to the devil by holding in anger (Eph. 4:26–27). And then he taught them to put on God's armor to stand firm against the entire host of demonic forces (6:10–17). James further exhorted believers to resist the devil (Jas. 4:7). If the devil does attack believers in their bodies and minds, and if it is necessary that Scripture warns us to resist and fight against the devil, what then happens if believers fail to do so? Nothing? Do they just go on with life completely free and happy as if they simply lost a board game like Monopoly or Candy Land?

I cannot imagine that is the case. Based on these texts, there must be consequences when Christians fail to resist demons. After all, Christians who are saved from sin can still sin. Though the Holy Spirit within us is holy, it is still possible to engage in unholy behavior—even though we are temples of the Holy Spirit. Indeed, we know that Christians in Scripture had to be corrected for ungodly behavior (e.g., 1 Cor. 5:1). If saints can sin, it also seems that saints can come under at least the temporary influence of demonic spirits.

Some teach a difference between being *possessed* and simply *oppressed*, or tormented. This distinction may be useful, but as I have already pointed out, demons do not possess anyone anyway—even someone they are in complete control of. Furthermore, I do not see how one is able to place different levels of demonic influence into neat categories. When someone manifests a demon, it is surely an extreme case, but not everyone demonized manifests. We simply do not know how all of this works.

It is possible for Christians to be influenced by demonic spirits in certain ways—we know this. On the other hand, I also believe true Christians indwelled by the Spirit are by nature and position liberated children of God. We belong to God as *His* house and cannot be possessed by demonic forces. If there is demonic influence, there is not full demonic control. Furthermore, and most importantly, if demonic spirits *can* influence Christians to some degree, they still *should* not influence Christians to any degree! As God's child and God's temple, even a Christian who comes under the temporary influence of demons has the higher ground. But he must do something with that higher ground! Therefore, though I admit I do not completely understand how demonic spirits can affect Christians, it seems that it can happen on some level. But when it does, we should do exactly what James told us to do. We should submit to God, *resist the devil*, and throw off demonic attack.

This is the practical approach I have adopted. If I see someone manifesting a demon, all I know is the demon has to go. Period. I am not going to look at a person clearly manifesting a demon and explain to him why it is impossible because Christians cannot be demonized according to Scripture. Wherever there is demonic influence, however you classify it, take authority over it and get it out or throw it off.

On the other hand, I don't think we should go hunting for demons without cause, and I don't assume every issue a person has is connected to demons. Neither do I believe a Christian should ever come under bondage to any demonic spirit on any level. Through the blood of Jesus we have the right to walk in total freedom. We should never settle for anything less.

FAITH, FEAR, AND UNBELIEF

The Gospels contain a fascinating and famous story of an exorcism performed by Jesus that has some important lessons for us in the ministry of deliverance.

> And when they had come to the multitude, a man came to Him, kneeling down to Him and saying, "Lord, have mercy on my son, for he is an epileptic and suffers severely; for he often falls into the fire and often into the water. So I brought him to Your disciples, but they could not cure him."
>
> Then Jesus answered and said, "O faithless and perverse generation, how long shall I be with you? How long shall I bear with you? Bring him here to Me." And Jesus rebuked the demon, and it came out of him; and the child was cured from that very hour.
>
> Then the disciples came to Jesus privately and said, "Why could we not cast it out?"
>
> So Jesus said to them, "Because of your unbelief; for assuredly, I say to you, if you have faith as a mustard seed, you will say to this mountain, 'Move from here to there,' and it will move; and nothing will be impossible for you. However, this kind does not go out except by prayer and fasting."
>
> —MATTHEW 17:14–21, NKJV

Notice that when the disciples asked Jesus why they were not able to cast out the demon, Jesus had a simple answer: "Because of your unbelief." Jesus then goes on to reiterate this statement by saying that faith as a grain of mustard seed can remove mountains. This brings us to a very important point: when dealing with demons, faith is an indispensable requirement.

In light of the theme I have been repeating throughout this book, it should not be difficult to understand why unbelief is so poisonous. Unbelief, as set in contrast to faith, is the agreement with the spirit of the age. It is the adoption of the demonic way of thinking rather than the Christlike way. Anyone who is in agreement with the devil is going to have a difficult time casting him out. Faith is agreement with the Word of God. It is not dictated by the senses. In God's economy it is substance and evidence (Heb. 11:1).

While God's power operates through faith, Satan thrives on fear. In deliverance ministry fear has got to go. Demons smell fear like sharks smell blood, and it will only embolden them. You must approach demons with a bold confidence in the power of the name of Jesus. You must know He has given you authority to "trample on snakes and scorpions and to overcome all the power of the enemy; nothing will harm you" (Luke 10:19). No demon is going to be able to attach itself to you. No curse is going to come upon you (Prov. 26:2). You have nothing to fear from them. You are covered in the blood of Jesus. You are a child of God. Jesus has already "disarmed the powers and authorities, he made a public spectacle of them, triumphing over them by the cross" (Col. 2:15). It is in His victorious name that you cast out devils. Inside of you dwells the Holy Spirit, the finger of God by which Jesus Himself drove out demons in His earthly life (Luke 11:20). In deliverance ministry arm yourself with a confident trust in God and a deep love for the person you are ministering to. Love drives out fear (1 John 4:18). A spirit of fear is demonic, but God has given us the perfect antidote—power, love, and a sound mind (2 Tim. 1:7, NKJV).

THIS KIND DOES NOT GO OUT EXCEPT BY PRAYER AND FASTING

Since we just discussed Matthew 17:14–21, I'll take this opportunity to address a common question related to deliverance. What does Jesus mean by His ending statement, "However, this kind does not go out except by prayer and fasting" (v. 21, NKJV)? I have already explained that unbelief is quite clearly the issue at hand. According to Jesus, unbelief is what prevented the disciples from being able to cast the demon out of that boy. But in verse 21 Jesus seems to be saying something quite different. He says that some demons will not come out without prayer and fasting. Many people have asked me about this verse, and I agree it is quite confusing in this context.

Others will find something even more perplexing: Matthew 17:21, the verse containing the sentence about prayer and fasting, might be completely missing from their Bibles. There is a good reason for this:

the earliest Greek manuscripts containing this passage do not include this statement.

Let me explain just a bit about the process that leads to our modern New Testaments. For those unfamiliar, *textual criticism* is the science that studies ancient manuscripts to determine what their original documents stated. This method is needed for the Bible because we do not actually have any of the original documents, called autographs, written by the biblical authors. Instead we have copies—and copies of copies—spanning from the second century into the Middle Ages. These are called manuscripts.[6] Of course, for thousands of years before the printing press was invented, biblical manuscripts had to be copied by scribes by hand.[7] Although scribes were often highly skilled and disciplined in their work, they were also human and subject to error. But we are fortunate. We have more than 5,600 Greek copies of all or part of the New Testament books. In fact, there are more copies of the books in the New Testament than any other documents from antiquity—by far![8] The New Testament is the best-preserved set of ancient documents in human history. Further, the vast majority of differences between manuscripts (called textual variants) are inconsequential. Most variations consist of simple spelling mistakes or differences in word choice, some as simple as the use of a different pronoun (e.g., *he* instead of *they*). Only a very small percent of the variants affect the meaning of a given passage, and none affect actual Christian doctrine.[9] Because most variants are extremely minor and because we possess thousands of manuscripts, scholars are mostly certain they know what the original New Testament autographs said. The science of textual criticism is both important and reliable. It provides the best manuscripts from which our modern Bibles are translated.

Still, in some cases scholars are less certain of the original wording. None of these cases affect actual Christian teaching or faith, as I said. But in these cases it requires a bit more scrutiny to get to the original wording. One of these cases is Matthew 17:21. The current consensus among New Testament scholars is that scribes at some point added the statement about prayer and fasting in Matthew 17:21.[10] They have three basic reasons for believing this:

1. This verse is not found in our oldest and best manuscripts.[11] Obviously, if manuscripts closer to the original
   autographs consistently leave out a phrase that more
   recent manuscripts have, it was probably added at some
   point.

2. The textual criticism principle called *lectio brevior*, or
   shorter reading, holds that the shorter version of a text
   is usually the more accurate one. It is far more likely
   that scribes added material than that they omitted it.[12]
   Bruce Metzger alludes to this principle when he makes
   this statement about Matthew 17:21: "Since there is no
   satisfactory reason why the passage, if originally present
   in Matthew, should have been omitted in a wide variety
   of witnesses, and since copyists frequently inserted
   material derived from another Gospel, it appears that
   most manuscripts [that include this verse] have been
   assimilated to the parallel in Mk 9:29."[13] And this leads
   us to the third reason.

3. In the parallel passage that tells this story in Mark 9:29,
   Jesus is recorded as saying, "This kind can come out
   by nothing but prayer and fasting." Metzger and many
   other scholars hold that the Mark passage seems to have
   been assimilated into the Matthew 17:21 passage.[14]

At this point you might wonder why we don't just accept the reference to prayer and fasting in Mark 9:29. But a similar problem exists
with this verse. The last two words ("and fasting") don't appear in some
of the earliest and best manuscripts for this passage either.[15] While
there is a bit more textual support for the originality of the Mark 9
passage, there is still a good argument to be made against it. That is
why some modern Bibles have left the words "and fasting" out (or perhaps put them in brackets or attached them with a footnote).

Here is what all this means to me. It is not certain whether or not
Jesus makes fasting a prerequisite for casting out certain demons. I
personally do not believe, based on the evidence I have seen, that the
original writings of Matthew and Mark contain this statement that

makes fasting a condition for driving out certain demons. On the other hand, as we discussed, fasting is a very important spiritual discipline—and very biblical. Fasting in general aligns with the teachings of Jesus, the apostles, and the early church. In fact, one of the best explanations for the addition of the words "and fasting" to Mark 9:29 is that the early church so emphasized—and assumed—fasting as a companion to prayer, it was most likely added accidentally[16] or to clarify something certain scribes considered obvious.[17] In the second or third century Tertullian said that Jesus "taught likewise that fasts are to be the weapons for battling with the more direful demons."[18] It is clear that many in the early church believed Jesus made this statement about fasting.

In any case I would certainly not discount the importance of fasting in spiritual warfare and deliverance ministry. I actually encourage those involved in deliverance ministry to fast as they are able. But I do not think fasting should be seen as some secret weapon against the devil or a way for Christians to get spiritual power. Our power comes from the outpouring of the Holy Spirit and from faith. Let's keep it simple.

My mentor, Reinhard Bonnke, was once invited on a television show to be interviewed by a man who had written books about fasting. Fasting was a big part of this man's ministry emphasis. He wanted to ask Reinhard Bonnke, a man who has seen amazing miracles and millions of salvations, what he thought about fasting. I am sure he thought Evangelist Bonnke would reinforce his fasting emphasis. Instead he said something no one expected: "I must be honest with you. I found the power switch on a different wall."

Now just to be clear, I know Evangelist Bonnke fasts, and he understands the value of fasting. But his point is important. Faith is the power switch to which he referred.[19] And it was Jesus' point in the passage above. Ironically, fasting is actually more effective to help us get authority over ourselves. Since bringing ourselves in alignment under God's authority results in authority both in our own lives and over demons, it is in fact quite valuable in deliverance ministry—just not for the reason many people assume.

Fasting and prayer help us bring ourselves into spiritual alignment. Part of this is getting the unbelief out and aligning our minds with

God's Word. This is what Jesus was talking about. As I wrote in my book *Live Before You Die*, "At first glance it may appear that the demon is the focal point of this account, but a closer look will reveal that the real antagonist in this story is not the demon but the spirit of unbelief. The disciples were concerned about the demon inside the boy, but Jesus was concerned about the unbelief inside His disciples. The disciples' question was about casting out demons, but Jesus's answer was about casting out doubt. Jesus knew that once unbelief has been cast out, exorcizing demons would be a piece of cake."[20]

THE CONCEPT OF GENERATIONAL CURSES

I have also noticed that some demonic spirits tend to torment family members in successive generations. This is often referred to as a generational curse. I don't like this terminology because it is not clear to me that we are dealing with a curse per se. Also, this terminology is highly ambiguous. If you ask ten people what they mean by *curse*, you will get ten different definitions. All I can say for sure is that spiritual and other kinds of issues seem to haunt multiple generations.

The disciples were concerned about the demon inside the boy, but Jesus was concerned about the unbelief inside His disciples. The disciples' question was about casting out demons, but Jesus's answer was about casting out doubt.

This is another area in which I think we ought to take a fairly nuanced approach. There is certainly a lot of nonsense surrounding the generational curses idea, and some people have certainly taken it too far. The concept definitely opens the door for odd and sometimes superstitious beliefs. It is also sometimes used as a crutch that gives people an excuse as to why they are struggling with their issues. I am not in favor of any of these things. The blood of Jesus transforms us into new creations, and everything we need is available at the cross.

Still, it is quite normal to observe that the issues in some people's lives seem to fit a pattern within their family history. For example, often those with alcoholism grew up with an alcoholic father or mother. This is a demonstrable fact.[21] People who have problems with pornography were often in a family environment where pornography was an issue. People who have problems with anger or rage will often tell you their fathers had the same problem. Could this be mere coincidence? Can it be attributed to merely biological factors? Many of those involved in deliverance ministry believe that whatever the natural explanations are, there is also a spiritual component. But is there any biblical support for this?

Here are some Scriptures to consider. When Jesus encountered a man blind from birth, the disciples asked Him an interesting question: "Rabbi, who sinned, this man or his parents, that he was born blind?" (John 9:2). This question clearly indicates the disciples believed physical ailments could be passed down because of the parents' sin. For some this would fit the definition of a *generational curse*.

God told Moses about the extension of His blessings to "a thousand generations of those who love me and keep my commandments" (Exod. 20:6). On the other hand, He punishes "the children for the sin of the parents to the third and fourth generation of those who hate [Him]" (v. 5). It seems obvious that a spiritual principle exists of both blessings and punishment being handed down to successive generations.

I tend to think that what is often described as a generational curse is either (1) something hereditary (more about this below) or (2) a demonic spirit that attaches itself to a family over generations. We read in the Old Testament about *familiar spirits*, a term often used in connection with divination (e.g., Lev. 19:31, NKJV). It seems these spirits are able to impersonate people who have died, giving relatives the impression they are hearing from their ancestors during a séance. This seems to indicate some demonic spirits are hanging around long enough to become "familiar" with members of a family. Also, their familiarity might give these demons a good idea about how to exploit hereditary weaknesses and proclivities within a family.

Interestingly, the only time demons are mentioned explicitly in the Old Testament is in connection with idol worship. For example, "They even sacrificed their sons and their daughters to demons" (Ps. 106:37, NKJV; see also Lev. 17:7, NKJV; Deut. 32:17, NKJV; 2 Chron. 11:15, NKJV). It seems noteworthy to me that several times when God forbids idol worship in the Old Testament, He also warns His people that the iniquity of the fathers will be visited upon the third and fourth generation (Exod. 20:5; 34:6–7; Deut. 5:9). Could it be that these sacrifices, essentially blood covenants cut with demons, caused those spirits to be joined to that family in some way for generations?

EPIGENETICS

The modern science of epigenetics has made this issue more relevant than ever before. For those who are not familiar with epigenetics, here is my layman's explanation. Your epigenome consists of chemicals that tell your genes what to do. Among other things your epigenome is influenced by your behavior and environment, which regulate certain genetic expressions. For example, if you have identical twins and one of them lives a healthy life but the other does not, later in life they will look very different from one another. Their DNA will still be the same, but the expression of that DNA will be different. In the past it was thought that everyone's epigenome started as a blank slate. But now we know these epigenetic expressions can be passed down from generation to generation. This means addictive behaviors, lifestyle choices, and activities can cause changes to the epigenome of one's children. Interestingly, these changes can persist for two or three generations.[22]

Even if you do not believe the concepts of spiritual curses or familial demonic ties are biblical, there is no question the choices parents make often affect their children in profound and life-altering ways. Children who were abused develop issues in adulthood linked to that abuse. Often they end up repeating that same abuse with their own children. Why does this happen? Is it a hereditary propensity for addiction? Is it the children picking up on the habits of their parents and repeating the same mistakes? Is it simply that parents and children are alike and will have similar struggles? Is it epigenetic? Maybe it's a mixture of all the above. Or maybe it's all the above plus a spiritual or demonic component.

I do not pretend to know all the answers. But I do know there is a pattern we can clearly observe all over the world. Whether it is due to a generational curse, a hereditary spirit, or just children opening the same doors to demonic influence their parents opened—to me it is quite irrelevant. If someone is demonized, even if it is something that has affected the same family for generations, we need to deal with it.

Regardless of your take on generational curses, given the above information, here are some solid points to take away:

- If you are looking for the root cause or entry point for some demonic influence, looking at the family situation can often contain helpful clues.

- If an issue has persisted for generations within a family, it is a good indication the issue might have a spiritual connection.

- People need to realize that getting free is not just about their own deliverance but also about the health and well-being of their entire family.

THE DELIVERANCE PROCESS

Just to bring all of these points together for the sake of simplicity, if you are confronted with a demonized person, here is what I suggest. These points are not rigid. You may not always need all of them. And you may change the order sometimes. But I think it is safe to say this is a good outline that will serve you well.

Take authority over the demon (or demons), and command it (or them) to be quiet in Jesus' name.

Yelling at the demon, pleading the blood of Jesus, and rebuking it will only make it more violent. You will get a reaction this way, but the goal is not to create a dramatic scene. The goal is to get rid of the demon. I have seen people have prolonged discussions with demons talking through their host. Those ministering will often get quite rattled and even become intimidated by these demons. I could tell some wild stories about this, but it is best just to emphasize that you do not want demons talking. They are liars, deceivers, and accusers. Instead tell the demon to shut up.

Tell the demon you want to talk to the person, and call the person to consciousness in Jesus' name.

Once you are talking to the demonized person (not the demon), ask him if he wants to be free. If he says yes, you can proceed. If he says no, there is nothing more you should do.

If the person tells you he wants to be free, share the gospel with him first.

This does not need to be a long, protracted sermon. The person needs to know his freedom can come only through Jesus Christ. Tell him how Jesus died on the cross for his sins and that by his accepting His sacrifice, every demonic claim will be canceled. Make sure he understands he needs to surrender his entire life to Christ and follow Him from this moment on. Also, tell him he will be required to completely forgive anyone who has wronged him—no exceptions.

It is possible that during this time the demons will start manifesting again. Just continue to take authority over them, tell them to be quiet in Jesus' name, call the demonized person forward, and continue. As long as he wants what you are doing, do not let the enemy stop it.

Lead the person in a prayer of salvation.

Ask the person to repeat after you as you pray with him to surrender his life to Christ and confess Him as Lord. I would normally lead a simple prayer of faith that goes something like this:

> *Lord Jesus Christ, I am a sinner. Have mercy on me. Forgive my sins. Make me a child of God. I confess with my mouth what I believe in my heart—that Jesus Christ is Lord, that God raised Him from the dead. I put my trust in You and surrender my life to You. From this day forward I am Yours and You are mine. In the name of Jesus, amen.*

Have the person specifically renounce any areas where he intentionally gave demons access.

You might not always be aware of these, but the Holy Spirit can give you insight. Also, it will often become apparent what you are dealing with. Finally, you can ask the person outright what doors he has opened—he may know. Many demonized people can point to something that seemed to start it all. C. J.'s problems began when his mother made him kill his dogs. The rage and hatred to which he gave himself seems to have been the catalyst. I did not know this at the time I ministered to him, but by the Spirit I knew that bitterness and unforgiveness were keys. It is important the person you are ministering to does this himself. You cannot renounce these on his behalf. It must be an act of the person's will.

Have the person forgive anyone he was holding bitterness or anger against.

Because I sensed C. J.'s situation was tied to anger and bitterness, I asked him to write the names of the people he hated on a piece of paper and forgive them. This might not always be necessary, but forgiveness is always important.

Take authority over every demonic spirit and command it to go in Jesus' name.

It is possible that there will be very little outward manifestation by this point. C. J. said that at this point he felt as if he were vomiting air. He described it as a wind coming out of his belly. I was not aware of that. In fact, to me the conclusion of that particular deliverance was pretty undramatic. But he was free—that's the point.

Lay your hands on the person, together with anyone else ministering with you, and pray for him to receive the fullness of the Holy Spirit.

This was the most dramatic and rewarding moment in C. J.'s case. He was filled with the Holy Spirit and immediately began speaking in tongues. After this experience there was no question that C. J. had been set free. He looked like a new person. His demeanor was totally different. He was able to communicate freely. He said that for the first time in more than twenty days he suddenly felt hungry. He described it as scales falling from his eyes. He said everything looked different after that experience!

After a person has been delivered, it is important that he get discipled and stay accountable.

Remember, deliverance is the easy part. The person must be fully immersed in the Word of God, the church, worship, prayer, and community. C. J. told me that he has had many temptations to go back to his old life in the nearly sixteen years since his deliverance. Following Jesus is not easy for anyone, especially someone who has carried such baggage. Walk with him, love him, and pray for him, and you will have fruit that remains.

QUESTIONS FOR DISCUSSION

- What are some key things to remember about deliverance ministry?

- What are some ways we can recognize demonic influence?

- Why is discipleship so important after someone has been delivered?

- Can a Christian be demonized?

- What are some of the ways we can be affected by unbelief?

- Is there a connection between epigenetics and generational curses? Explain.

CHAPTER 11

WALKING IN VICTORY

"I'm here, Satan," he said. "I can't see you, and maybe you can move faster than I can, but I'm still here, and by the grace of God and the power of the Holy Spirit I intend to be a thorn in your side until one of us has had enough!"

—FRANK E. PERETTI, *THIS PRESENT DARKNESS*

So comes snow after fire, and even dragons have their ending!

—J. R. R. TOLKIEN, *THE HOBBIT*

A s WE REACH the final chapter of this book, I realize there is still so much to be said about spiritual warfare. In fact, this theme could be applied to virtually every area of the Christian life, as we have already seen. At the end of the day it is the Holy Spirit who will continue to train and teach you. As David said, "Blessed be the LORD my Rock, who trains my hands for war, and my fingers for battle" (Ps. 144:1, NKJV). Jesus gave us the incredibly reassuring promise that He would be with us always, even to the end of the world (Matt. 28:20). Your great confidence should be in this—no matter what you face, the great dragon slayer Himself is at your side, teaching you to fight and backing you up at every turn. In the end He is the One who will deal the fatal blow to the dragon and crush Satan under your feet (Rom. 16:20).

With that said, I would like to leave you with a few miscellaneous parting words for the spiritual battles you will encounter. Each of these topics could easily fill a chapter or even a book by themselves. I mention them here briefly because this book would be incomplete without them.

THE POWER OF ATTENTION

Given all of the time we have spent talking about spiritual warfare, this point might seem contradictory. In reality I don't think it is healthy to be obsessed with spiritual warfare, angels, demons, curses, and the devil. It is good to understand the context of the battle in which our spiritual lives take place. The military metaphor is also used quite extensively through Scripture, as we have seen, and is completely valid. But the best thing for us to focus on is not the devil but Jesus.

An article in the *New York Times* carried the following headline, "Long-Married Couples Do Look Alike, Study Finds." Dr. Zajonc, a psychologist at the University of Michigan, proposed that "people, often unconsciously, mimic the facial expressions of their spouses in a silent empathy and that, over the years, sharing the same expressions shapes the face similarly."[1] It seems modern science is discovering something Scripture revealed a long time ago— you will become like what you behold. Paul said that as we behold the glory of the

Wherever your heart, eyes, and mind are set is where the rest of you will end up eventually. You will become like what you behold.

Lord, we are changed into His own image from glory to glory (2 Cor. 3:18). There is an incredible, transformational power in what we set our eyes, minds, and hearts on, and I believe it goes much deeper than we even realize.

I can remember when my father taught me as a young boy to mow our lawn; he told me to set my eyes on a target straight ahead down the yard and aim for it. Wherever I put my eyes was where I would end up going. The same thing is true when you are driving down the road. If you watch the white line on the side of the road, you tend to drift to that side. If you watch the broken yellow lines, you gravitate toward the middle. But if you want to go straight ahead, that is where you should set your eyes. Wherever you look is where you will end up going. If our eyes, hearts, and minds are on Jesus, then we will be conformed into His image. But there is a flip side to the coin—a dark side.

In Matthew 5:28 Jesus said, "Whosoever looketh on a woman to lust after her hath committed adultery with her already in his heart" (KJV). Jesus understood the principle that where you look is where you will go. Adultery and fornication begin with lust. Murder begins with hate. Robbery begins with covetousness and greed. Wherever your heart, eyes, and mind are set is where the rest of you will end up eventually. You will become like what you behold.

Whatever you focus on, whatever you give your attention to, is what will grow in your life. If you are focused on demons and darkness, your life will be filled with fear. You will see demons in every corner, even when they aren't there. I have met people who are always talking about principalities and warring against spirits of this and spirits of that. Meanwhile they never seem to get any victory but only find themselves endlessly battling. This can be in itself a demonic distraction—to get you so focused on the demonic that you cannot get victory over it.

One of Satan's most powerful weapons is fear. Hebrews 2:15 tells us that fear can bring bondage. Satan thrives on fear, and evil depends on it. The antidote to fear is love, which comes from God. Paul tells us plainly, "For God has not given us a spirit of fear, but of power and of love and of a sound mind" (2 Tim. 1:7, NKJV). If you are focused on the demonic, fear will rule your life. This is not from God. If you focus on God, love will rule your heart. First John 4:18 tells us, "There is no fear in love. But perfect love drives out fear, because fear has to do with punishment. The one who fears is not made perfect in love." As Smith Wigglesworth said, "If you have a great God, you will have a little devil; if you have a big devil, you will have a little God."[2]

SAFETY IN NUMBERS

When contemplating the armor of God listed in Ephesians 6 on one occasion, it suddenly occurred to me that all of the protection it provided faced forward. It seemed that armor provided no protection for its wearer's back. This seemed strange to me since a sword in the back will kill you as quickly as a sword in the front. As I usually do whenever I don't understand something in Scripture, I asked the Lord about it. Suddenly I saw something I had never seen before. I had always seen the passage on the armor of God as Ephesians 6:10–17, ending with "the sword of the Spirit, which is the Word of God." Now the next verse jumped off the page.

> And pray in the Spirit on all occasions with all kinds of prayers and requests. With this in mind, be alert and always keep on praying for all the Lord's people.
> —Ephesians 6:18

I heard the voice of the Holy Spirit in my heart. *You are your brother's back armor.* And suddenly I saw it. We are supposed to have each other's backs. We are supposed to be praying for each other and looking out for each other. This is part of the armor God intended. This means none of us are intended to go into battle alone. We need our brothers and sisters. But unfortunately we often see Christians stabbing the very backs they are supposed to be protecting. I believe this grieves the heart of God and makes all of us more vulnerable to the enemy.

There are two important takeaways from this. First, it is important that you are plugged in to a spiritual community. You need the support, accountability, and love of the body of Christ. You need to be submitted in love to your spiritual family and be loyal to them. This is one of the best safeguards you can have in spiritual warfare.

I watched a nature documentary recently that followed a pride of lions hunting in the Maasai Mara in Kenya. As the pride approached a herd of wildebeests, the frightened animals began to run together as one, almost as though they were being directed. The massive herd caused the earth to rumble, and the lions, moving as a unit, found no opportunity for attack. Then on the edge of the herd one lone wildebeest separated itself from the group. It decided to make a run for it all on its own and began running a different direction. Immediately the pride focused in on the lone wildebeest and ran him down.

We are called the body of Christ, the family of God, and the ecclesia, or the assembly. All of these names describe a group. There is a great lesson here. This thing we call Christianity is intended to be done in community with others of like-minded faith. There is safety in numbers. Those who separate themselves and strike out alone become easy prey for the devil, who walks around like a roaring lion looking for someone to devour.

The second takeaway is this: make sure you are looking out for your brothers and sisters in Christ the way you want them to look out for you. Rather than gossiping and slandering, uphold your spiritual family in prayer. Fight for them. Be loyal to them. Be generous, be kind, be patient, and above all be loving.

WALKING IN FORGIVENESS

One of the revolutionary themes of Jesus' preaching was forgiveness. This is the topic of the vivid parable He told in Matthew 18. A certain king decided to collect debts that were due him. One servant was found who owed a whopping ten thousand talents (v. 24, NKJV). I think most modern readers brush past this detail without realizing what they are reading. When used in reference to money, a talent was a weight measure of gold or silver. A talent of silver weighed between forty-seven and one hundred pounds. A talent of gold weighed twice as much—between ninety-four and two hundred pounds, or between forty-two and ninety-one kilograms.[3]

As of April 2, 2019, the international price of gold was $41,491.34 per kilogram.[4] This means one talent of gold would be the equivalent of between $1.7 million and $3.8 million! The servant owed his master ten thousand of these (equivalent to between $17 billion and $38 billion today)! It should be obvious that Jesus was referring to a massive, absolutely hopeless debt.

Nowadays if someone cannot pay his debts, he can just declare bankruptcy and have a fresh start. But in Jesus' time the debtor himself, his possessions, and his family were collateral for the debt. Therefore, if the debtor could not pay, the creditor could take his wife and children as slaves, seize his property, and throw him in prison in lieu of repayment.

With consequences this severe most people would have been careful when borrowing money. But this particular servant had allowed his debt to accrue beyond any conceivable remedy for repayment. It is no wonder, then, in light of the servant's foolishness and utter irresponsibility that the king felt justified in having this reckless servant sold, along with his wife, children, and possessions, so at least some of the loss could be recuperated.

This is a picture of us. We are all guilty before God of a debt we can never repay and for which we have no one to blame but ourselves. Our own sins, our own irresponsibility, and our own foolishness have made us hopeless debtors.

As you can imagine, the servant was devastated. He was beyond assistance and out of options. He was hopeless, helpless, and powerless to do anything but beg for mercy. He fell on his knees and cried like a child. He was blubbering and pleading in utter despair, and the king was moved with compassion.

In Jesus' story what this king did next was something absolutely unheard of. Remember, there were no bankruptcy courts where debts were discharged in those days. Survival for creditors depended on cold pragmatism. Any successful businessman had to be ruthless. Defaulting on a loan of this size would have been a devastating blow to the lender, and he would have been compelled by reason to collect what he could and cut his losses. But for some inexplicable reason this king decided to personally absorb the debt and forgive it completely!

To those who heard Jesus tell it, this story must have sounded like a fairy tale. A king forgiving a common servant of such a huge debt? Unthinkable!

There is no other way to illustrate the utter absurdity of what God has done for us than with a wild story like this. Why would God forgive our sins? Why would He discharge our debt? What's more, why would He pay the debt Himself at such an inconceivably high personal cost? We have no idea how painful Calvary was, how

We are all guilty before God of a debt we can never repay and for which we have no one to blame but ourselves.

those nails pierced not only the precious hands of Jesus but also the heart of God. I am sure we will never fully understand just how personal was the loss and intimate the agony of the cross. And we cannot appreciate forgiveness unless we appreciate Calvary and what our debt cost God personally.

There are those who say they don't believe in the Christian way of salvation because it's too cheap. My friend, salvation may be free for us, but it was not cheap for the One who purchased it with His own blood! The amazing wonder of forgiveness is that our debt—all of it—was totally covered and completely pardoned for Jesus' sake! The unthinkable wonder of redemption is what Jesus was trying to communicate with His parable. Those who heard this story would have shaken their heads incredulously. A $17 billion debt totally forgiven? It was beyond unlikely. But that is not the end of the story—it gets more bizarre still.

The servant who was forgiven of a $17 billion debt left the king's courthouse and was walking home. He had just been given a new lease on life. One would have thought he floated home on a cloud of joy. But something was wrong. It seems this servant was on edge, temperamental, and testy. He saw someone across the street "who owed him a hundred denarii" (Matt. 18:28, NKJV).

Now, I've heard preachers say this was about twenty dollars (or some other tiny amount). They probably assume that since the debt the first man owed was so huge, the rhetorical antithesis would be a small amount, such as twenty dollars. But in fact a denarius was about a day's wage.[5] So one hundred denarii was not an insignificant amount of money. In fact, in John 6:7 a similar amount was enough to feed 2,500 men! In other words, the debt this second man owed was also substantial.

When the first servant saw this man who owed him several thousand dollars, he flew into a rage. He crossed the street with a swift stride, grabbed the other man by the throat, and shouted, "Pay me what you owe me!"

This fellow attendant fell on his knees and pleaded, "Give me time, and I will pay you all!" But the first servant's heart was as cold as stone. He dragged that fellow attendant to the local authorities and had him thrown in prison.

This part of the story might seem hard to understand at first, but if you think a little more deeply about human nature, it soon becomes clear. The first servant had been forgiven, but truth be told, he had never thought the debt fully his responsibility to begin with. After all, if that other servant had paid what he owed in a timely manner, he probably figured he would not have been in this mess in the first place, at least not as badly. Maybe he thought he would have been able to keep making payments on his loan had this other servant paid him on time. It seems he lost sight of the big picture while contemplating his own grievance.

Many times we think our debt to God has been caused by someone else's debt to us. People say, "If I hadn't been abused as a child, I wouldn't have this problem." When people have this attitude, they keep trying to collect on debts that God has already forgiven. How easy it is to blame others for our own problems. You can blame your parents, teachers, childhood, neighborhood, uncles, aunts, friends, or enemies. You can blame others to the point that you have in a sense excused yourself while holding everyone else accountable for your problems. And here we find a profound principle about bitterness. Unforgiveness is steeped in self-righteousness. This is one reason unforgiveness blocks the grace of God—because self-righteousness is a form of pride, and God resists the proud but gives grace to the humble.

It didn't take long for word to get back to the king about what this servant had done. The king summoned him back to the royal court for another hearing. This time the king was not so merciful. "His lord said to him, 'You wicked slave, I forgave you all that debt because you pleaded with me. Should you not also have had mercy on your fellow slave, in the same way that I had mercy on you?' And his lord, moved with anger, handed him over to the torturers until he should repay all that was owed him" (Matt. 18:32–34, NASB).

The unforgiving servant was handed over to the torturers. This is the fate of all who refuse to forgive. The place of unforgiveness is a dungeon of internal torture. When you hold resentment and animosity in your heart, you condemn yourself to a prison of torment. Unforgiving people drink from their own bitter fountains. They hurt themselves first and most. It has been said that holding a grudge is like drinking poison and waiting for the other person to die.

Jesus concluded the story by saying, "My heavenly Father will also do the same to you, if each of you does not forgive his brother from your heart" (Matt. 18:35, NASB). In Matthew 6:12 Jesus taught us to pray, "And forgive us our debts, as we also have forgiven our debtors."

And in Mark 11:26 Jesus says plainly, "But if you do not forgive, neither will your Father who is in heaven forgive your transgressions" (NASB).

Think for a moment about the amazing power forgiveness has. Jesus poured out His blood on the cross to wash your sins away. His blood

Many times we think our debt to God has been caused by someone else's debt to us. When people have this attitude, they keep trying to collect on debts that God has already forgiven.

has the power to break through every barrier, destroy all bondage, wash away every stain, and transform a heart of stone into a heart of flesh. On the other hand, unforgiveness has the power to block that amazing grace from flowing to our lives. Unforgiveness brings us into spiritual bondage (the servant was locked in prison) and possibly even gives demonic spirits a right to torment us (he was handed over to the torturers).

Wherever I go in the world preaching the gospel, I always pray for the sick as well. Some people are literally unable to receive a physical healing and deliverance because of unforgiveness. This root of bitterness has blocked the blessing of God from flowing into their lives on every level and has given the enemy a legitimate stronghold. I also have seen how simple forgiveness has resulted in miraculous healing and deliverance for so many. I am an eyewitness of the power of both bitterness and forgiveness.

Just like a deadly cancer that begins with only a few wayward cells behaving erratically, bitterness usually starts small. It begins with an offense, a criticism, a look, or just a small slight. But it will start to fester and grow, and it eventually takes on a life of its own. It starts to multiply and invade other healthy areas of a person's life. It gives rise to anger and resentment. Over time, if allowed to continue, it will feed on itself until it gives rise to other resentments over totally unrelated things, and soon a person's entire life is filled with offense, bitterness, resentment, and ultimately death—emotionally, mentally, spiritually, and even physically.

Cancer and bitterness will both lead to death if they are not aggressively attacked and removed. Surgery, radiation, and chemotherapy are the standard treatments most often used today to kill cancerous tumors. But love and forgiveness are the antidotes God has designed to attack and destroy the cancer of bitterness in the human heart. For the Christian there is no alternative—we must forgive. Jesus does not make any concessions for particular offenses. No matter how severe the injustice, no matter how painful the wound, no matter how monstrous the violation, we have not been given a preference in the matter. We must forgive unconditionally from our hearts—always!

Corrie ten Boom was a Christian Dutch woman who was imprisoned in a Nazi concentration camp for hiding Jews in her house during the Holocaust. She suffered unimaginable horror at the hands of the Nazis. Her dear sister Betsie died in the concentration camp. In the November 1972 issue of *Guideposts* magazine Corrie tells an incredibly powerful and heart-wrenching story. It was 1947, and she had been traveling around Germany, speaking about God's forgiveness. At the end of one service she looked up and saw one of her former guards approaching. Her memories of being arrested for hiding Jews and sent to Ravensbrück concentration camp came flooding back. Now the guard stood with his hand extended, saying, "How good it is to know that, as you say, all our sins are at the bottom of the sea!" Corrie dug in her purse rather than take the guard's hand. She knew the guard did not remember her, but she remembered—the dresses and shoes piled in the floor, the shame of walking naked past the guard, the leather crop that hung from his belt, and the skull and crossbones on his cap. Then the guard said he had become a Christian and he knew God had forgiven him. Then he stuck out his hand again and asked, "*Fräulein*, will you forgive me?"

Corrie stood there frozen for what seemed like hours, unable to shake the guard's hand. She knew she need to forgive him. She had seen firsthand how bitterness affected the Holocaust victims who could not forgive their enemies. But Corrie knew that forgiveness is an act of the will, not an emotion:

> "Jesus, help me!" I prayed silently. "I can lift my hand. I can do that much. You supply the feeling."
> And so woodenly, mechanically, I thrust my hand into the one stretched out to me. And as I did, an incredible thing took place. The current started in my shoulder, raced down my arm,

sprang into our joined hands. And then this healing warmth seemed to flood my whole being, bringing tears to my eyes. "I forgive you, brother!" I cried. "With all my heart!"[6]

I like the picture of biblical forgiveness John W. Nieder and Thomas M. Thompson give in their book *Forgive and Love Again*:

- To forgive is to turn the key, open the cell door, and let the prisoner walk free.

- To forgive is to write in large letters across a debt, "Nothing owed."

- To forgive is to pound the gavel in a courtroom and declare, "Not guilty!"

- To forgive is to shoot an arrow so high and so far that it can never be found again.

- To forgive is to bundle up all the garbage and trash and dispose of it, leaving the house clean and fresh.

- To forgive is to loose the moorings of a ship and release it to the open sea.

- To forgive is to grant a full pardon to a condemned criminal.

- To forgive is to relax a stranglehold on a wrestling opponent.

- To forgive is to sandblast a wall of graffiti, leaving it looking like new.

- To forgive is to smash a clay pot into a thousand pieces so it can never be pieced together again.[7]

It is said that the famous Confederate General Robert E. Lee called on a woman who lived near Lexington, Virginia, shortly after the Civil War. The woman took the general to see what had once been a beautiful tree in her yard. Now the tree was decimated. During a battle it had been barraged by artillery fire. Broken limbs dangled from the trunk, which had been torn by cannonballs. The woman's prized tree was now a pitiful eyesore, and she expected sympathy from the general. She thought that of all people Lee would understand her feelings of indignation and affirm her in her hatred for the North. Instead, after a brief silence the general said, "Cut it down, my dear Madam, and forget it."[8]

Just as that woman did, many people have broken trees in their front yards. They let them stand because they attract pity. They love to tell their stories and be comforted in the midst of their bitterness and resentment for some injustice. But if you want to see a tree of injustice, look at the cross. It was there on those bloody limbs that Jesus suffered unimaginable cruelty and injustice because of *your* offense. From the cross He looked down and said with love, "Father, forgive them" (Luke 23:34). My friend, Jesus comes to you today and says of your tree of bitterness, "Cut it down!"

Forgiveness can be a painful process, but like a surgical procedure to remove a malignant growth, it is absolutely imperative. Once the cancer of bitterness is removed, God's blessing will flood a person's life, and health will return to the soul and spirit and in many cases even the body.

Since this book is about spiritual warfare, I draw attention once again to what the king commanded in Matthew 18:34: "And his lord was wroth, and delivered him to the tormentors, till he should pay all that was due unto him" (KJV). Notice this servant was handed over to tormentors. Could it be that unforgiveness actually gives a legal right to tormenting spirits? It is a terrifying thought, and yet since unforgiveness actually prevents us from being able to receive God's forgiveness, as Jesus said in Matthew 6:15, it would seem demonic torment is only the beginning of sorrows for the one who will not forgive. It is wise to remember this both personally and when ministering to those under demonic torment. Often unforgiveness will play a critical role.

NEVER GIVE UP

This is my final encouragement to you in this book, and it is perhaps the most important one. Years ago during our ministry's School of

Evangelism a student asked evangelist Reinhard Bonnke an interesting question: "What is the number one key to your success?" Evangelist Bonnke's answer surprised me. I thought he would say something about prayer or faith or holiness or anointing. But he said none of those things. Instead he answered with one word: "Perseverance."

Earlier in this book when we talked about the armor of God, I highlighted the fact that Paul says that after "having done all, to stand. Stand..." (Eph. 6:13–14, NKJV). In other words, after you have done everything to prepare for the battle—you have read this book, you have prayed and fasted, you have put on the armor of God—there is still something you need to do if you want to be victorious. You have to actually stand! You have to hold your ground. You have to fight this battle. Anyone can fight for twenty minutes or a few days, but Jesus said, "The one who stands firm to the end will be saved" (Matt. 24:13).

If you want to see a tree of injustice, look at the cross. It was there on those bloody limbs that Jesus suffered unimaginable cruelty and injustice because of *your* offense.

Life is difficult, and we know that in this world we will have trouble—Jesus assured us of it. But He also told us we can be of good cheer because He has already overcome the world (John 16:33). Sometimes you will be wounded. You might even lose battles from time to time. That is the nature of war. But the prize goes not to the one who fights perfectly but to the one who keeps fighting. Proverbs 24:16 tells us that "though the righteous fall seven times, they rise again."

As we have pointed out so often in this book, we fight from a place of victory. Jesus has already crushed that dragon under His heel, and we have His promise that soon He will crush Satan under ours as well (Rom. 16:20).

Be the one who gets back up. Be the one who endures to the end. Be the one that overcomes and wins the prize. In the words of that great fighter Winston Churchill, "Never give in, never give in, never, never, never—in nothing, great or small, large or petty—never give in except to convictions of honour and good sense. Never yield to force; never yield to the apparently overwhelming might of the enemy."[9]

I leave you now with the words of the apostle Paul in Romans 8:35–39:

> Who shall separate us from the love of Christ? Shall trouble or hardship or persecution or famine or nakedness or danger or sword? As it is written: "For your sake we face death all day long; we are considered as sheep to be slaughtered." No, in all these things we are more than conquerors through him who loved us. For I am convinced that neither death nor life, neither angels nor demons, neither the present nor the future, nor any powers, neither height nor depth, nor anything else in all creation, will be able to separate us from the love of God that is in Christ Jesus our Lord.

QUESTIONS FOR DISCUSSION

- You will become like what you behold. What are you paying attention to? Do you need to change your focus?

- How does unforgiveness keep us from walking in victory?

- To whom can you offer a word of encouragement to never give up?

NOTES

INTRODUCTION

1. "Serpents and Dragons in British Folklore," *Atlantic Religion* (blog), September 29, 2015, https://atlanticreligion.com/2015/09/29/serpents-and-dragons-in-british-folklore/.
2. Gerald Massey, *The Natural Genesis*, vol. 1 (New York: Cosimo Classics, 2007), 294, https://books.google.com/books?id=IDCju2TrweMC&q.
3. Aaron J. Atsma, "Drakon Kholkikos," Theoi Project, accessed March 11, 2019, https://www.theoi.com/Ther/DrakonKholkikos.html.
4. Wikipedia, s.v. "Fafnir," last edited January 25, 2019, 20:30, https://en.wikipedia.org/wiki/Fafnir.
5. Wikipedia, s.v. "Kukulkan," last edited March 10, 2019, 23:23, https://en.wikipedia.org/wiki/Kukulkan.
6. Wikipedia, s.v. "Vritra," last edited March 1, 2019, 06:23, https://en.wikipedia.org/wiki/Vritra.
7. Wikipedia, s.v. "Druk," last edited January 17, 2019, 03:28, https://en.wikipedia.org/wiki/Druk.
8. John Gill, "Psalms 91," *Exposition of the Whole Bible*, StudyLight.org, accessed March 11, 2019, https://www.studylight.org/commentaries/geb/psalms-91.html.
9. Matthew Henry, "Psalms 91," *Matthew Henry's Commentary on the Whole Bible*, Blue Letter Bible, accessed March 11, 2019, https://www.blueletterbible.org/Comm/mhc/Psa/Psa_091.cfm, emphasis in the original.

CHAPTER 1

1. "The Harmattan is a season in the West African subcontinent, which occurs between the end of November and the middle of March. It is characterized by the dry and dusty northeasterly trade wind, of the same name, which blows from the Sahara Desert over West Africa into the Gulf of Guinea.... In some countries in West Africa, the heavy amount of dust in the air can severely limit visibility and block the sun for several days, comparable to a heavy fog. This effect is known as the Harmattan haze." Wikipedia, s.v. "Harmattan," last edited January 7, 2019, 18:38, https://en.wikipedia.org/wiki/Harmattan.

2. See also 2 Chronicles 36:15; Haggai 1:13; Malachi 3:1; and Matthew 11:10. In Malachi 2:7 a priest who teaches Torah is called "the messenger [angel] of Yahweh of hosts" (LEB).

3. One Old Testament scholar believes that the word *angel* is not an all-inclusive term for God's servants who inhabit the spiritual realm. Rather, an angel, or messenger, is only one kind among many kinds of spiritual beings created by God to serve Him. See Michael S. Heiser, *Angels: What the Bible Really Says About God's Heavenly Host* (Bellingham, WA: Lexham Press, 2018), xiii, 16–18, 164.

4. Michael S. Heiser, *The Unseen Realm: Recovering the Supernatural Worldview of the Bible* (Bellingham, WA: Lexham Press, 2015), 26, https://www.amazon.com/Unseen-Realm-Recovering-Supernatural-Worldview/dp/1577995562.

5. For example, in Deuteronomy 32:17 the word *elohim* refers to unknown "gods" who were also called "demons" earlier in the same verse: "They sacrificed to demons who were not God, to [*elohim*] whom they have not known" (NASB). Compare 1 Corinthians 8:4–6 and 10:18–22.

6. Heiser, *The Unseen Realm*, 28–32.

7. This one verse uses the term *elohim* both as a singular reference to the Most High God and as a plural reference to angelic beings. But since both God and angels dwell in the same spiritual realm as superhuman beings, the same term applies to both—though in different ways.

8. See Genesis 6:1–4; Job 1:6 (NKJV); 2:1 (NKJV); 38:7 (NKJV); Psalm 29:1 (LEB); 82:6; and 89:6 (LEB) for references to the "sons of God" or "sons of the Most High."

9. Hebrew words that end with -*im* are plural forms of masculine words, the way English words end in *s*. (Feminine Hebrew words end with -*oth* in their plural forms.)

10. Heiser, *Angels*, 26. Assuming the cherubim of Ezekiel's visions are the same as the four living creatures in Revelation, they are actually distinguished from angels in Revelation 5:11 and 7:11. Yet it seems elsewhere the term *angels* is a word that encompasses all of the spiritual beings created by God (Matt. 22:30; Heb. 1:1–14). So the word's meaning depends on its context.

11. Isaiah 37:16; Ezekiel 1; 9:3; 10:1; 11:22; 41:18–20.

12. Exodus 25:17–22; 26; 36–37; 1 Kings 6–8.

13. Psalm 18:10; 80:1; 99:1.

14. R. Laird Harris, s.v. "שׂרף (śārāp)," in *Theological Wordbook of the Old Testament*, eds. R. Laird Harris, Gleason L. Archer Jr., and Bruce K. Waltke (Chicago: Moody Press, 1980), 884. See also Heiser, *Angels*, 25–27.

15. Harris, s.v. "כרוב (kᵉrûb)," *Theological Wordbook of the Old Testament*, 454; Heiser, *Angels*, 26.

16. According to Old Testament scholar Gary Cohen, definitions of the Hebrew term include "prince, chief, captain, ruler, governor, keeper, chief captain, steward, master." See Gary Cohen, s.v. "שׂרר (śārar)," *Theological Wordbook of the Old Testament*, 884.

17. New Testament scholars do not all agree that Jesus is referring to angelic beings here. Some believe He is referring

to human beings in positions of leadership. Since, however, the psalm clearly refers to the angelic council of the Lord, and since it makes sense that Jesus would refer to that council to make the point about His own sonship and divinity, I hold that Jesus is embracing this view of the elohim. See also Michael S. Heiser, "Jesus' Quotation of Psalm 82:6 in John 10:34: A Different View of John's Theological Strategy," (paper presentation, Pacific Northwest Regional Meeting of the Society of Biblical Literature, Gonzaga University, Spokane, WA, May 13–15, 2011), http://www.thedivinecouncil.com/Heiser%20 Psa82inJohn10%20RegSBL2011.pdf.

18. Paul and John share a similar perspective of the church's gathering. That is why Paul gives certain instructions about church gatherings "for the sake of the angels" (1 Cor. 11:10, AMP) and why John could write a letter to a city church that simultaneously addressed that church's "angel" (e.g., Rev. 2:1).

19. See David Aune, *Word Biblical Commentary: Revelation 1–5*, vol. 52A (Waco, TX: Word Books, 1997), cxxxi, 268–269, https://www.amazon.com/Revelation-1-5-Word -Biblical-Commentary/dp/0849902517.

20. See Mike Bickle, "The Father's Throne and Jesus' Exaltation," *Studies in the Book of Revelation*, 2014, https://ihopkcorg-a.akamaihd.net/platform/ IHOP/812/47/20140321_Father_s_Throne_and_Jesus_ Exaltation_Rev.4-5_BOR05_study_notes.pdf.

21. Notice how this context puts Michael again in specific relationship to the nation of Israel. See Revelation 12:1–6.

22. See a similar passage that addresses both an evil world ruler (the king of Babylon) and his corresponding evil spiritual ruler in Isaiah 14:9–15.

23. Matthew adds the detail that there was a second demonized man (Matt. 8:28). The two demonized men acted

together, but clearly one took the lead in word and action. Therefore, he received singular attention in Mark and Luke (Luke 8:26–37).

24. Craig S. Keener, *The IVP Bible Background Commentary: New Testament* (Downers Grove, IL: InterVarsity Press, 1993), 147, https://books.google.com/books?id=cnAAOuN2_JIC&q.

25. English Bibles usually translate these phrases as "demon-possessed."

CHAPTER 2

1. Alia E. Dastagir, "'Born This Way'? It's Way More Complicated Than That," *USA Today*, June 15, 2017, https://www.usatoday.com/story/news/2017/06/16/born-way-many-lgbt-community-its-way-more-complex/395035001/.

2. C. S. Lewis, *Mere Christianity* (New York: HarperCollins, 2001), 47–48, https://books.google.com/books?id=p1Pbhy6SugwC&q.

3. *Expelled: No Intelligence Allowed*, directed by Nathan Frankowski (Chicago: Rocky Mountain Pictures, 2008).

4. Blaise Pascal, *The Thoughts, Letters, and Opuscules of Blaise Pascal*, trans. O. W. Wight (New York: Hurd and Houghton, 1864), 327, https://babel.hathitrust.org/cgi/pt?id=mdp.39015005273464;view=1up;seq=9.

5. Francis Bacon, "Of Atheism," *The Essays or Counsels, Civil and Moral* (Oxford: Clarendon Press, 1890), 111, https://babel.hathitrust.org/cgi/pt?id=hvd.32044090286774;view=1up;seq=9.

6. J. Barton Payne, s.v. "שָׂטָן (śāṭan)," *Theological Wordbook of the Old Testament*, 874–875.

7. Zvi Ron, "Wordplay in Genesis 2:25–3:1," *The Jewish Bible Quarterly* 42, no. 1 (2014), http://jbqnew.jewishbible.org/assets/Uploads/421/JBQ_421_1_wordplay.pdf.

8. Leon R. Kass, *The Beginning of Wisdom: Reading Genesis* (New York: Free Press, 2003), 82, https://books.google.com/books?id=H9RxCpsBPPsC&q.

9. Ed Nelson, "Yeshua in the Torah: Genesis 3:15: The Serpent, Dusty Feet and the Messiah" (unpublished article, 2010), 5.

10. Nelson, "Yeshua in the Torah," 24.

CHAPTER 3

1. Sun Tzu, *The Art of War*, trans. Lionel Giles, 3.18, http://classics.mit.edu/Tzu/artwar.html.

CHAPTER 4

1. *Merriam-Webster*, s.v. "zeitgeist," accessed March 19, 2019, https://www.merriam-webster.com/dictionary/zeitgeist.

2. Elijah P. Brown, *The Real Billy Sunday: The Life and Work of Rev. William Ashley Sunday, D. D., the Baseball Evangelist* (New York: Fleming H. Revell, 1914), 281–282, https://archive.org/details/realbillysunday100brow/page/280.

3. Richard Dawkins, *The God Delusion* (Boston: Houghton Mifflin, 2006), 383–385, https://books.google.com/books?id=yq1xDpicghkC&q.

4. Richard Dawkins, "Why I Want All Our Children to Read the King James Bible," *The Guardian*, May 19, 2012, https://www.theguardian.com/science/2012/may/19/richard-dawkins-king-james-bible.

5. Fyodor Dostoevsky, *Notes From Underground* (West Valley City, UT: Waking Lion Press, 2006), 27, https://www.amazon.com/Notes-Underground-Fyodor-Dostoevsky/dp/1600960839.

CHAPTER 5

1. Dennis Rockstroh Knight-Ridder, "'Wonder Woman' Gets Perfect SAT," *Daily News*, March 10, 1996, https://www.

thefreelibrary.com/%27WONDER+WOMAN%27+GETS +PERFECT+SAT.-a083922467.
2. This section is an excerpt from *Experiencing the Supernatural* by Rabbi K. A. Schneider, copyright © 2017. Used by permission of Chosen Books, a division of Baker Publishing Group.
3. *Westminster Shorter Catechism*, 1.

CHAPTER 6

1. This quote is often wrongly attributed to Calvin Coolidge. It was actually text used as filler material in newspapers from as early as 1910. Many people attribute it to Coolidge because it sounds like him and because of the way he is often associated with perseverance. See Amithy Shlaes, *Coolidge* (New York: HarperCollins, 2013), 5, https://www. amazon.com/Coolidge-Amity-Shlaes/dp/0061967599.

CHAPTER 7

1. Adam Clarke, *Memoirs of the Wesley Family* (London: J. Kershaw, 1823), 270, https://books.google.com/ books?id=dmQUAAAAQAAJ&vq.
2. For a thorough exploration of the spirit, soul, and body construction of humanity I refer you to Watchman Nee, *The Spiritual Man* (New York: Christian Fellowship Publishers, 2014).
3. C. S. Lewis, *The Screwtape Letters* (New York: HarperOne, 2009), 16, https://books.google.com/ books?id=cTqsF2XCMR8C&q.
4. Dallas Willard, *The Spirit of the Disciplines*: *Understanding How God Changes Lives* (New York: HarperCollins, 1988), chap. 9, https://books.google.com/books?id=W9KF_I-DB9EC&q.
5. Wikiquote, s.v. "Yogi Berra," last edited March 16, 2019, 18:11, https://en.wikiquote.org/wiki/Yogi_Berra.

6. For a more advanced study on spiritual disciplines I recommend the modern classic by Richard Foster, *Celebration of Discipline: The Path to Spiritual Growth* (San Francisco: Harper, 1978).

CHAPTER 8

1. Jack Kent, *There's No Such Thing as a Dragon* (New York: Dragonfly Books, 2009), https://www.amazon.com/Theres-No-Such-Thing-Dragon/dp/0375851372.
2. Sarah Gibbens, "Why an 8-Foot Pet Python May Have Killed Its Owner," *National Geographic*, January 26, 2018, https://news.nationalgeographic.com/2018/01/snake-owner-killed-pet-python-aspyxiated-spd/.
3. Aleksandr Solzhenitsyn, *The Gulag Archipelago 1918–1956: An Experiment in Literary Investigation* (Boulder, CO: Westview Press, 1998), 168, https://www.amazon.com/Gulag-Archipelago-1918-1956-Experiment-Investigation/dp/0813332893.
4. It is estimated that between one billion and two billion babies have been aborted worldwide in the past fifty years. Colin Mason and Steven Mosher, "Earth Day: Abortion Has Killed 1–2 Billion Worldwide in 50 Years," LifeNews.com, April 21, 2011, https://www.lifenews.com/2011/04/21/earth-day-abortion-has-killed-1-2-billion-worldwide-in-50-years/.
5. Philip Schaff, *History of the Christian Church, Volume III: Nicene and Post-Nicene Christianity. A.D. 311–600*, Christian Classics Ethereal Library, accessed March 26, 2019, http://www.ccel.org/ccel/schaff/hcc3.iii.vii.x.html.
6. Paschal Robinson, "St. Francis of Assisi," *The Catholic Encyclopedia*, vol. 6 (New York: Robert Appleton Company, 1909), http://www.newadvent.org/cathen/06221a.htm.
7. Regis J. Armstrong, J. A. Wayne Hellmann, and William Short, eds., *Francis of Assisi: Early Documents—The Saint,*

vol. 1 (New York: New City Press, 1999), 227, https://books.google.com/books?id=vwVsEM8mXWYC&pg.

8. Schaff, *History of the Christian Church*, http://www.ccel.org/ccel/schaff/hcc3.iii.vii.viii.html.

9. See "Translation of the Shema," Chabad-Lubavitch Media Center, accessed March 27, 2019, https://www.chabad.org/library/article_cdo/aid/3217840/jewish/Translation.htm.

10. Charles H. Spurgeon, *Morning and Evening: Daily Bible Readings*, "June 11—Morning Reading," Blue Letter Bible, accessed March 27, 2019, https://www.blueletterbible.org/devotionals/me/view.cfm?Date=06/11&Time=am.

11. Basilea Schlink, *My All for Him: Fall in Love With Jesus All Over Again* (Bloomington, MN: Bethany House, 2001), 22.

12. Thomas Doolittle, *Love to Christ: Necessary to Escape the Curse at His Coming*, A Puritan's Mind, accessed March 27, 2019, https://www.apuritansmind.com/puritan-evangelism/love-to-christ-necessary-to-escape-the-curse-at-his-coming-by-thomas-doolittle/.

13. Saint Augustine, *Confessions*, trans. F. J. Sheed, 2nd ed. (Indianapolis: Hackett Publishing, 2006), 3, https://books.google.com/books?id=_wusCvC4yOcC&pg.

CHAPTER 9

1. William Arndt et al., *A Greek-English Lexicon of the New Testament and Other Early Christian Literature* (Chicago: University of Chicago Press, 2000), 543–544.

2. Arndt et al., *A Greek-English Lexicon of the New Testament and Other Early Christian Literature*, 402.

3. Tom Wright, *Matthew for Everyone: Part 1, Chapters 1–15* (London: Society for Promoting Christian Knowledge, 2004), 212, https://books.google.com/books?id=DRipJ92cCZQC&pg.

4. Gilbert Cruz, "Juneteenth," *Time*, June 18, 2008, http://content.time.com/time/nation/article/0,8599,1815936,00.

html; Henry Louis Gates Jr., "What Is Juneteenth?," WNET, accessed March 28, 2019, https://www.pbs.org/wnet/african-americans-many-rivers-to-cross/history/what-is-juneteenth/; Stephanie Hall, "Juneteenth," *Folklife Today* (blog), Library of Congress, June 17, 2016, https://blogs.loc.gov/folklife/category/holidays/juneteenth/.

5. Arndt et al., *A Greek-English Lexicon of the New Testament and Other Early Christian Literature*, 262.

6. Arndt et al., *A Greek-English Lexicon of the New Testament and Other Early Christian Literature*, 263.

7. Daniel Kolenda, *Unlocking the Miraculous: Through Faith and Prayer* (Orlando: Christ for all Nations, 2016).

8. Blue Letter Bible, s.v. "*dikaios*," accessed March 28, 2019, https://www.blueletterbible.org/lang/lexicon/lexicon.cfm?Strongs=G1342&t=KJV.

9. "Human Language," Lumen: Boundless Psychology, accessed March 28, 2019, https://courses.lumenlearning.com/boundless-psychology/chapter/human-language/. See also Steven Pinker and Ray Jackendoff, "The Faculty of Language: What's Special About It?," *Cognition* 95, no. 2 (2005), 201–236, https://doi.org/10.1016/j.cognition.2004.08.004.

10. Amy Marshall, "Talk It Over: Language, Uniquely, Makes Us Human," The Conversation US, Inc., February 24, 2013, http://theconversation.com/talk-it-over-language-uniquely-makes-us-human-12242.

11. Eric William Gilmour, *Union: The Thirsting Soul Satisfied in God* (Winter Springs, FL: Sonship International, 2013), 103, 106.

12. Daniel Kolenda, *Live Before You Die* (Lake Mary, FL: Passio, 2013), 193–195.

CHAPTER 10

1. Carlos Annacondia, *Listen to Me, Satan!* (Lake Mary, FL: Charisma House, 2008), 81.

2. Wiktionary, s.v. "bloodlust," last edited March 18, 2019, 10:36, https://en.wiktionary.org/wiki/bloodlust.

3. "Have You Had an Encounter With a Seemingly Autonomous Entity After Taking DMT?," Qualtrics, accessed April 1, 2019, https://web.archive.org/web/20180330180538/https://jhmi.co1.qualtrics.com/jfe/form/SV_eqvCfk2u19kSzm5.

4. Roger Barrier, "Why Don't Pastors Preach and Teach More on Demons?," Crosswalk.com, February 12, 2015, https://www.crosswalk.com/church/pastors-or-leadership/ask-roger/why-don-t-pastors-preach-and-teach-more-on-demons.html.

5. Annacondia, *Listen to Me, Satan!*, 71.

6. F. F. Bruce, "Biblical Criticism," *New Bible Dictionary*, 1st ed., ed. J. D. Douglas et al. (Grand Rapids, MI: Wm. B. Eerdmans, 1962), 151.

7. Elizabeth Palermo, "Who Invented the Printing Press?," LiveScience, February 25, 2014, https://www.livescience.com/43639-who-invented-the-printing-press.html. Palermo dates the printing press to "sometime between 1440 and 1450."

8. Josh McDowell, *The New Evidence That Demands a Verdict* (Nashville: Thomas Nelson, 1999), 34, https://www.amazon.com/New-Evidence-That-Demands-Verdict/dp/0785242198.

9. McDowell, *The New Evidence That Demands a Verdict*, 33–68.

10. Charles Pope, "Prayer and Fasting or Just Prayer? A Consideration of a Biblical 'Disagreement,'" *Community in Mission* (blog), February 16, 2016, http://blog.adw.org/2016/02/

prayer-and-fasting-or-just-prayer-a-consideration-of-a-biblical-disagreement/.

11. Pope, "Prayer and Fasting or Just Prayer?" See also Donald A. Hagner, *Word Biblical Commentary: Matthew 14–28*, vol. 33B (Dallas: Word, 1995), 501.

12. Eberhard Nestle, *Introduction to the Textual Criticism of the Greek New Testament*, trans. William Edie (New York: G. P. Putnam's Sons, 1901), 323.

13. Bruce M. Metzger, *A Textual Commentary on the Greek New Testament*, 2nd ed. (London: United Bible Societies, 1998), 35, https://www.amazon.com/Textual-Commentary-Greek-Testament-Ancient/dp/1598561642.

14. Metzger, *A Textual Commentary on the Greek New Testament*, 35. See also, for example, Leon Morris, *The Gospel According to Matthew* (Grand Rapids, MI: Wm. B. Eerdmans, 1992), 449; and Hagner, *Word Biblical Commentary: Matthew 14–28*, 501.

15. Metzger, *A Textual Commentary on the Greek New Testament*, 85; and Charles John Ellicott, ed., *A New Testament Commentary for English Readers*, vol. 1 (New York: E. P. Dutton & Co., 1878), 213–214, https://archive.org/details/newtestamentcomm01elli.

16. "In light of the increasing emphasis in the early church on the necessity of fasting, it is understandable that ["and fasting"] is a gloss that found its way into most witnesses." Metzger, *A Textual Commentary on the Greek New Testament*, 85.

17. Luke Wayne, "Was Matthew 17:21 Removed From Modern Bibles?," Christian Apologetics and Research Ministry, October 31, 2018, https://carm.org/was-matthew-17-21-removed-from-modern-bibles.

18. Tertullian, "On Fasting in Opposition to the Psychics," *The Sacred Writings of Tertullian*, vol. 2, trans. Peter Holmes and Sidney Thelwall (Loschberg, Germany:

Jazzybee Verlag, 2012), 429, https://books.google.com/books?id=3uoqDwAAQBAJ&pg.

19. Reinhard Bonnke (Evangelist Reinhard Bonnke - Official Page), "The key to the power switch is faith. Just that. Go believing and God goes with you. Faith is faith when it rests on the Word, not on experience, or paperback stories...," Facebook, July 20, 2015, 9:55 a.m., https://www.facebook.com/evangelistreinhardbonnke/posts/10155823005470258.

20. Kolenda, *Live Before You Die*, 144.

21. R. D. Mayfield, R. A. Harris, and M. A. Schuckit, "Genetic Factors Influencing Alcohol Dependence," *British Journal of Pharmacology* 154, no. 2 (May 2008), 275–287, https://doi.org/10.1038/bjp.2008.88.

22. Tim Spector, "How Your Grandparents' Life Could Have Changed Your Genes," The Conversation US, Inc., October 14, 2013, https://theconversation.com/how-your-grandparents-life-could-have-changed-your-genes-19136.

CHAPTER 11

1. Daniel Goleman, "Long-Married Couples Do Look Alike, Study Finds," *New York Times*, August 11, 1987, https://www.nytimes.com/1987/08/11/science/long-married-couples-do-look-alike-study-finds.html.

2. Smith Wigglesworth, *Smith Wigglesworth on Manifesting the Divine Nature: Abiding in Power Every Day of the Year* (Shippensburg, PA: Destiny Image, 2013), 197, https://books.google.com/books?id=fsZtXFKru0IC&pg.

3. "Verse-by-Verse Bible Commentary: Matthew 18:24," StudyLight.org, accessed April 2, 2019, https://www.studylight.org/commentary/matthew/18-24.html; Blue Letter Bible, s.v. *"talanton,"* accessed April 2, 2019, https://www.blueletterbible.org/lang/lexicon/lexicon.cfm?Strongs=G5007&t=KJV.

4. Gold Price, accessed April 2, 2019, 12:21:28, https://goldprice.org.
5. Ellicott, *A New Testament Commentary for English Readers*, 114.
6. Corrie ten Boom, "Guideposts Classics: Corrie ten Boom on Forgiveness," *Guideposts*, November 1972, https://www.guideposts.org/better-living/positive-living/guideposts-classics-corrie-ten-boom-on-forgiveness.
7. John W. Nieder and Thomas M. Thompson, *Forgive and Love Again* (Eugene, OR: Harvest House, 2010), 58–59, https://books.google.com/books?id=rDJfIhmqn98C&pg.
8. Charles Bracelen Flood, *Lee: The Last Years* (Boston: Mariner, 1981), 136, https://books.google.com/books/about/Lee.html?id=s7sv58JnA94C.
9. Winston Churchill, "Never Give In," Harrow School, London, October 29, 1941, https://winstonchurchill.org/resources/speeches/1941-1945-war-leader/never-give-in/.

Your stamp on this envelope is an additional contribution to the outreach.

PRODUCT REQUEST
13306

BUSINESS REPLY MAIL
FIRST-CLASS MAIL   PERMIT NO 4877   FORT WORTH TX

POSTAGE WILL BE PAID BY ADDRESSEE

LIFE
OUTREACH INTERNATIONAL
J A M E S   R O B I S O N
PO BOX 982000
FORT WORTH TEXAS 76182-9986

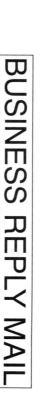

NO POSTAGE
NECESSARY
IF MAILED
IN THE
UNITED STATES